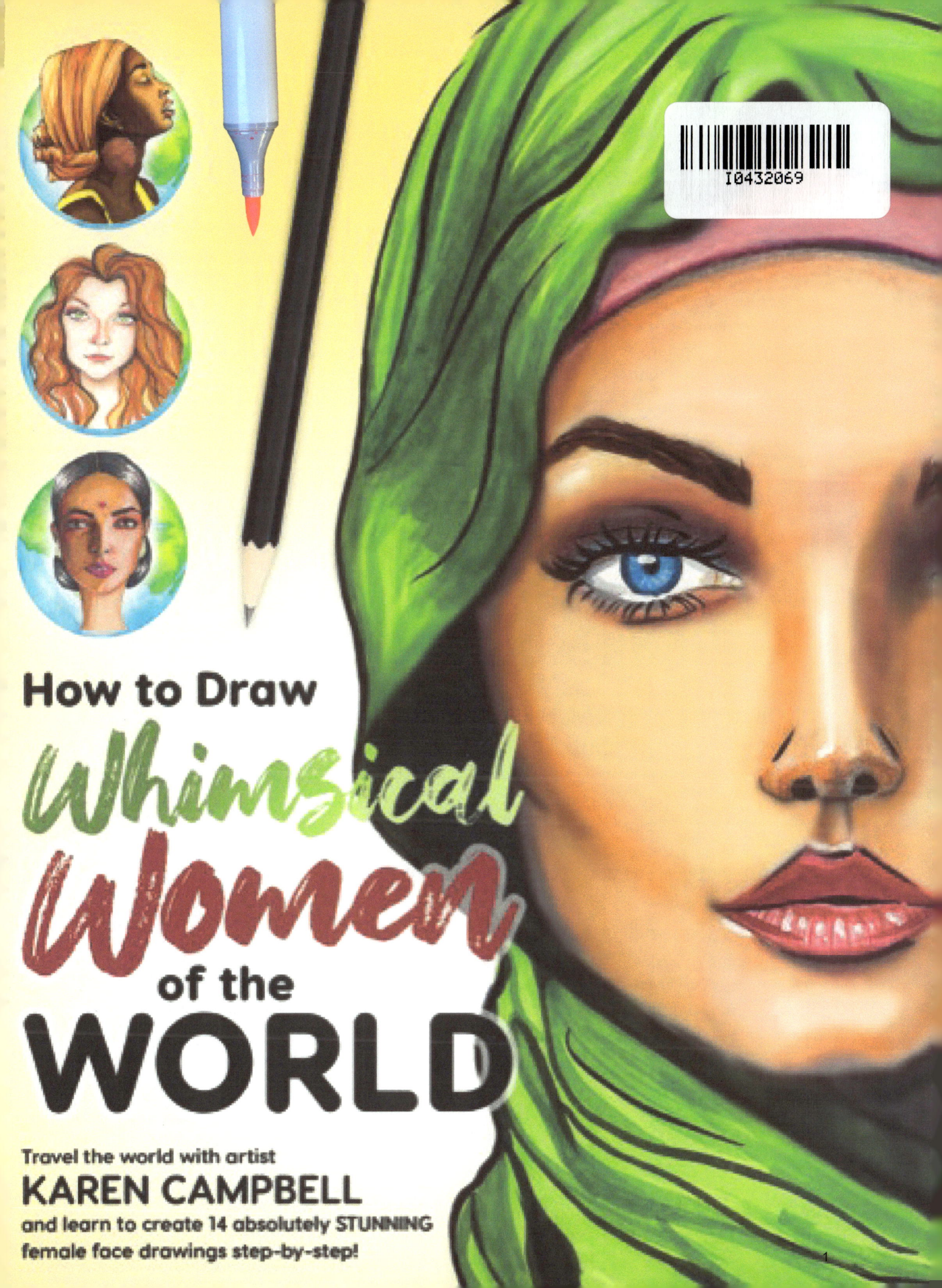

A quick note from the author...

This book is dedicated to all my students, fans and followers who purchase my art books, tune into my YouTube channels or log into AwesomeArtSchool.com to get creative with me everyday! It's YOU who inspire me to keep on creating, teaching and having so much fun. It's YOU all, to whom I am most grateful. Thank you for joining me on this particularly special, epic, world-wide art adventure! I'm so proud to be able to feature your masterpieces along side mine in this book. Keep up the fabulous work, and never forget that YOU ARE AWESOME!!!

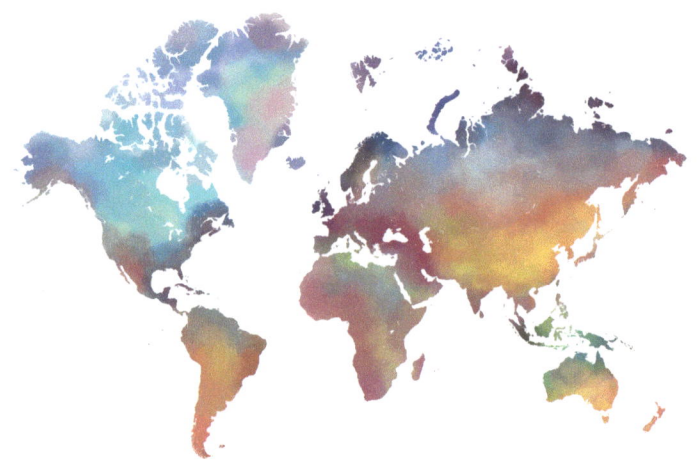

To access the free video series that accompanies this book visit:
http://bit.ly/whimsicalwomen

Text and Illustrations Copyright © 2021 by Karen Campbell. All rights reserved.
Author, Illustrator, Publisher: Karen Campbell, Artist, LLC **karencampbellartist.com**
Cover Design: KT Design, LLC **ktdesignllc.com**
Editors: Linda Duvel and Mandi Brown **trianglecreativegroup.com**
Compiler: Taylor McLean

This book has been written and designed to aid the aspiring artist. Reproduction of work for at-home practice is permissible. Any art produced, electronically reproduced, or distributed from this publication for commercial purposes is forbidden without written content from the publisher, Karen Campbell, Artist, LLC. If you would like to use material from this book for any purpose outside of private use, prior written permission must be obtained by contacting the publisher at **karen@awesomeartschool.com**. Thank you for supporting the author's rights.

Have so much fun! KAREN

Are these faces whimsical?

When first glancing at the title of this book, you may be wondering why I used the term "whimsical" especially since the faces in this book appear to be very realistic!

After a decade of teaching thousands of people of all ages how to draw both in person and online, my most significant observation is that in order to achieve fabulous drawing results the **ATTITUDE** of the artist is simply most important!

Those students who relax and have fun while they draw get better results faster.

Those who only strive for perfection and realism tend to get more easily discouraged, quit sooner, are harder on themselves and see less progress over time.

Therefore, I use the term "whimsical" with all my students, to help them shift their mind-set *away* from the stress of having to draw someone perfectly or realistically and towards the goal of getting it "close enough" or simply "whimsical".

Whimsical here simply means NOT totally realistic. If your drawing winds up being realistic than awesome!! And if not, whimsical will ALWAYS be welcome and beautiful, especially if this was the goal from the onset. Most people can achieve whimsical and thus most people experience what they themselves consider to be drawing success!!

Keeping the goal on having fun and getting the facial proportions approximate or "whimsical" (rather than perfect) helps my students feel less stressed and more confident when approaching their practice.

Without the stress of perfectionism I also find my students anxious to dive in and to just GO FOR IT (which may also have something to do with the fact that I'm their biggest and loudest cheerleader)!!

Can you then guess what happens after that?
Yep, you guessed it, they practice MORE, because their practice time truly is fun! But it's more than just that, my students practice sessions yield results far better than they'd expected! Which leads to even MORE practice, which leads to better and better (and faster) results!

So whimsical, in this book, refers much more to a carefree mindset when drawing realistic faces, and very little to do with a specific artistic style.

I hope this mindset shift helps you become a better artist too! Give it a try and see for yourself! I think you'll be happily surprised.

Supplies

Make no mistake, this is the book that will teach you how to draw some of the most beautiful women around the world! I will teach you step-by-step, how to create each fabulous face. All you need for each and every lesson here is a simple pencil. If you like precise, razor sharp lines then definitely work with a mechanical pencil.

Pentel GraphGear 1000's are my favorite mechanical pencils (shown here). They are weighted and feel important when I hold them and, because of that, I feel confident when making each stroke on my paper! Sounds weird, right? But it's true!

Truthfully? Any old pencil will do, even a yellow school pencil can do an amazing job, so if that's all you have, you're in good shape to draw!

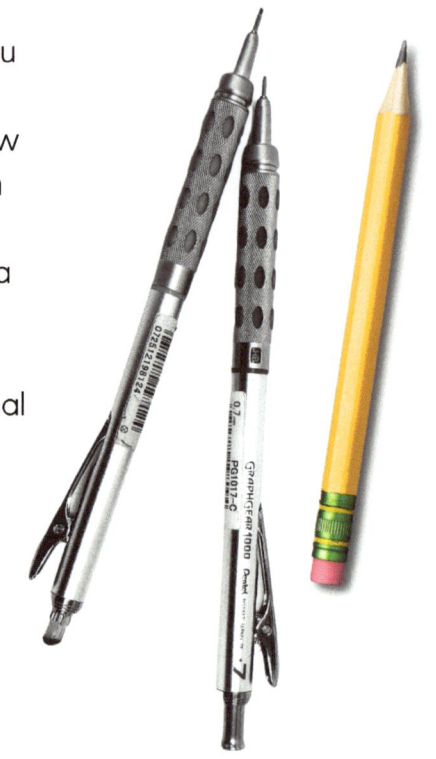

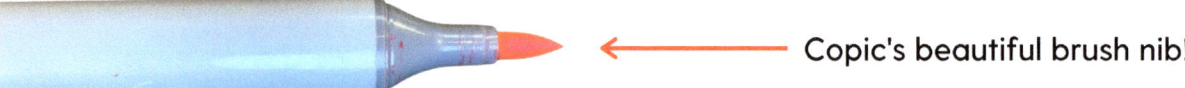

← Copic's beautiful brush nib!

When it comes to coloring my whimsical faces I love to use alcohol based markers.

Alcohol markers are fast drying and permanent and really fun to use. They are also produced by many different companies and come in a large array of styles, colors and price points. I own alcohol markers from probably a dozen different companies and use them all! The good news is that all brands work the same way and you can mix and match them to your hearts content.

My favorite markers are Copic Sketch markers because they have a really lovely brush nib on one end that makes drawing feel like painting! I also recommend Ohuhu brand alcohol markers. The also have that great brush nib and come with a much lower price tag (phew!).

Alcohol markers can be tricky to use if you're new to them. Turn the page for some great tips to help you if you're just getting started.

Marker Coloring Tips

1 Color quickly. The best blending occurs when the layers that are applied are wet. Alcohol markers dry pretty quickly so you need to move fast if you want them to blend seamlessly.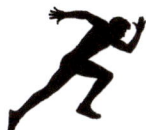

2 Work a little smaller. Drawing on a smaller scale enables you to move more quickly, which results in improved blending and less streaking. My drawings are huge and you will see my streaks as a result!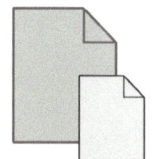

3 To help "fix" streaks, work systematically in two directions using the same color. For your first layer, color using very uniform horizontal strokes. Then apply the second layer of the same color in vertical strokes. The two layers often cancel each other out to create a more blended appearance.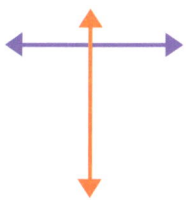

4 Test, test, test and test some more. Before you start coloring, check the marker color on a separate piece of scratch paper. There's nothing worse than a surprise!! Marker cap colors are notorious for not being a true representation of the actual color.

5 Invest in a separate Skin Tone Set of markers. After having drawn so many faces I can tell you with certainty that you cannot own too many skin tones! I must use dozens of different skin tones (by various brands) to create the projects in this book! Ohuhu makes a wonderful set of 24 for under $30.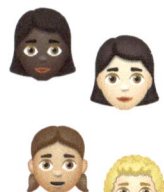

6 Use the right paper. Paper is **AS IMPORTANT** as the markers you're working with. My favorite marker paper to use is actually a very inexpensive, really heavy duty, slippery smooth coverstock that you can buy from Amazon or most any office supply store. It is by Hammermill. You can find links to all my favorite art supplies here:
www.amazon.com/shop/karencampbellartist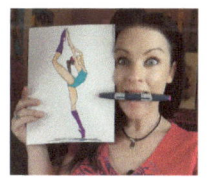

Additional Supplies

As I've mentioned, markers can leave a streaky look. Sometimes you can also have large, undesirable areas of high contrast between shades. I like to use colored pencils to help blend out the marker streaks and to soften the transitions between those troublesome, high contrast areas.

The trick is pretty easy! Pick shades of colors that match your markers and lightly sketch to see if you can help in those areas.

Primsacolors and Polychromos by Faber-Castell are my favorite colored pencil brands but any brand will do!

Choose skin colors that roughly match your marker skin colors.

You can also use colored pencils to add texture to clothing and to create the look of individual hair strands!

As you move through the projects in the book you'll see how to use them.

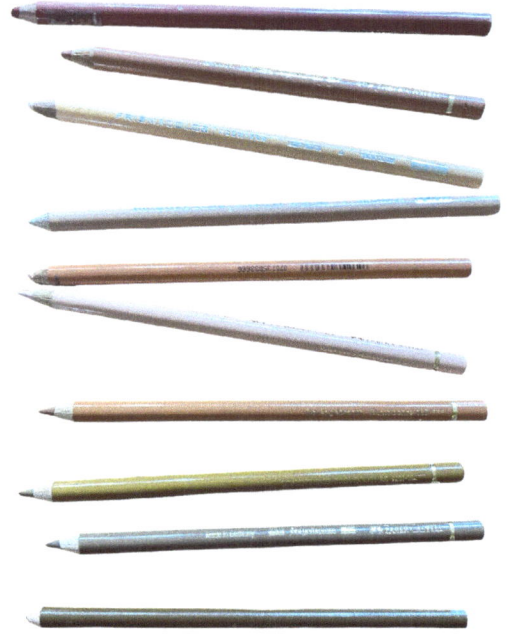

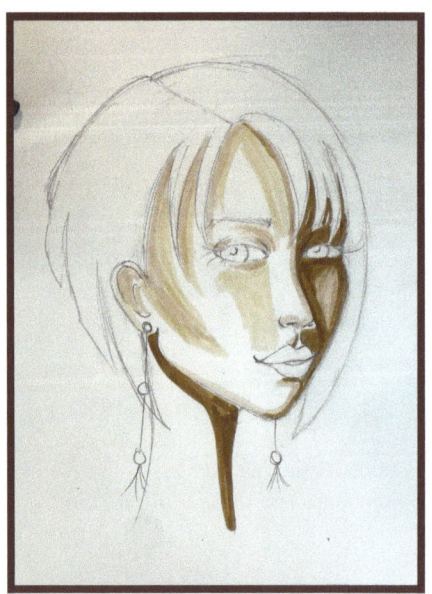

This is a great example of how a drawing can start off. As you can see, the transitions between the different areas of skin are marked by a definitive line.

You can use your colored pencils to sketch right along those lines thereby easing the transition from one color to the next.

This is especially useful if you don't have a lot of skin tone marker colors. Use your colored pencils to fill in the blanks!

Additional Supplies

Some people love to outline things as they draw. Some people don't! There is no right or wrong when it comes to outlining your drawings; it is simply an artistic choice that you get to make!

Personally? I'm an outliner. I used to try and fight it. At one point (because an art teacher told me that there are no outlines anywhere on a human body) I used to feel bad or guilty when I outlined my faces or facial features!!

After many years of creating and teaching I've decided "to heck with that philosophy!" If you want to outline, go for it. If you don't want to because you have an unsteady hand or you don't care for the look, then simply don't.

Whatever decision you make, own it! Your drawings will look awesome either way.

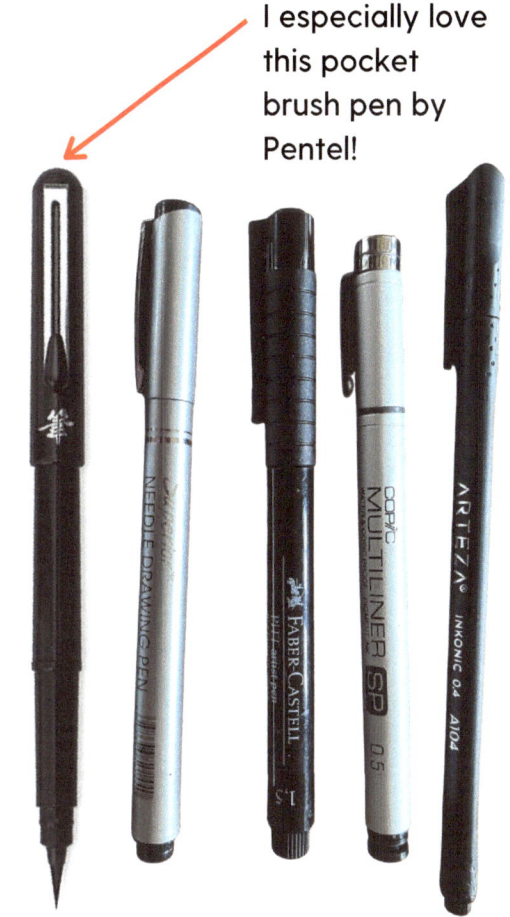

I especially love this pocket brush pen by Pentel!

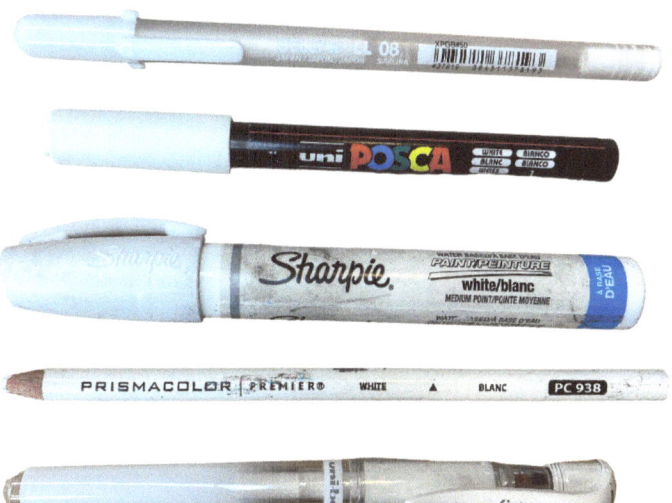

Lastly, make sure you have some good white drawing utensils in your art arsenal! Here is a collection of my top favorites.

When I want to create a soft highlighted region I reach for my white colored pencils.

When I want to pack more of a punch on a tiny area I get out my gel pens.

And when I really want to create some drama or make a good, solid SPARKLE, I don't hesitate to bust out my paint markers! Posca and Sharpie make the best (in my opinion)!

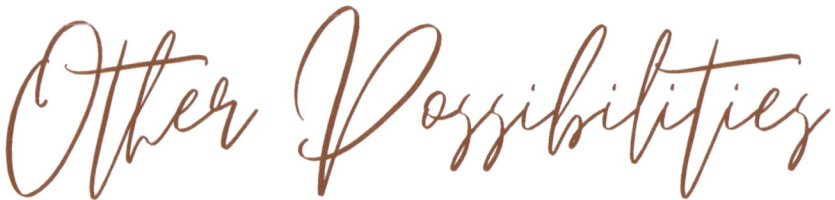

Other Possibilities

With all that being said about markers, pencils and pens...the truth is, that when it comes to coloring in your drawings, the sky truly is the limit!!

I'm actually a mixed media artist and I teach many mediums to my students. My philosophy is always to use what you love! So...

If you love colored pencils, markers, watercolors, use them!!

More of a crayon kinda person? Go for it!!

While I'm teaching marker techniques in this book, to me, every art supply is fair game to use!

You can also use the same color layering method I teach you here for lots of other mediums!! Colored pencils, watercolors, even acrylics, can all be layered and blended to achieve similar effects to what you'll see in this book.

To prove it (and to inspire you too!), I've invited a slew of my students to submit THEIR unique works for publication in this book. After each lesson you'll get to see their interpretations! Everything from graphite to acrylics, mixed media, collage, watercolors, pastels and more show up in these works.

As an extra fun resource, in case you'd like to learn more about the drawing steps and color methods I'm using for each project in this book, here is a link to the fun (and completely FREE) video series I hosted on YouTube that will guide you through each lesson - every step of the way!
Visit **http://bit.ly/whimsicalwomen** to watch them all!

All 14 lessons are in video format at the link PLUS a bonus Asian male face as well.

Regardless of what mediums you decide to use, I only hope that you have FUN with it!!

Now without further ado, let's officially begin!

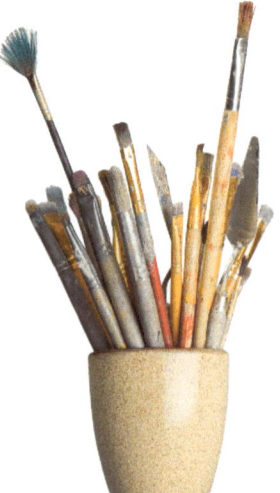

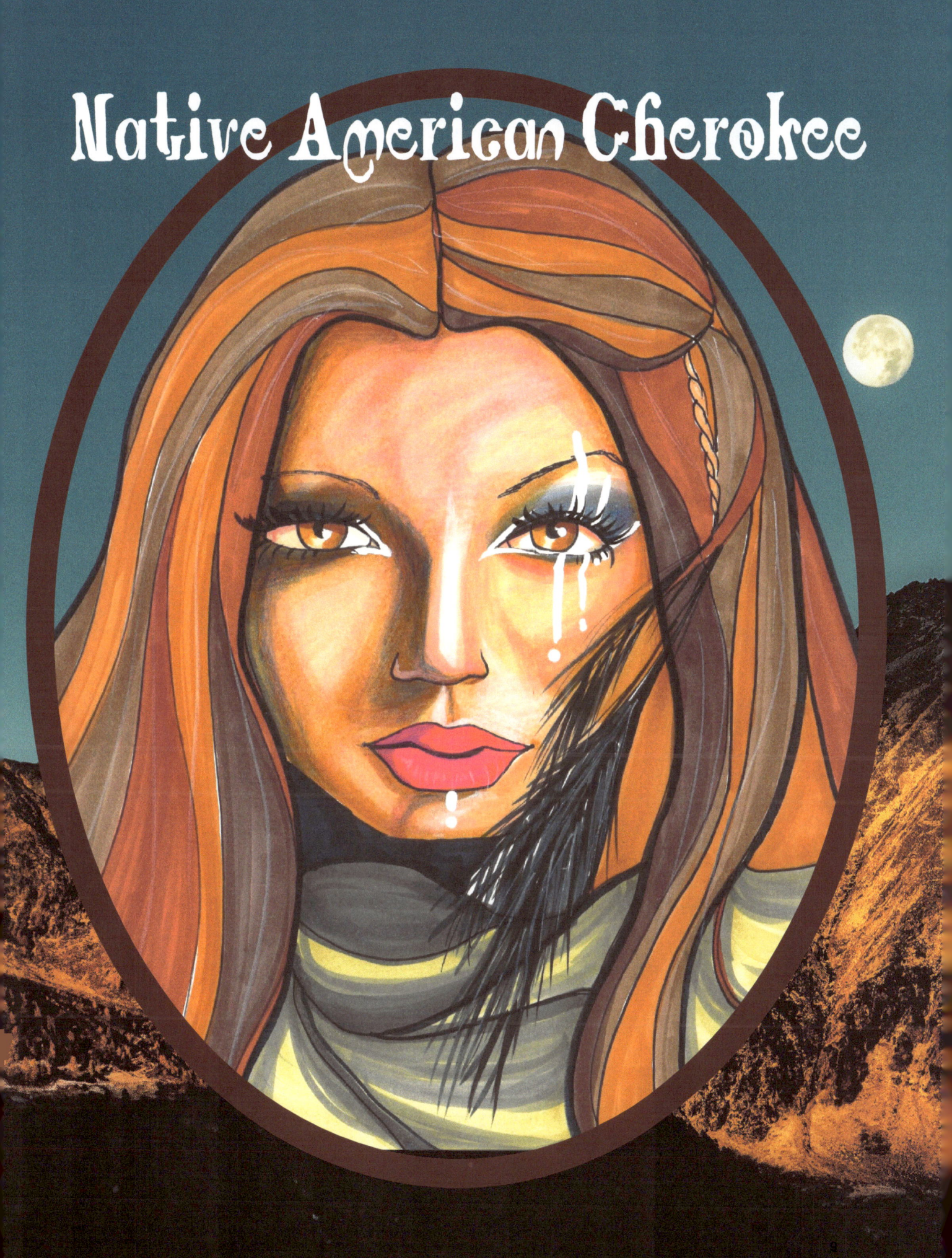

Native American

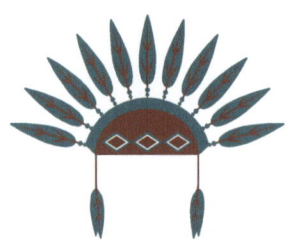

Begin with a simple oval.

If you need to draw many of them to get a good shape, go for it!

Vertical line helps keep things symmetrical

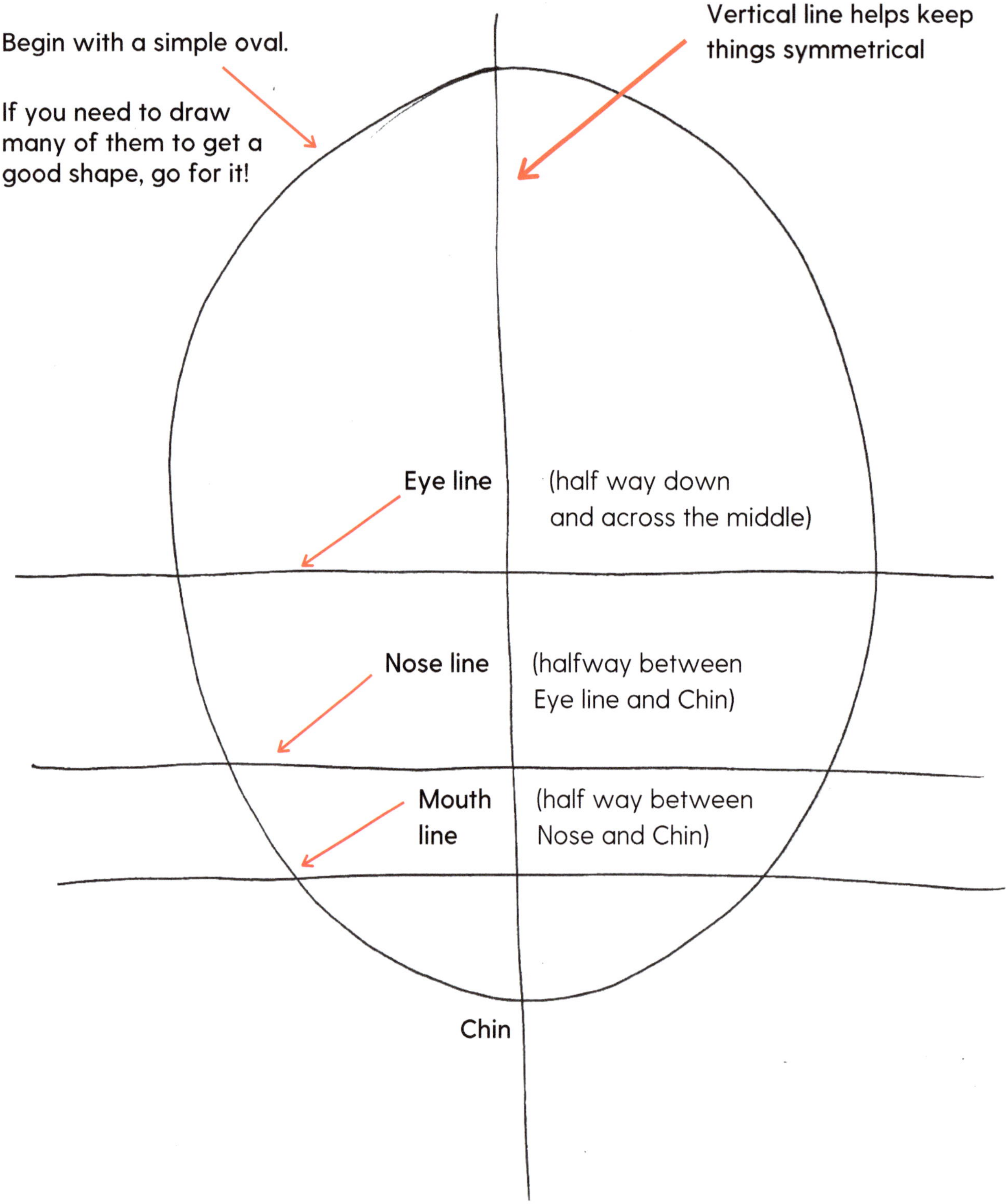

Eye line (half way down and across the middle)

Nose line (halfway between Eye line and Chin)

Mouth line (half way between Nose and Chin)

Chin

Native American

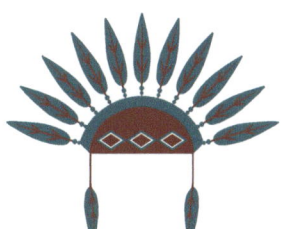

Sketch in facial feature "placeholders".

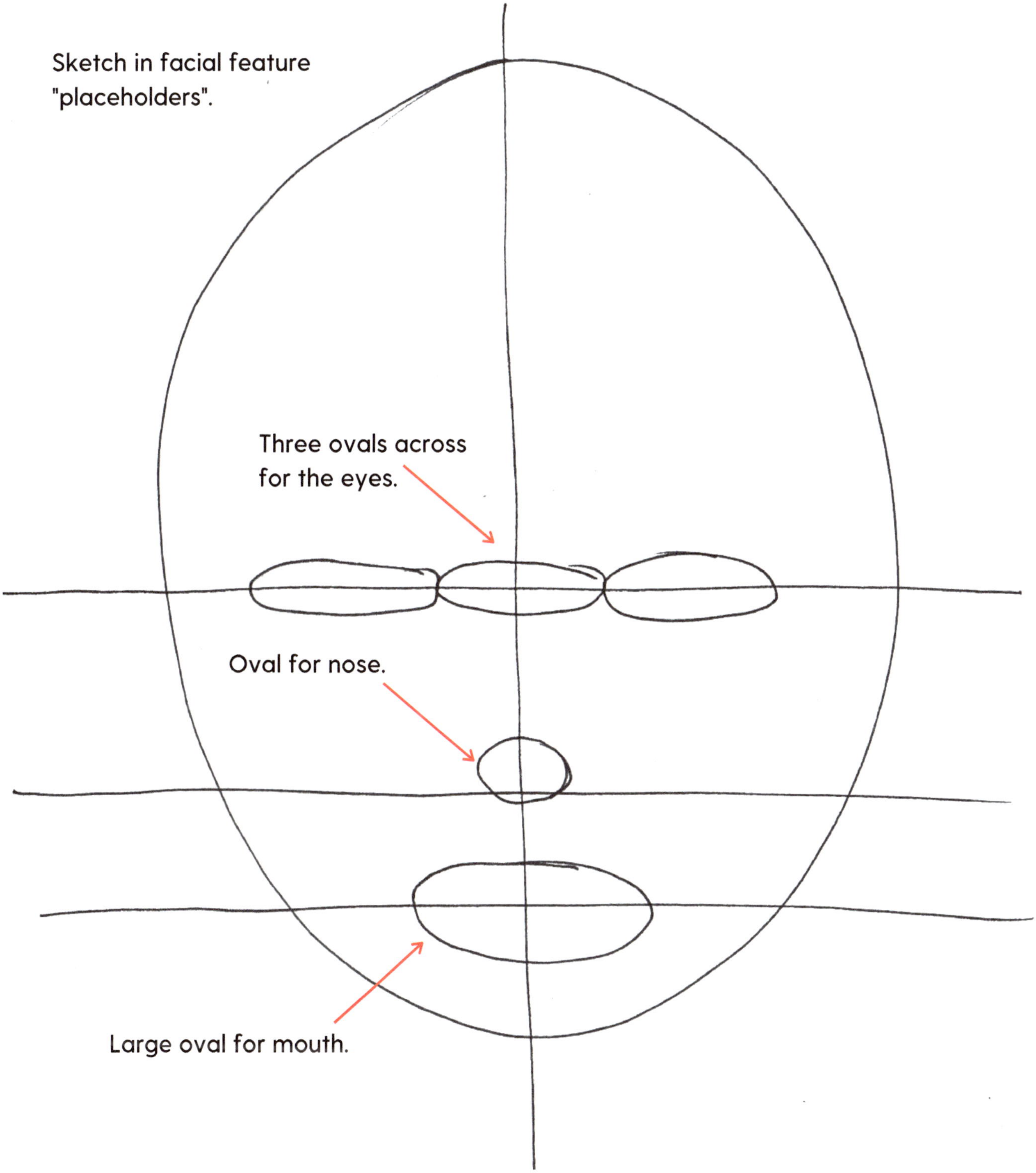

Three ovals across for the eyes.

Oval for nose.

Large oval for mouth.

11

Native American

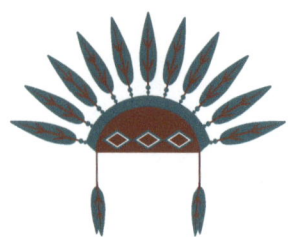

Draw the outline for the hair. Note how it goes ABOVE the head oval AND INTO the area that will be the face.

head oval

Now you can add the eyebrows over the eye place-holders.

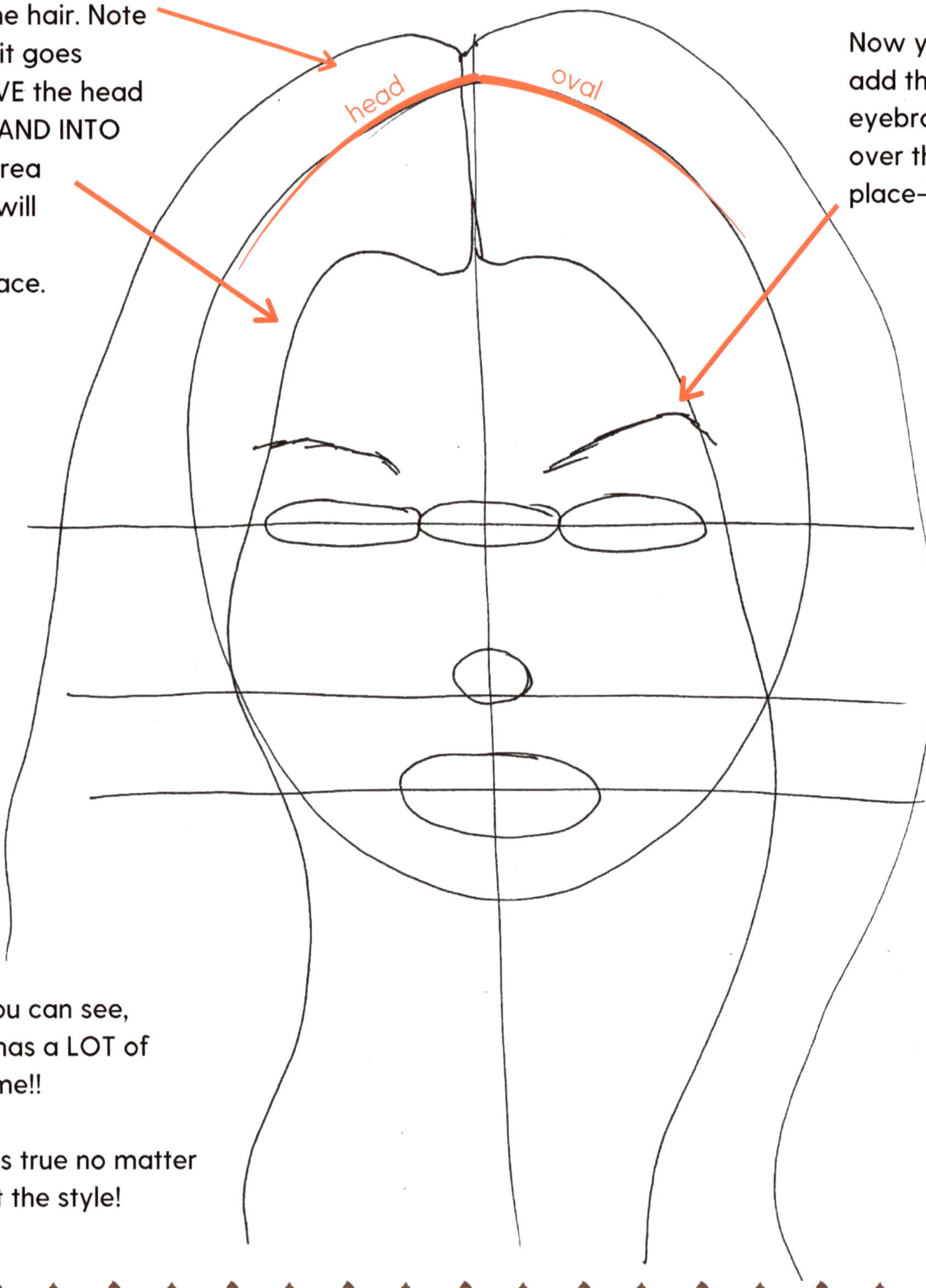

As you can see, hair has a LOT of volume!!

This is true no matter what the style!

12

Native American

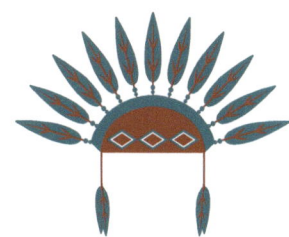

It's perfectly okay for your outlines to be different than mine. These are "whimsical faces" afterall!

Refine the shapes of the facial features a bit.

Add small eyelids.

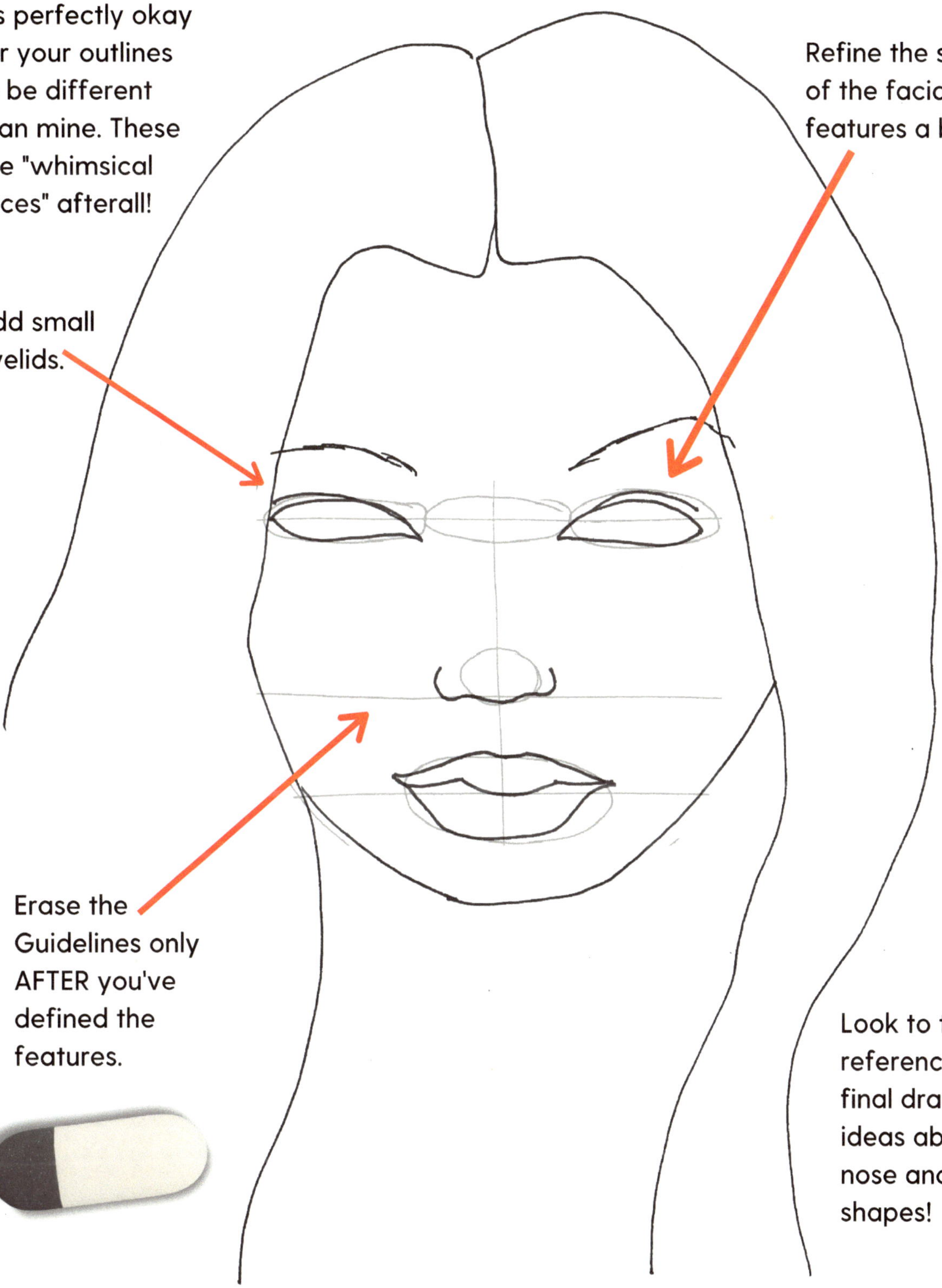

Erase the Guidelines only AFTER you've defined the features.

Look to the reference (my final drawing) for ideas about lip, nose and eye shapes!

Native American

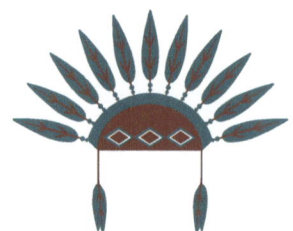

Add a few more sections of hair.

Add a braid detail.

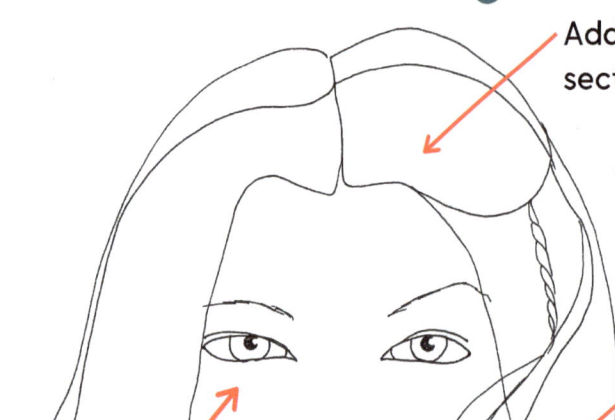

Rough in some feather shapes.

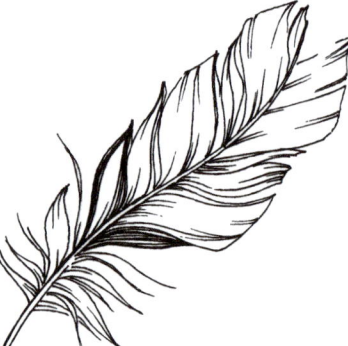

Add irises and pupils to the eyes.

Add more feather details.

Add more hair sections.

Color as desired!

For every whimsical woman in this book, I'm using a combination of Copic markers and colored pencils! However, you'll see my students are far more creative than I and used lots of different art supplies!

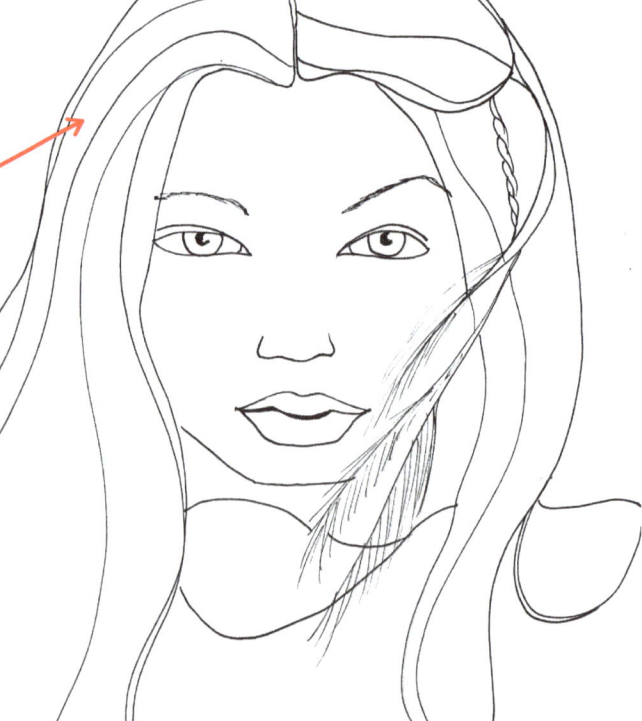

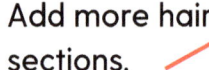

Native American

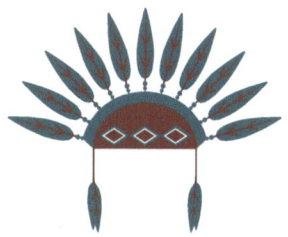

For each portrait in this book, I'll show you my step-by-step coloring process. For this first one though, I'm going one step further by taking you behind-the-scenes so you can see my ENTIRE process which begins long before I even put marker to paper!

1. First, take a moment and stare at the reference (Page 9). Try to really get a good handle on the colors you see! Can you find markers in your collection that look like the colors in the picture?
If so, pull them out and set them aside.

2. Then, just to make sure the markers you choose are going to work, start testing them out on a separate sheet of paper. Do they look like the skin colors (and clothes colors) you'll be coloring? If yes, great! Make sure you have 3-6 colors for the skin. The more shades you use creates a look that has more dimension (plus it's fun!).

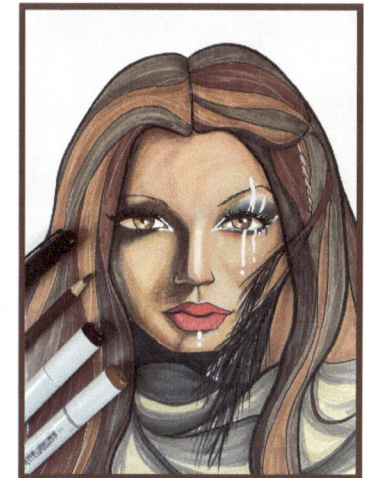

3. Then swatch them all next to each other to see how they overlap. Will they blend well? Are the colors close enough together in value that they'll segue nicely from one shade to the next?

The coolest part is that crayons, pencils, watercolors and paints can all be layered just like I'm showing you here with my Copic markers and colored pencils. All you have to do is substitute your favorite art supply and follow the steps I lay out for you in this book. If you're still unsure, you can watch all the lessons on YouTube! So fun! And it's 100% free! To see all 15 video lessons, simply visit https://bit.ly/whimsicalwomen

Native American

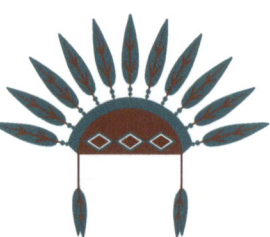

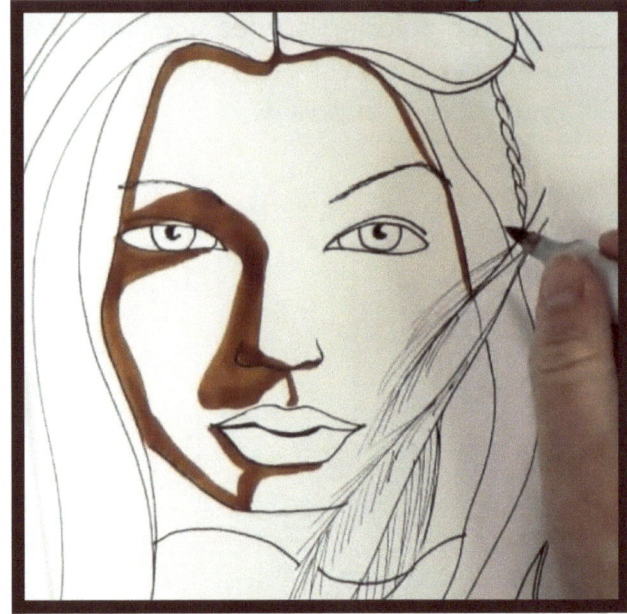

Step 1. Once you have selected your 3-5 skin colors from dark to light, apply the darkest color first. I am using a photographic reference so I am careful to copy where the darkest parts are.

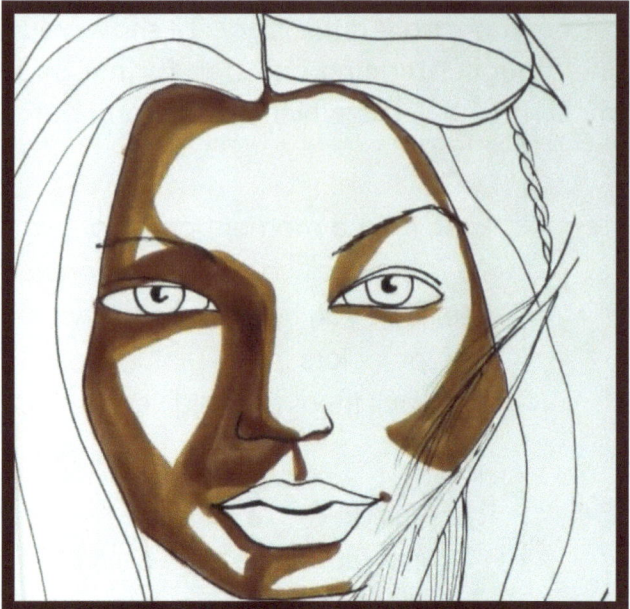

Step 2. Apply the second darkest color next. Notice it blends really well with the first color. The shift from one value to the next is so subtle you hardly notice it! That's how closely your colors should relate.

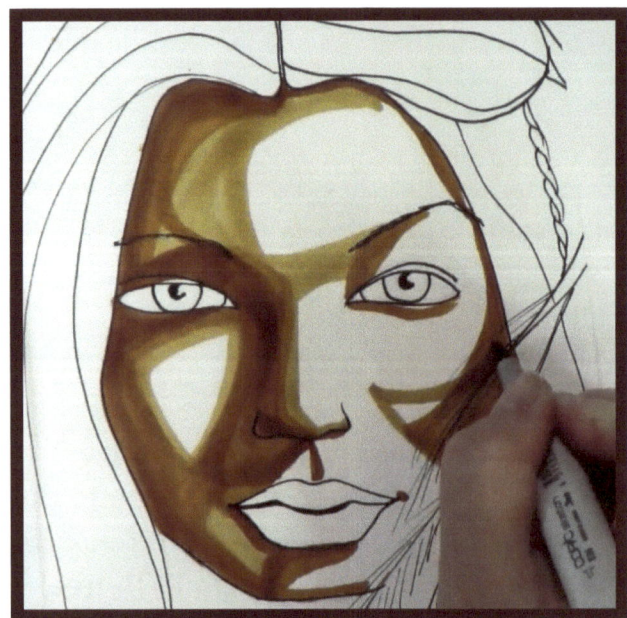

Step 3. Now add the 3rd darkest shade.

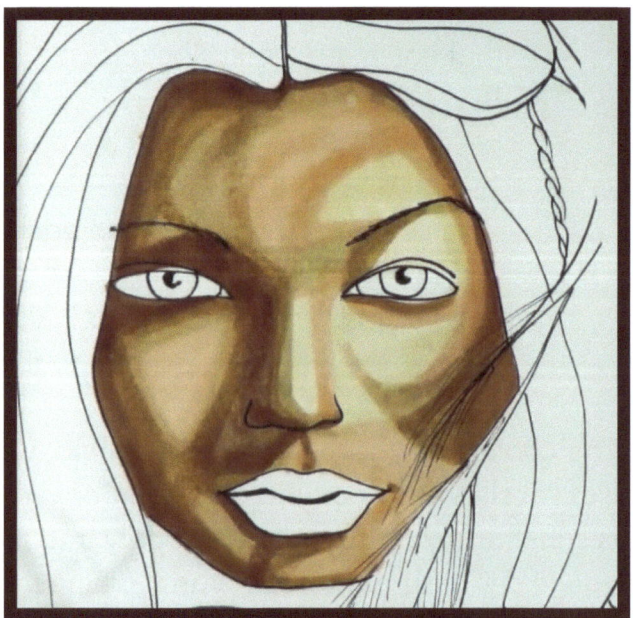

Step 4. Then add the lightest shade.

Native American

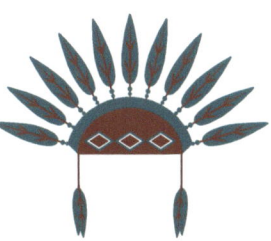

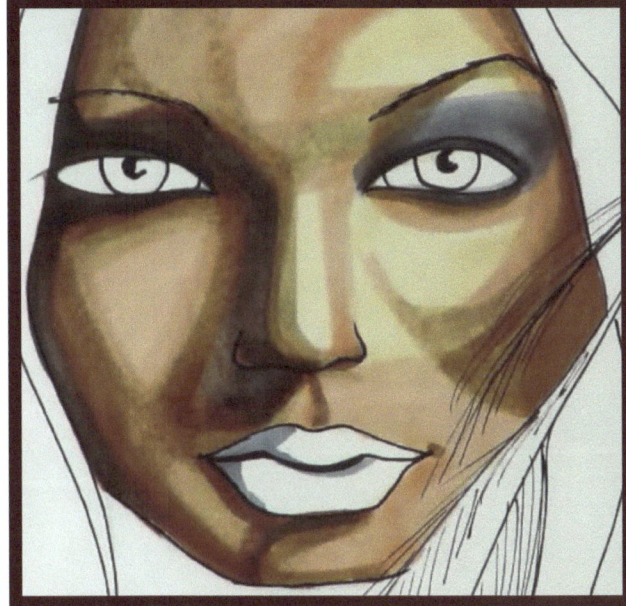

Step 5. Use a medium grey shade to add more shading in the darkest areas: around eyes and to the left side (in shadow).

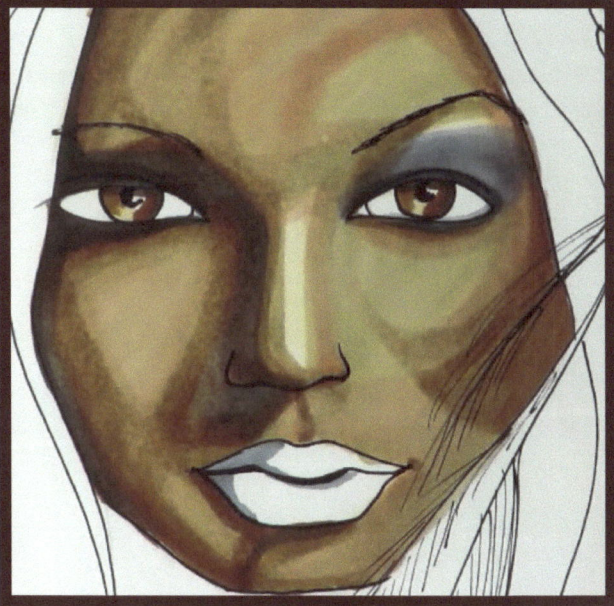

Step 6. Go over the ENTIRE face with a light shade (this would be the 5th and final shade) to blend all the colors together. Color eyes in with different shades of brown.

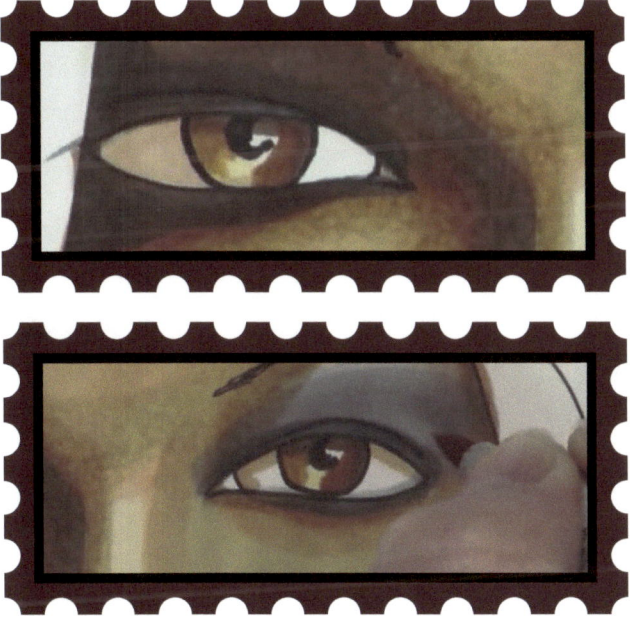

Step 7. Add shading to whites of the eyes.

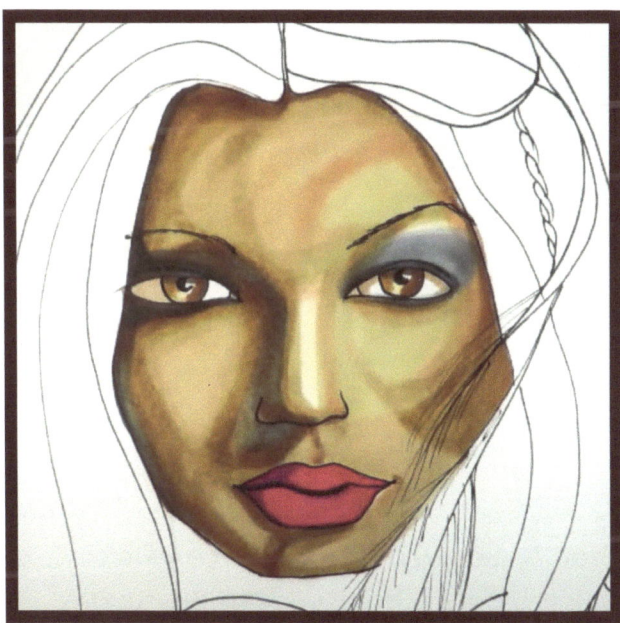

Step 8. Color in the lips.

Native American

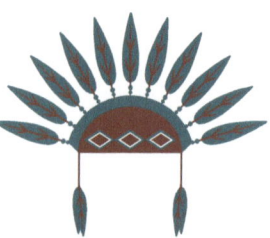

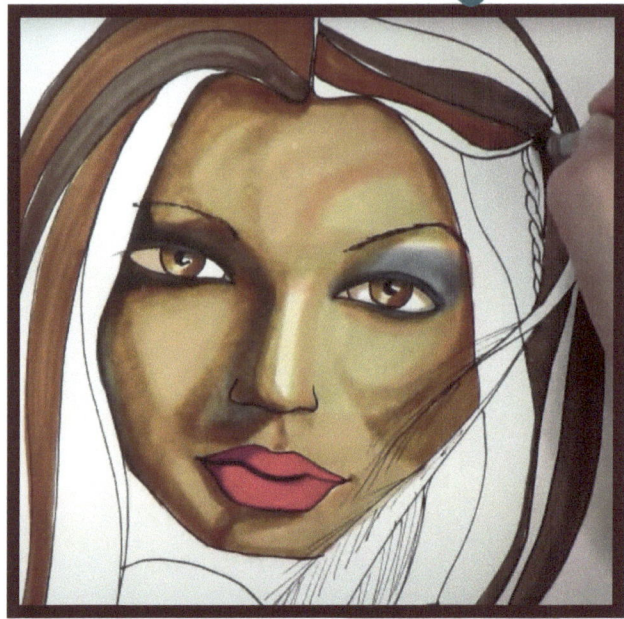

Step 9. Color in the different sections of hair in alternating shades of brown.

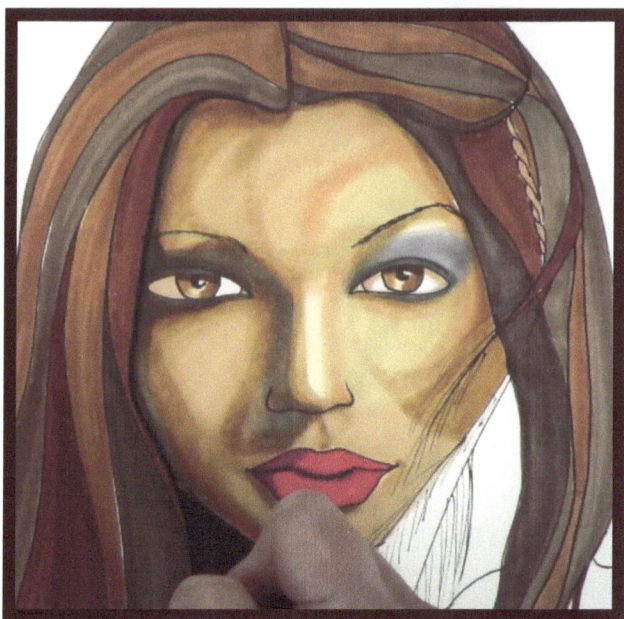

Step 10. Use a thick, bold, black marker to define and outline the overall hair shape.

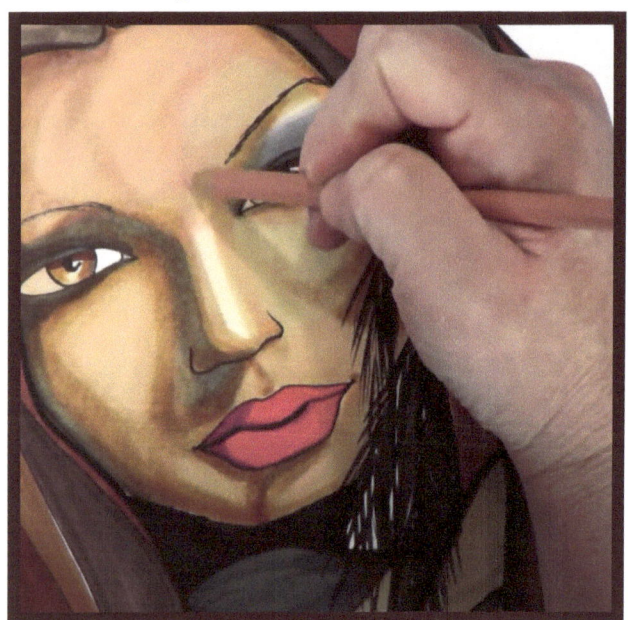

Step 11. Go over the entire face with a colored pencil. This blends all the shades and helps ease the transition between the shades of marker colors underneath.

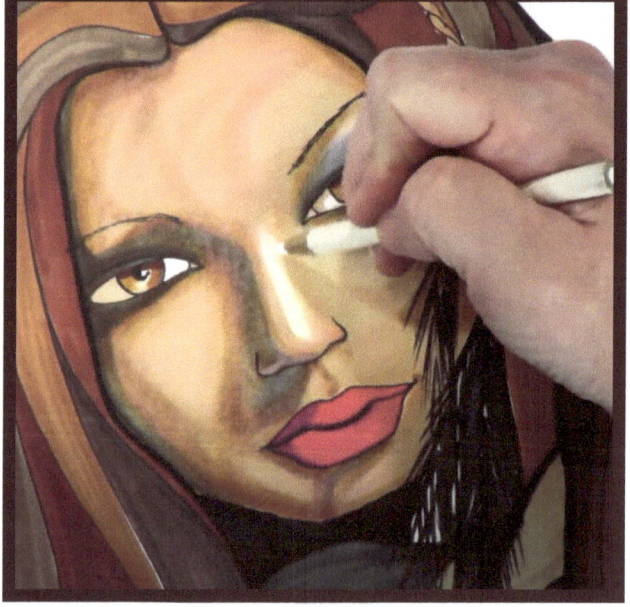

Step 12. Use a white colored pencil to accentuate any highlighted areas. In this case that is the nose bridge and the right brow bone.

Native American

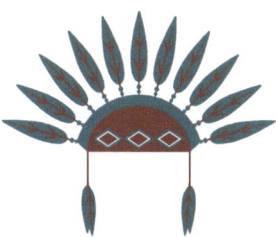

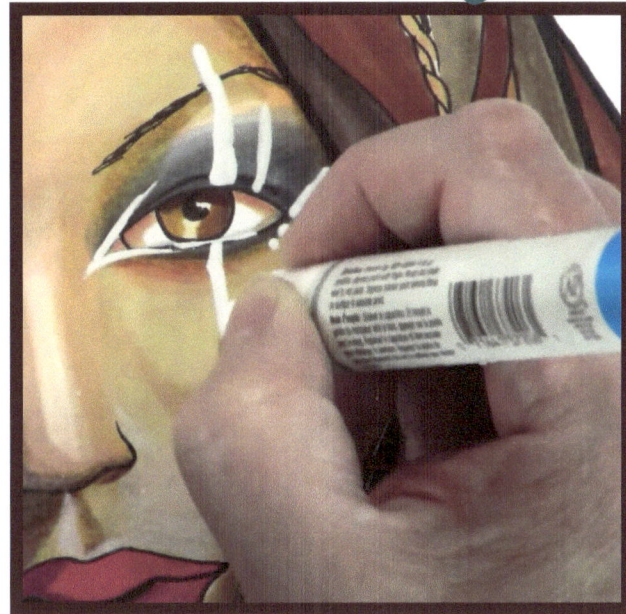

Step 13. With a paint pen, draw on the tribal paint design and the eye sparkle!

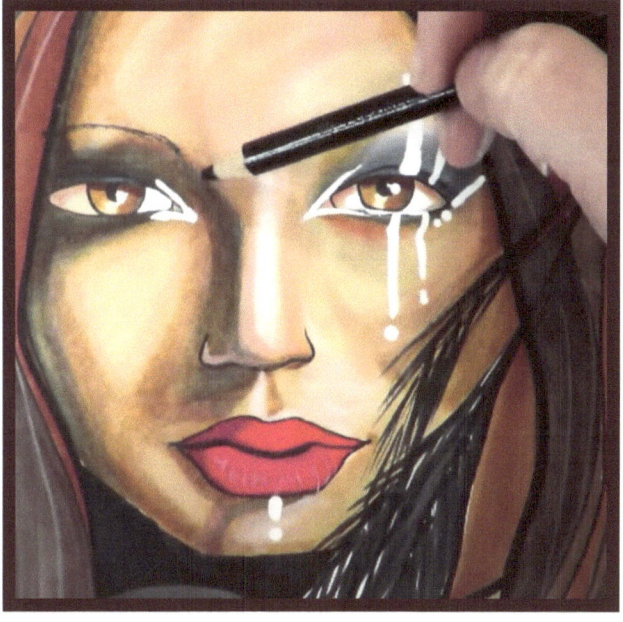

Step 14. Add any last minute shading with a dark pencil. I'm using Indigo.

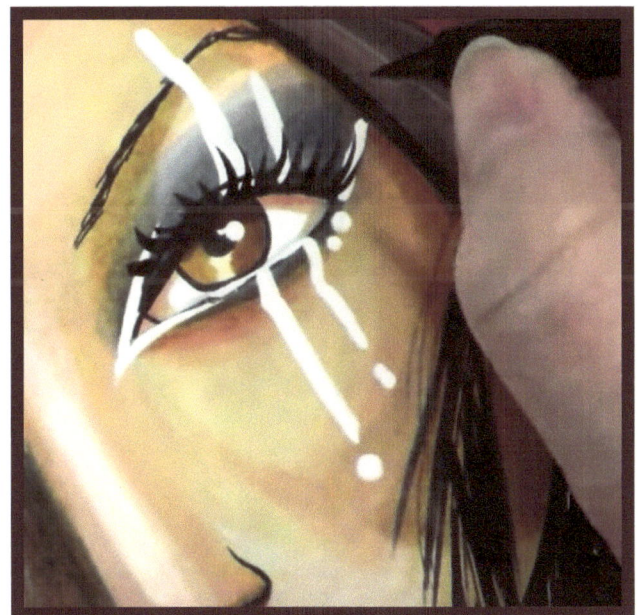

Step 15. Apply lashes. My favorite art supply for drawing eyelashes in the Pentel Pocket Brush Pen! Results are stunning and fast!

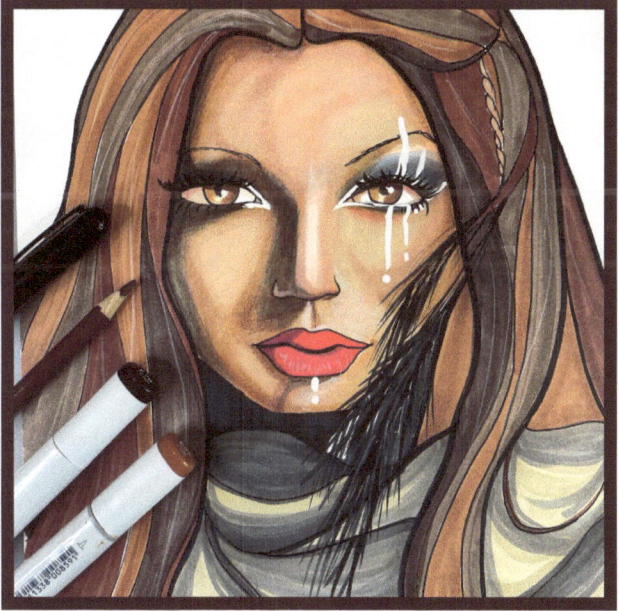

Step 16. Color in her wrap with shades of grey and gold/green. Turn to page 20 to see how others chose to bring their drawings to life!

Student Spotlight

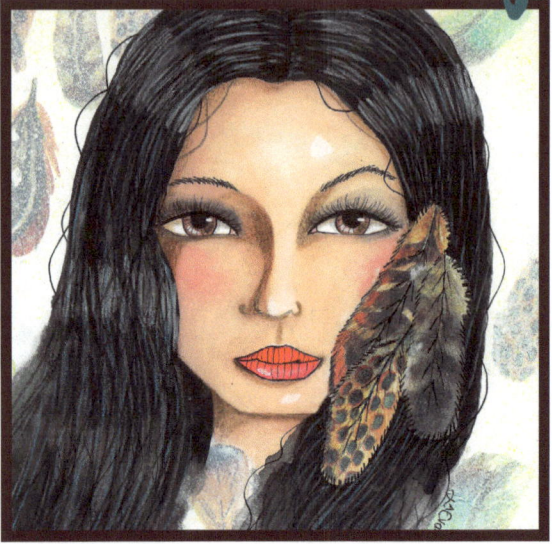

Leigh-Ann Evans. Created with watercolour paint and pencils with colored pencils on top. *"I love the flow and blend-ability of water-soluble mediums."*

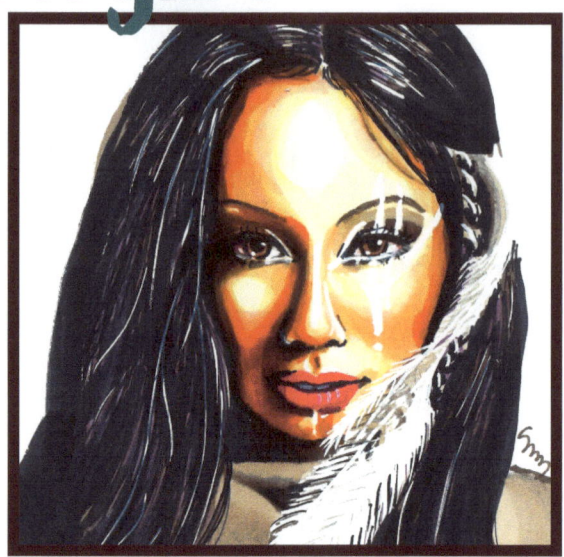

Zsuzsanna Bimbo. Created with Promarkers and White Sharpie. *"I chose these mediums after I had some lessons with Karen and I was surprised how my drawings turned out!"*

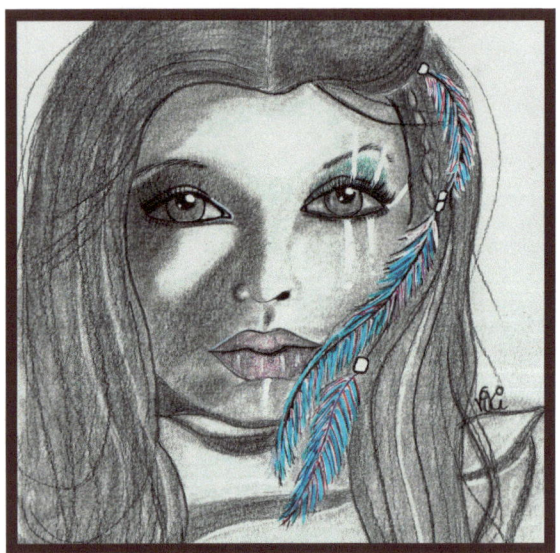

Viki Colonna. Graphite and acrylic paint. *"I am such a beginner and I am using what I have at this point."*

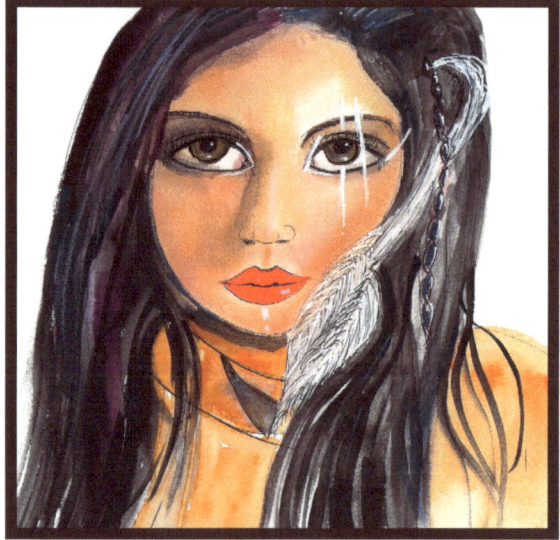

Felicia Boros. *"I used Pan pastels for her face because of the texture, watercolors and other mixed media."*

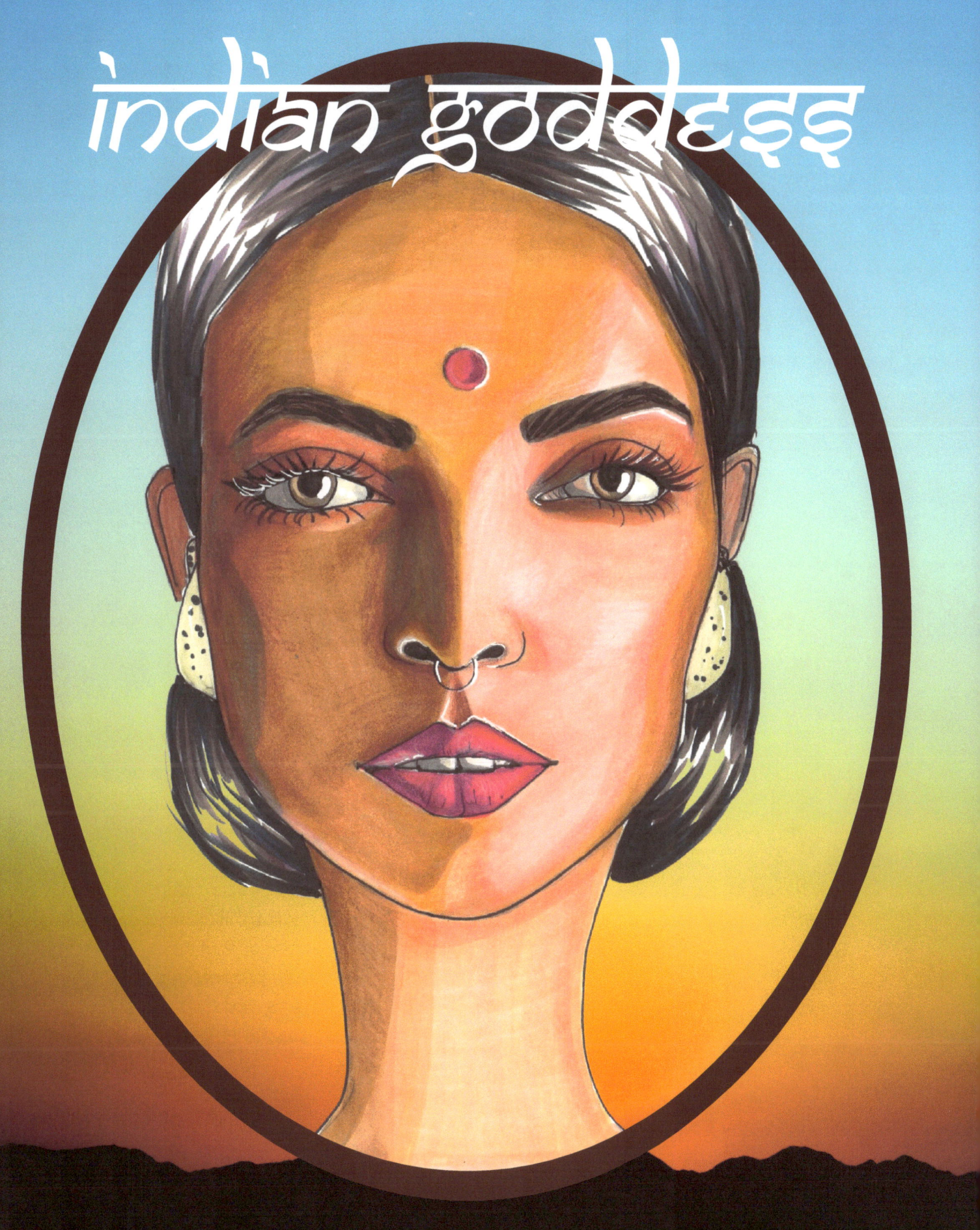

indian

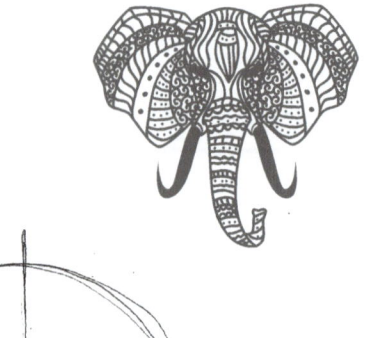

Begin with a simple oval. Add the guidelines in the exact same way we did for the Native American.

eye

nose

mouth

Add lines for the neck.

I love a thinner neck for my whimsical women!

Add the squished ovals or "place-holders" for all the features of the face.

The three ovals positioned this way for this woman sets up us for the correction proportions of the nostrils and gets us ready for the nose ring later!

indian

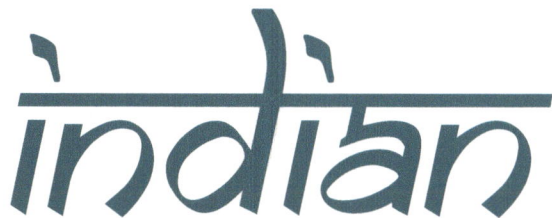
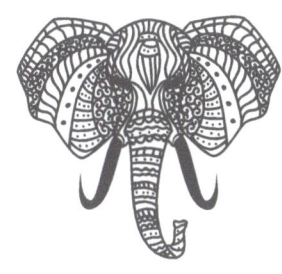

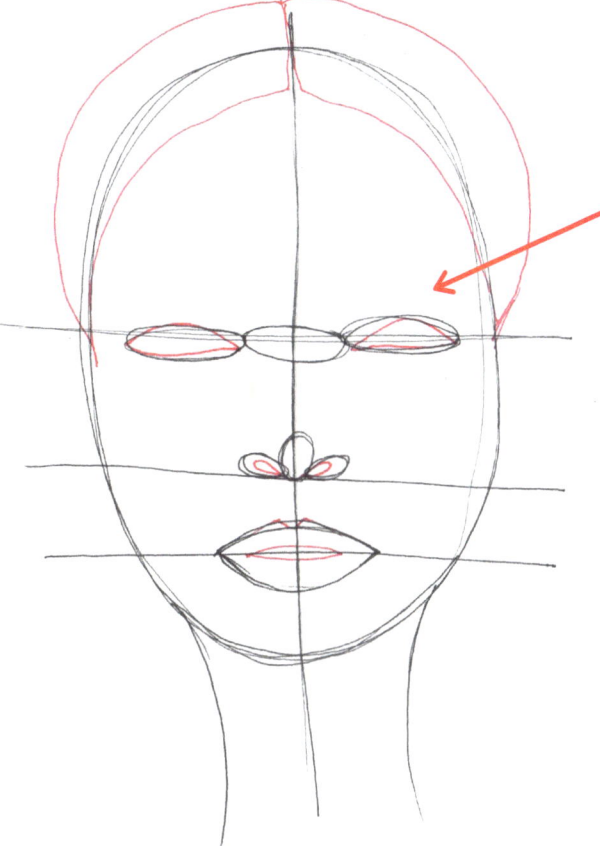

Refine the eye shapes.

Be careful to create the shapes within these original ovals so they don't end up being too large.

Add the outline for the hair. As always, the hair has volume so make sure your lines go above and into the head oval shape!

When you're happy with the shape of things, erase your guidelines.

Notice how uneven the ears are. That's okay! When you're learning to draw faces, you'll often find little things "off" here and there.

Don't worry about it! These little differences happen when drawing and is part of the learning process.

Plus, this is the "whimsy" I love so much and real humans have these exact kinds of discrepancies so it's perfectly okay!

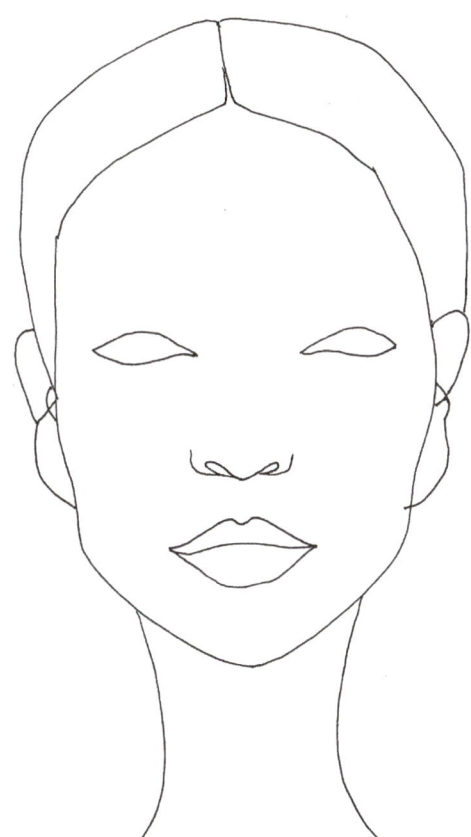

indian

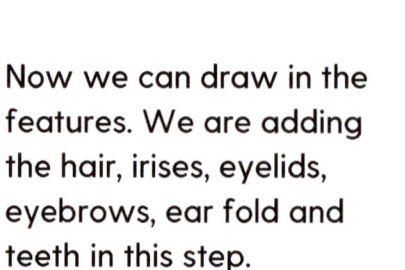

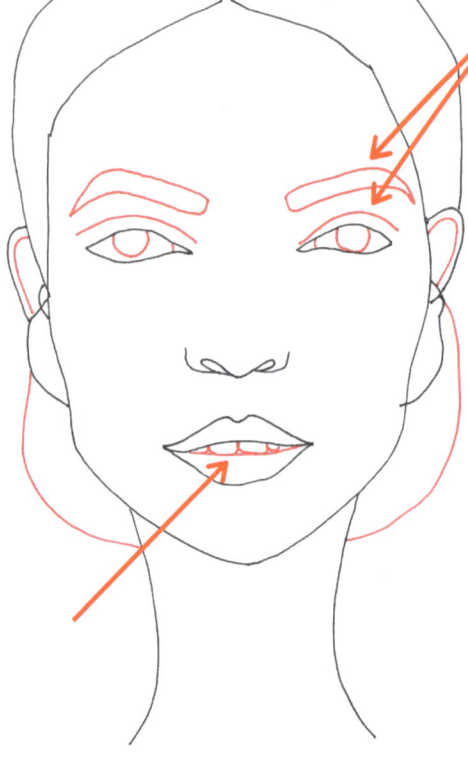

Now we can draw in the features. We are adding the hair, irises, eyelids, eyebrows, ear fold and teeth in this step.

You got this!!

Feel free to use a little circle template to help you draw the circles for her bindi (dot), irises, nose ring and pupils!

That's what I do!

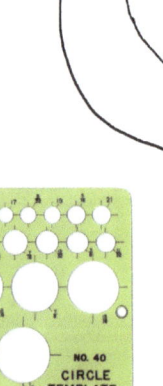

indian

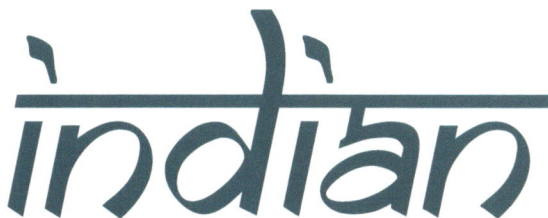

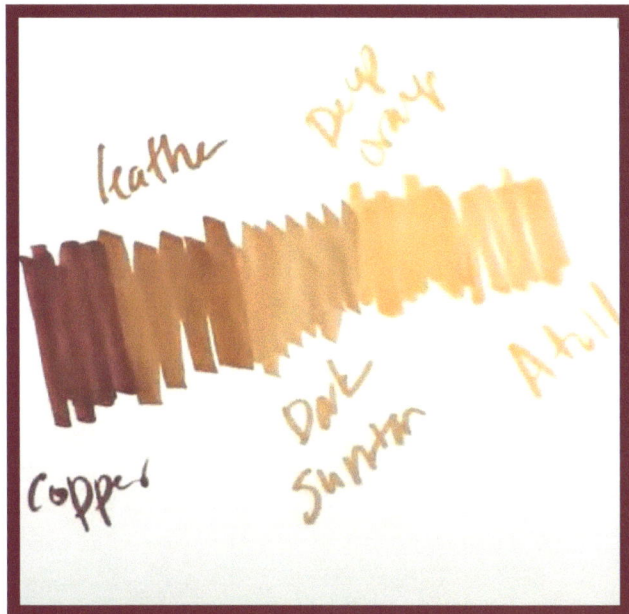

Step 1. Have a color plan ahead of time. Pick out 3-6 skin tones.

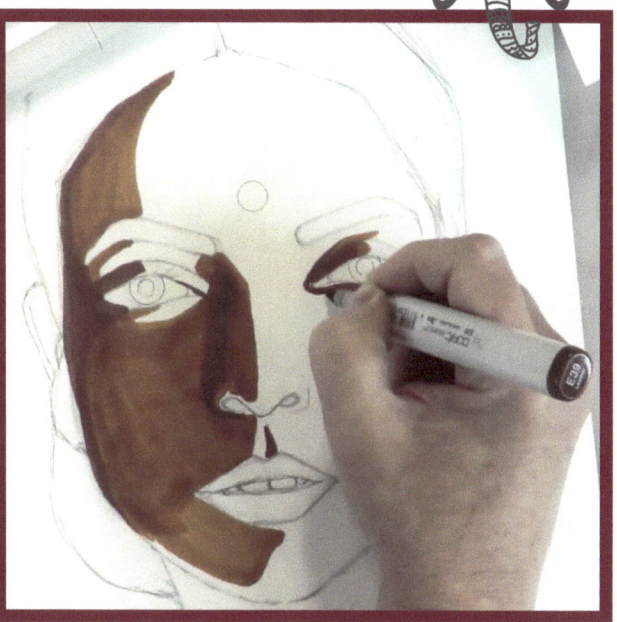

Step 2. Add the 2 darkest shades first. Only apply it to the darkest areas in shadow.

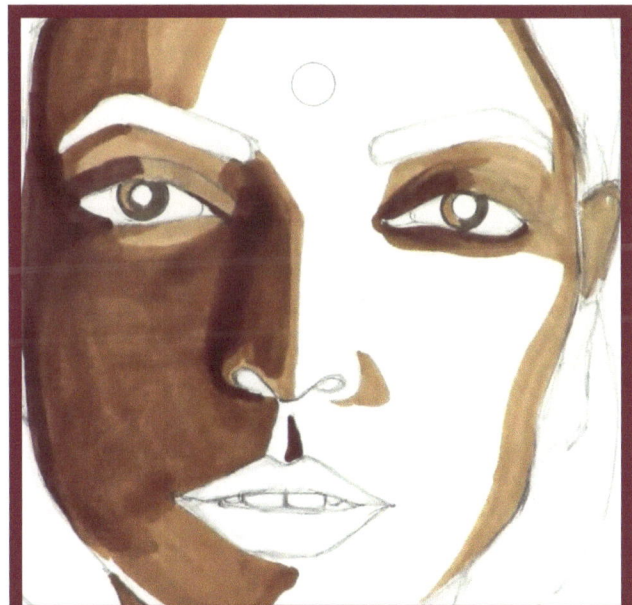

Step 3. Add the 3rd shade next. Careful to blend into the first 2 shades. Add the same colors to the irises.

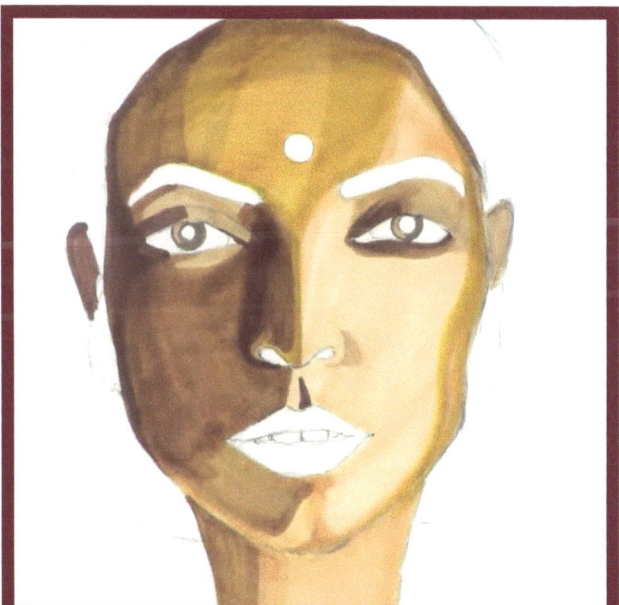

Step 4. Color in the entire face with the lightest shade. Add even a 5th shade for added drama! Here I'm adding it to the forehead and along the right side only.

indian

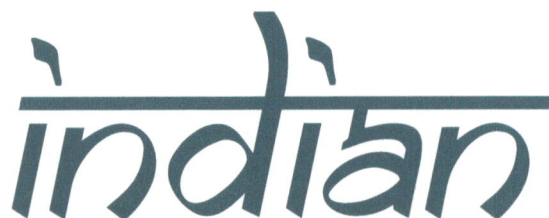

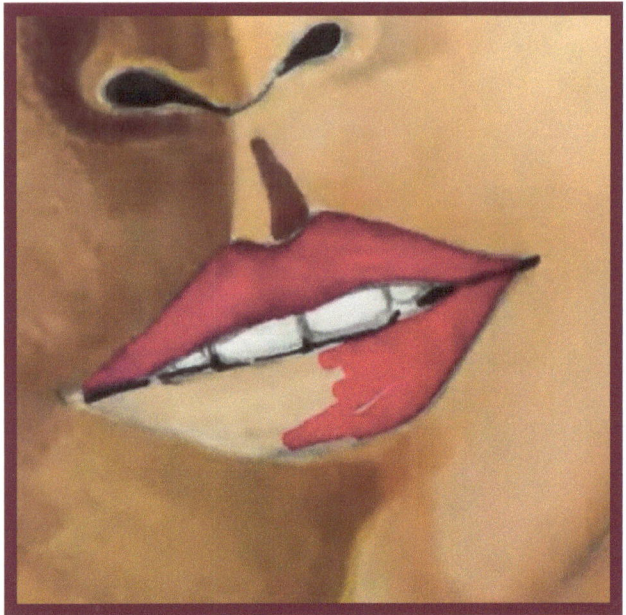

Step 5. Color the lips in red (or however you like)!

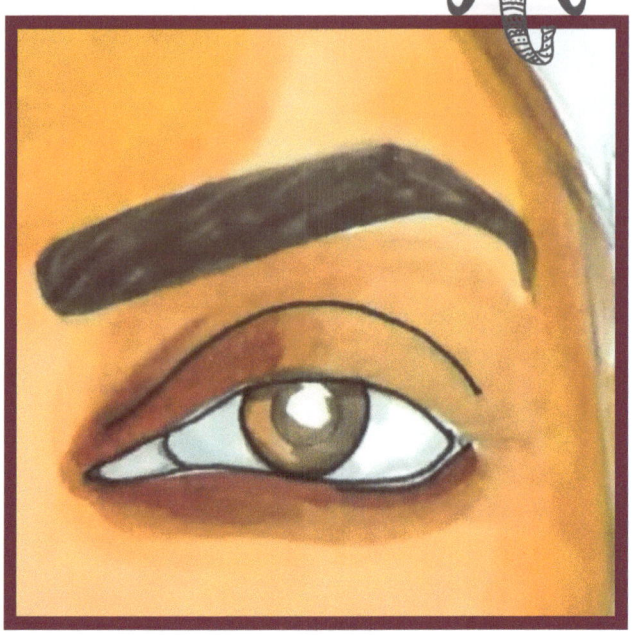

Step 6. Add Grey to the whites of the eyes. Color in brows. Outline everything in black.

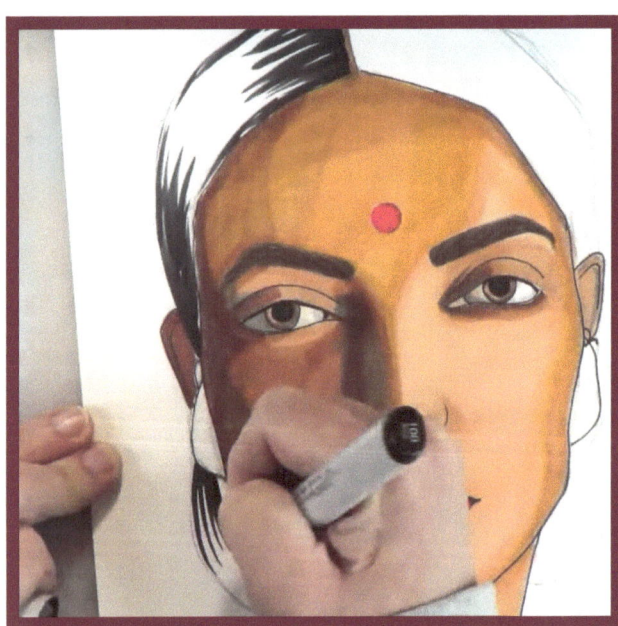

Step 7. Color the roots and ends of the hair with black. Leave a large area of white in the middle for a highlight.

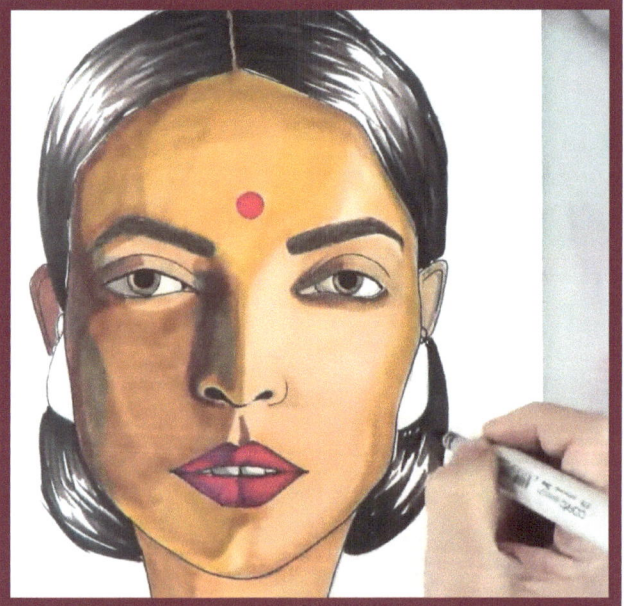

Step 8. With a brown (or just lighter color), color in the same sections of hair again only this time, go a bit further into the white space, but still leaving some white space.

indian

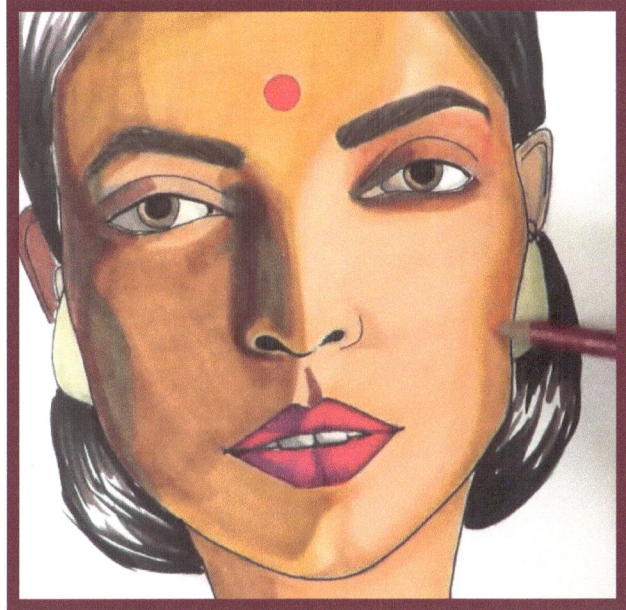

Step 9. Use colored pencils to add shading, highlights and to help blend between colors.

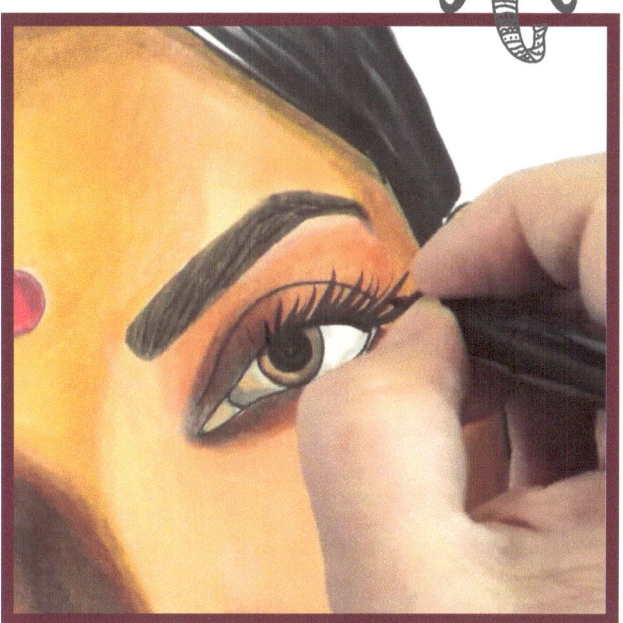

Step 10. Use a brush pen to draw eyelashes! Go slow, practice lots and have fun!

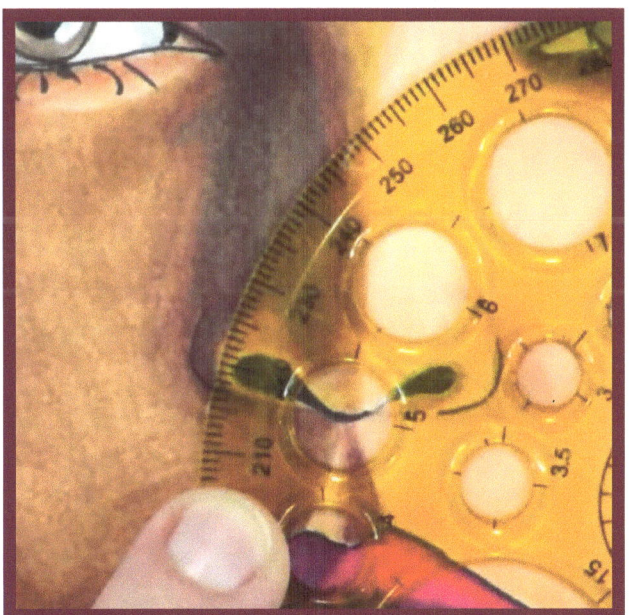

Step 11. Use a circle template to draw the nose ring with a pencil.

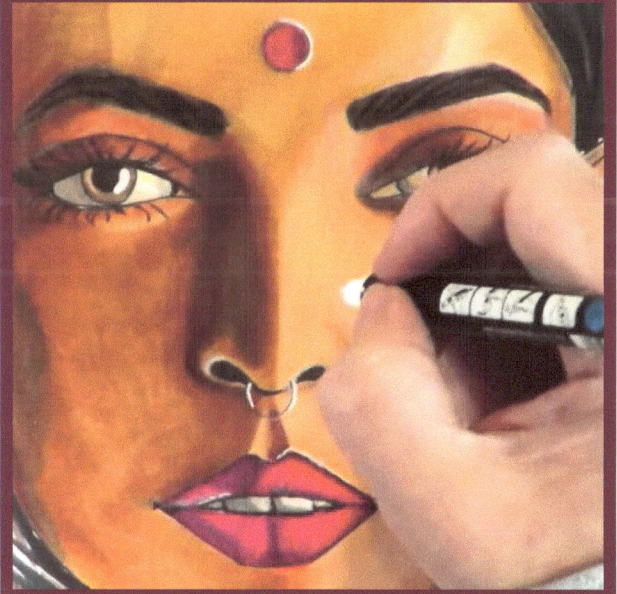

Step 12. Use a paint pen to add highlights to the eyes, nose ring, upper lip and bindi.

student work

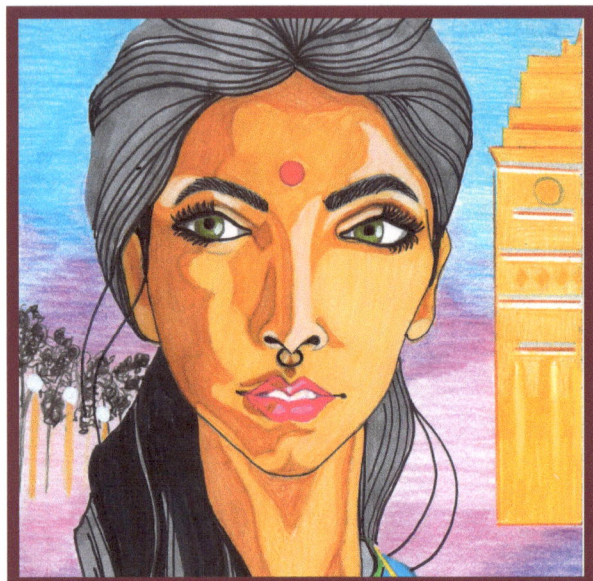

Pam Burns. Used HB pencil, alcohol markers, colored pencils and paint marker. *"I've been so happy (and surprised!) with what I am learning and hope to improve!"*

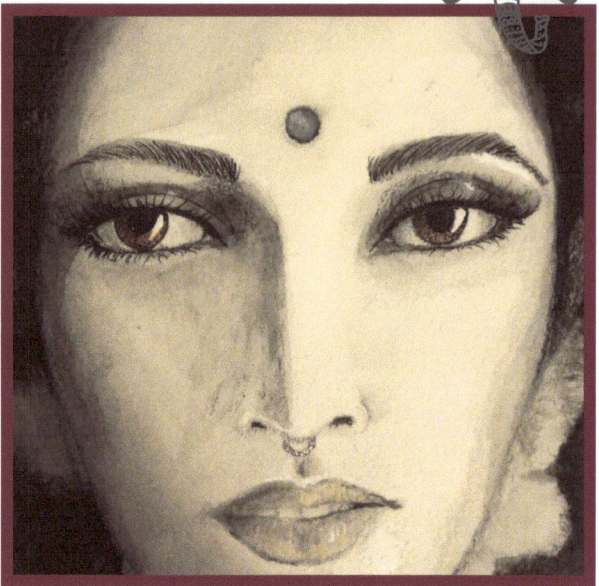

Darlene Hanna. Stabilo, water crayon and fine liner. *"Stabilo is amazing when water is applied and so much fun!!"*

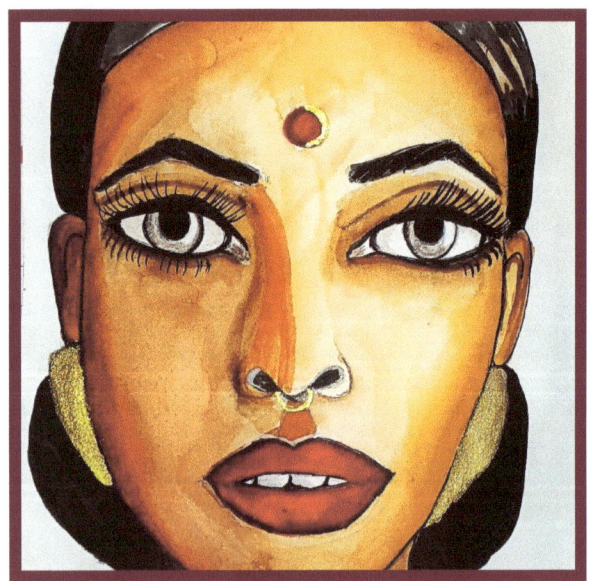

Jhilmil Jain. *"I used primarily watercolors since I love the fluidity of the medium, and a broad nib fountain pen for the outline of the face and lashes."*

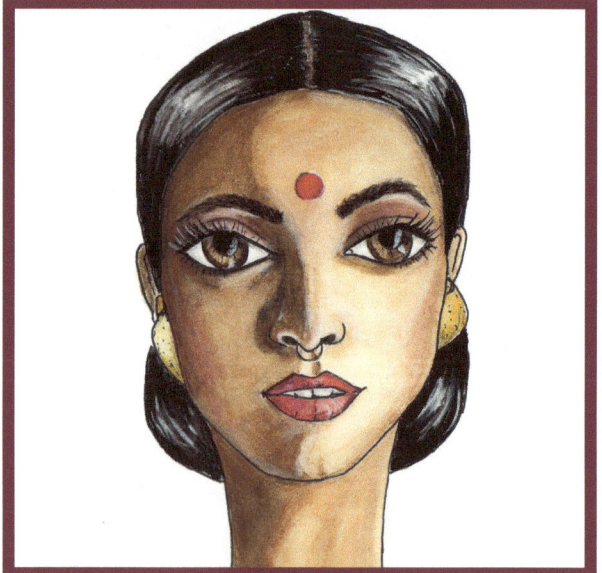

Jamie Drake. Watercolors and Prismacolor colored pencils and black Sharpie. *"I love getting the base color with watercolor and it works so well with colored pencils."*

Scottish Lass

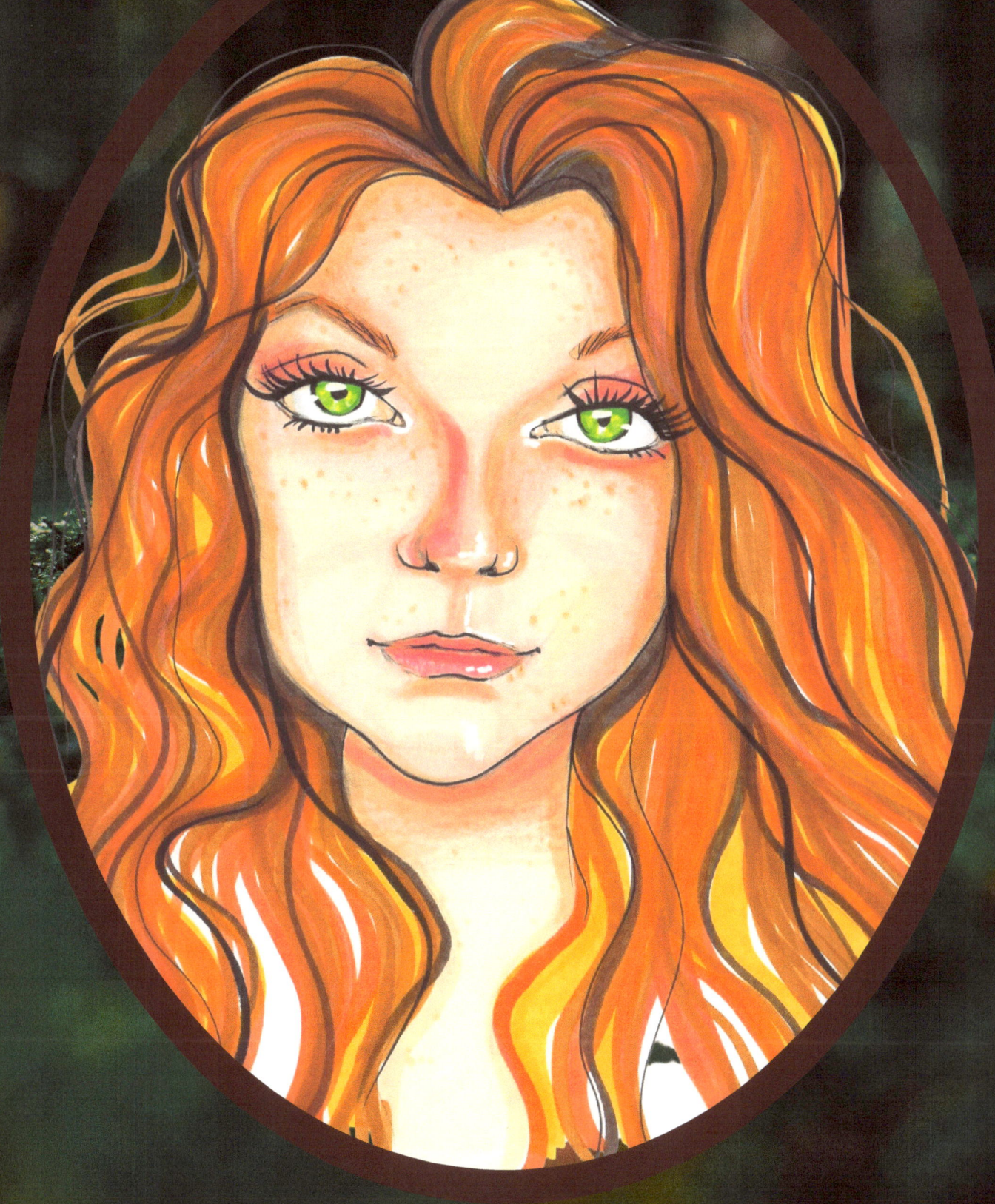

Scot

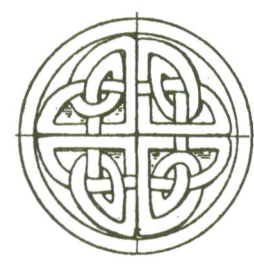

As always, start with an oval.

Place the guidelines as shown. It is okay if things are approximate at this stage. We will fine-tune soon!

Make three ovals across for the eyes. This fiery red-head has large eyes so they can be a little less squished than before!

Her nose is a bit broader so draw three circles to help you this time!

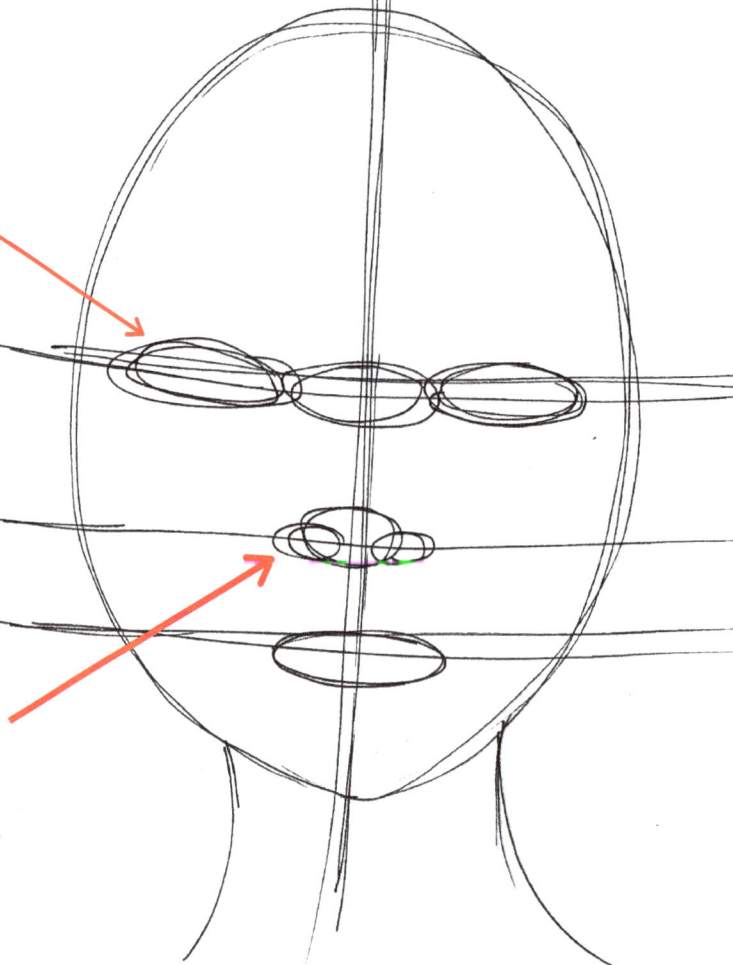

Scot

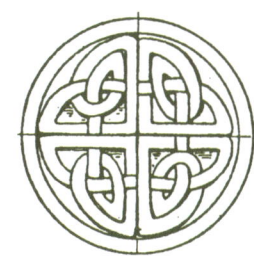

Before you erase the guidelines, sketch in the hair outline and refine the features.

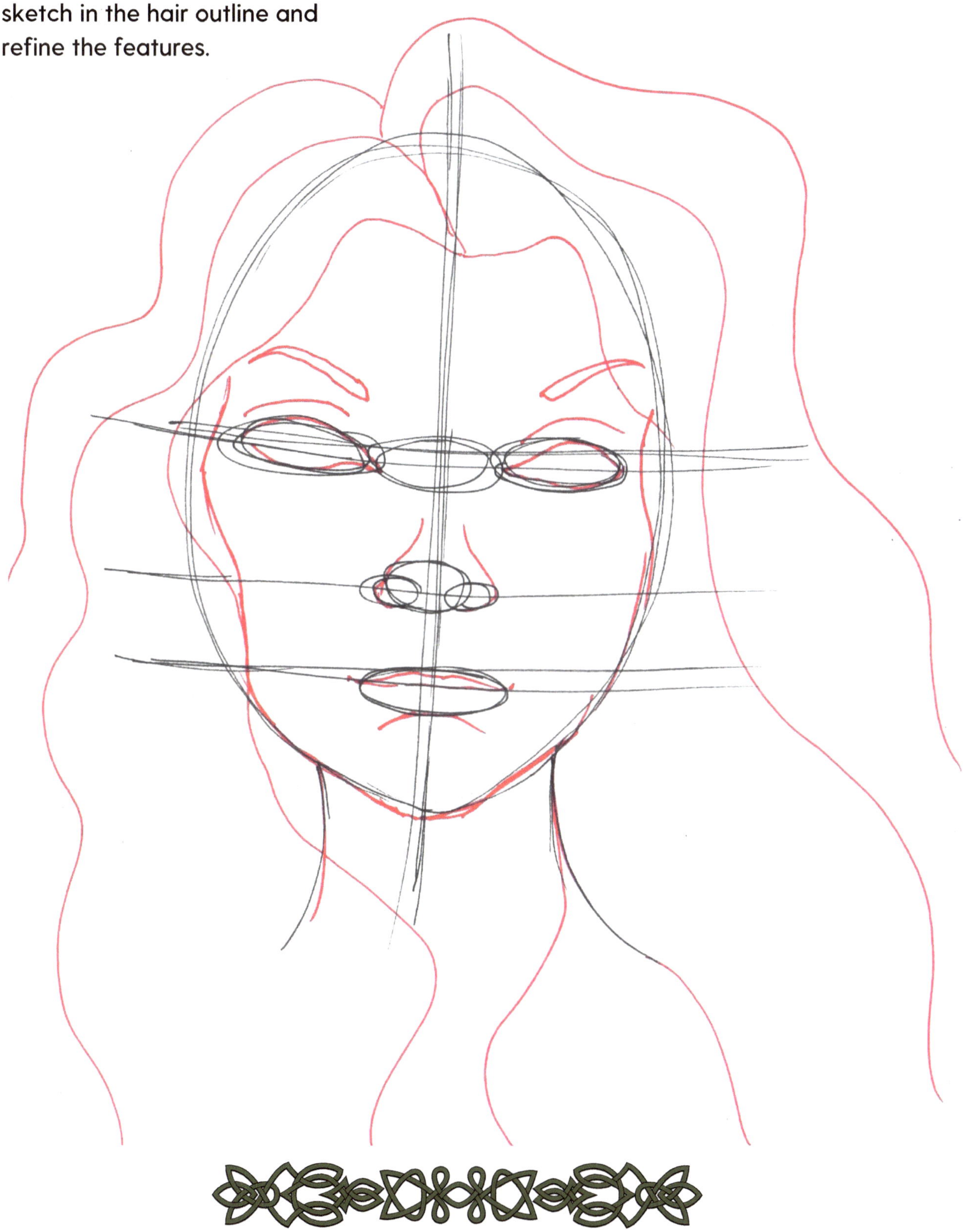

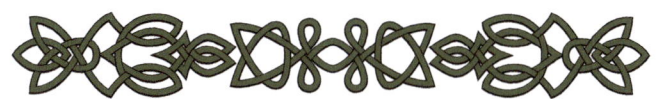

Scot

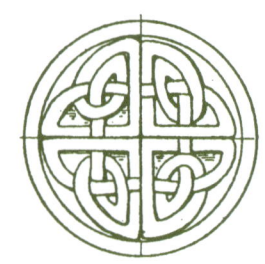

Let's take a closer look at the nose to get a better understanding of how we go from just ovals to a drawing....

It's the outside of the small ovals (on the left) that let you know where to place the small outline on the outside (on the right).

At the end of the day, it's all about the shading. Shading brings your faces and features to LIFE!

Step 1.   Step 2.   Step 3.

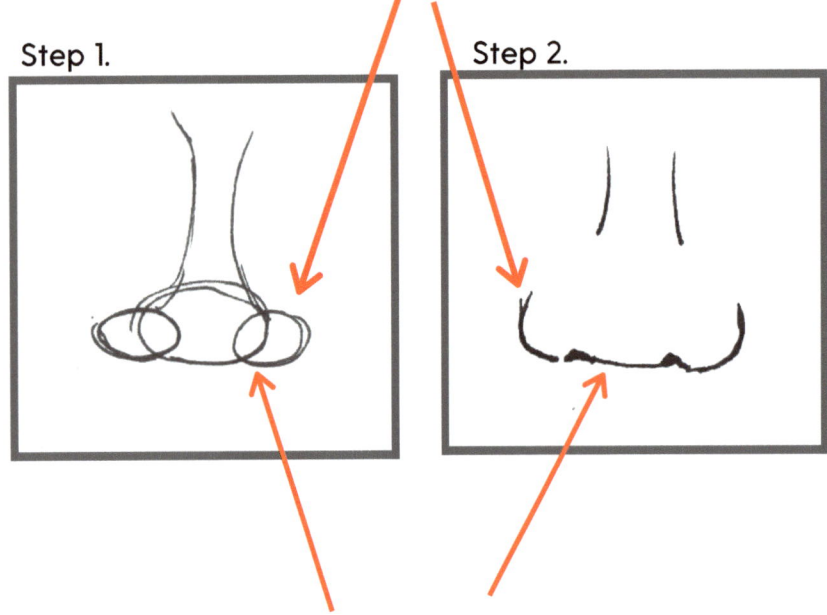

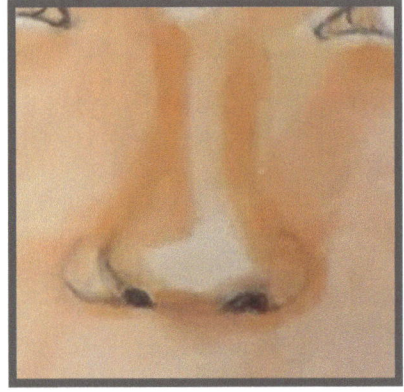

It's the little in-between areas (the intersection of the ovals) that let you know where to put the nostrils when it's time to erase the guidelines.

Instead of drawn lines for the nose bridge, we create the 3D illusion of the bridge by slowing building up a little extra color on either side.

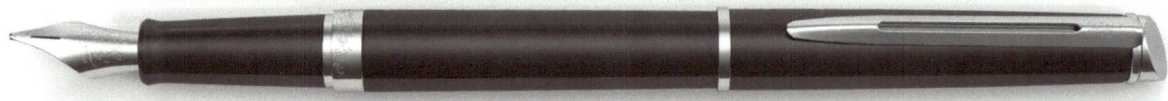

How much or how little you want to outline your drawings and selecting which lines to leave in or take out is entirely up to YOU! That's the freedom that drawing "whimsically" gives you. You have complete permission to create as you please! Whimsical faces are the best!

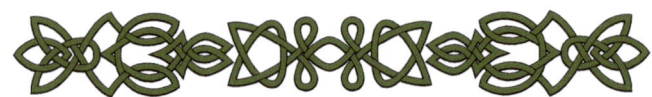

Scot

Erase the guidelines and add the irises and pupils.

You can add the chin line and nose lines VERY LIGHTLY to help you figure out where the subtle shading will go but those lines will disappear as you add color :)

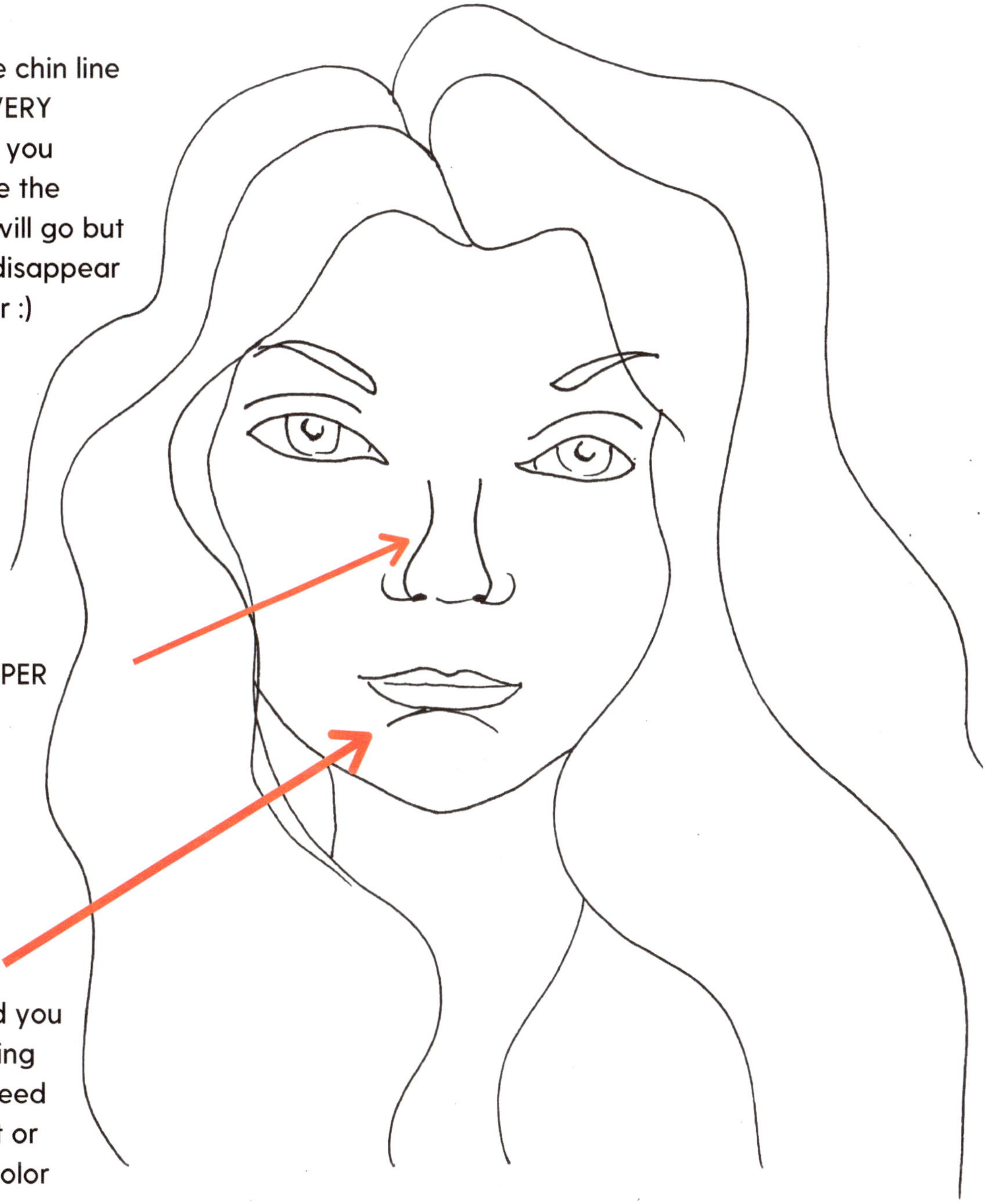

Sketch these SUPER lightly!

These lines are guidelines that help remind you where the shading will go! They'll need to be super light or erased before color is added.

Scot

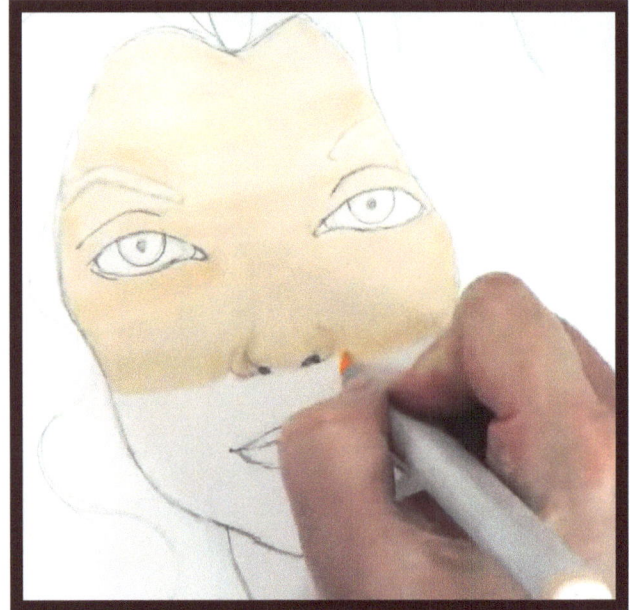

Step 1. Color in the entire face with the lightest peach tone skin color you can find.

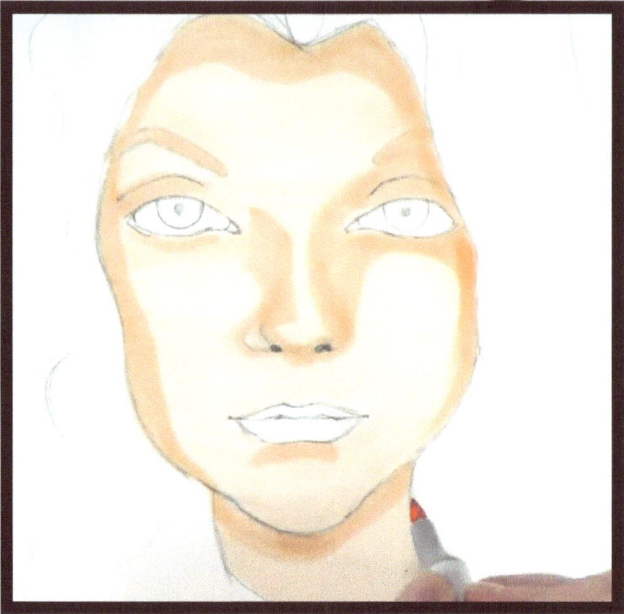

Step 2. Add one shade darker around the hairline, eyes, nose and under mouth & chin.

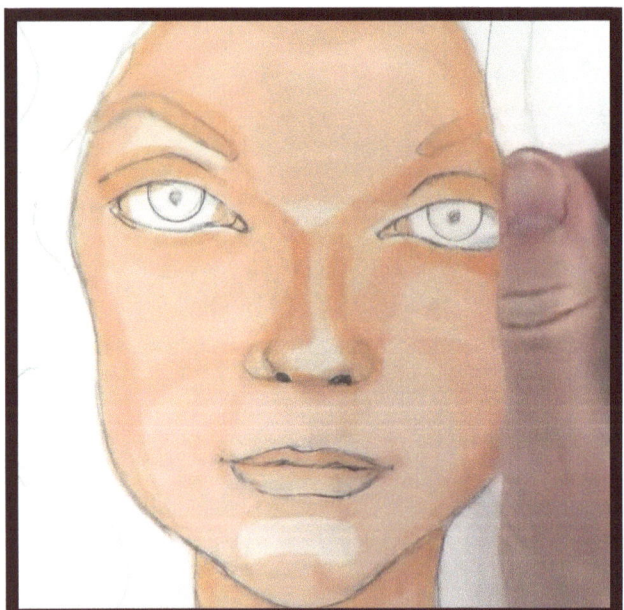

Step 3. Color the whole face again with another shade of light skin color (peach or pink).

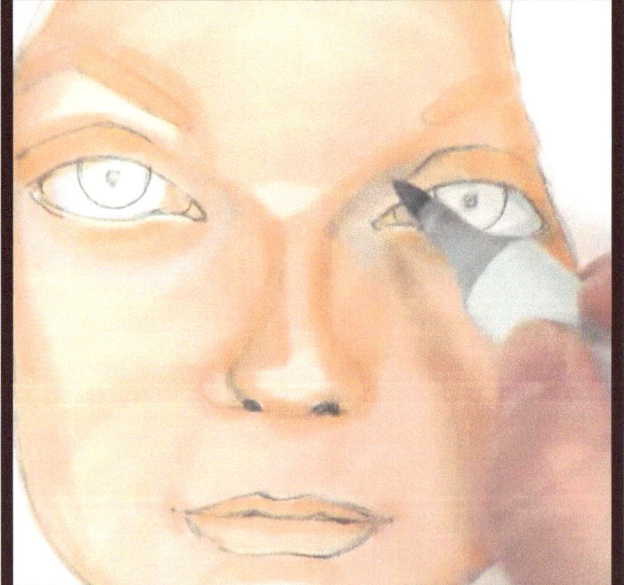

Step 4. Use a light grey to add shadow around the eyes and along nose bridge, under mouth and under chin.

Scot

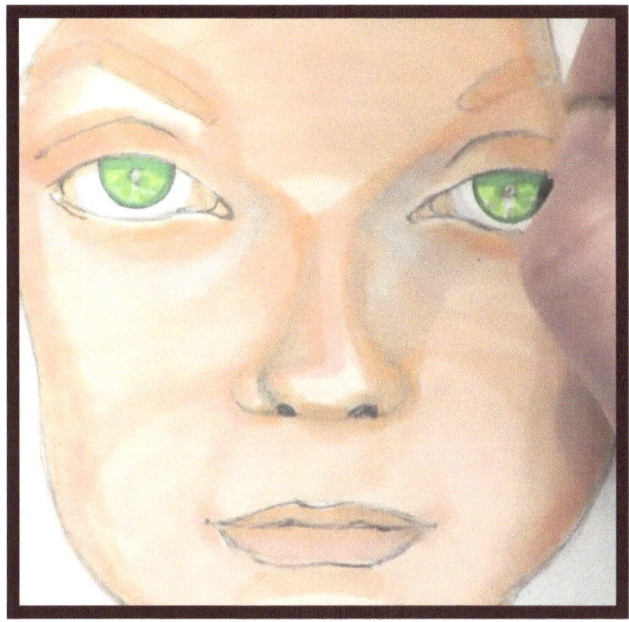

Step 5. Color the eyes with multiple shades of green!

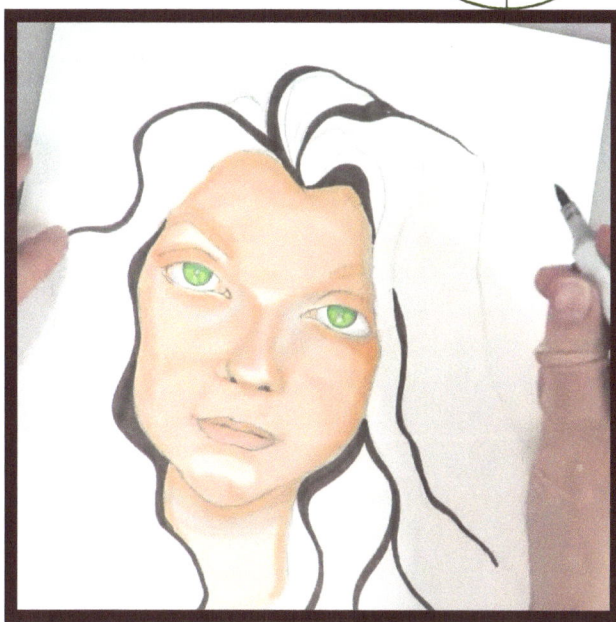

Step 6. Choose 3-6 shades of orange and brown for the hair. Begin with darkest first.

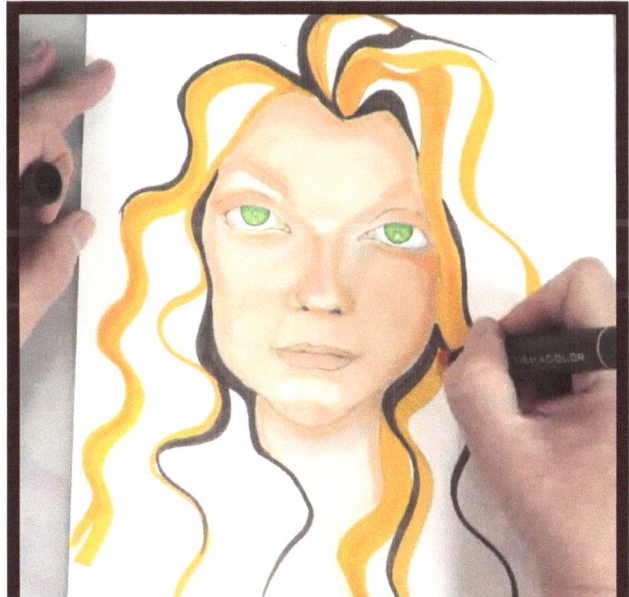

Step 7. Now add some light orange in sections. Follow the same waves throughout. This is whimsy style! Have fun!

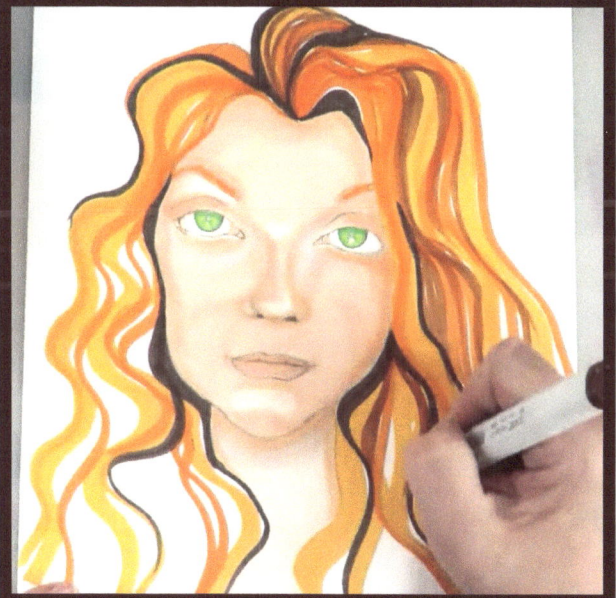

Step 8. Alternate your colors throughout, following the same waves as you go!

Scot

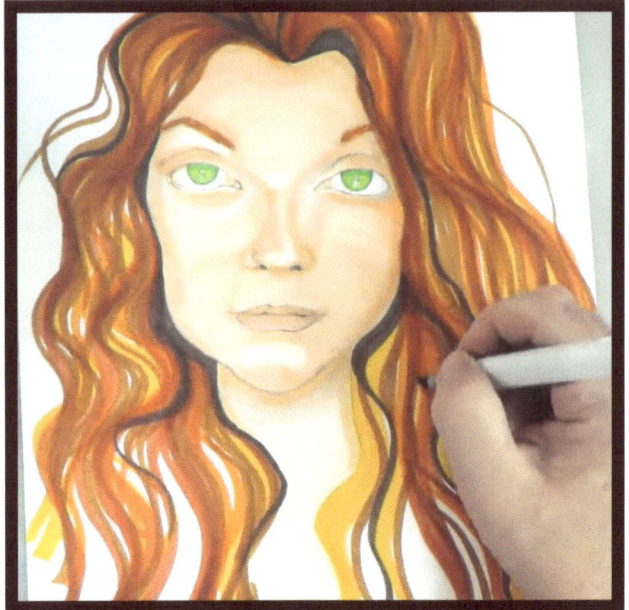

Step 9. Use all 3-5 colors and keep taking turns drawing the curvy hair strands!

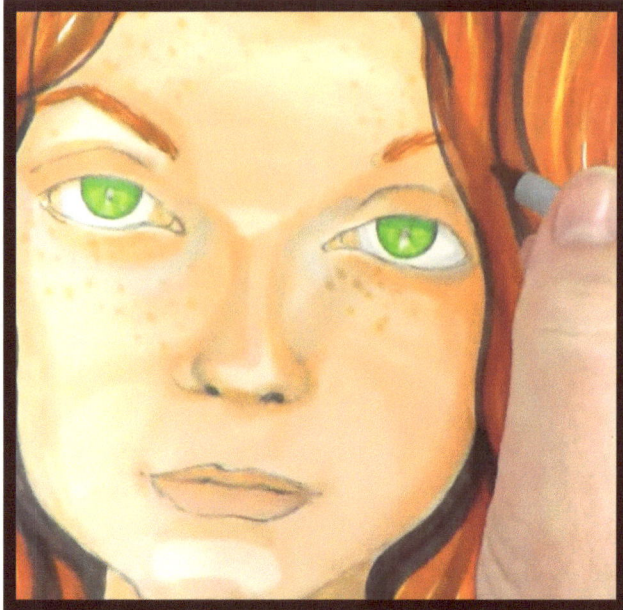

Step 10. Add light grey to the whites of the eyes and freckles in a light beige skincolor.

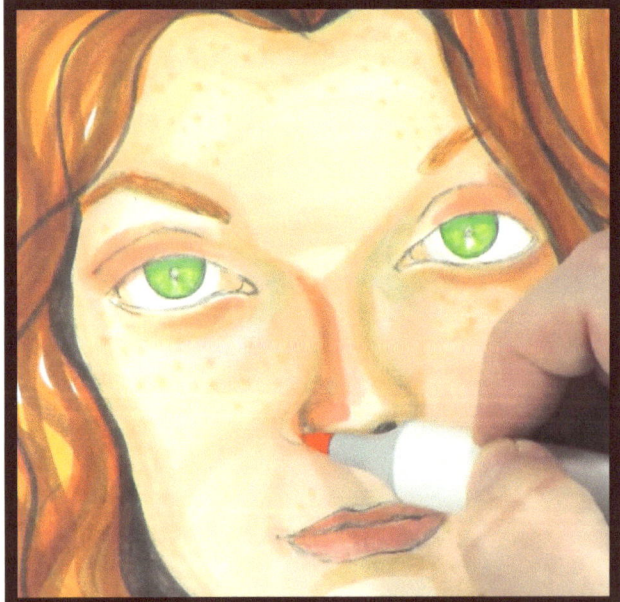

Step 11. Using a peachy-pink, apply sweeps of color to the outsides of the eyes, along the nose bridge and onto the lips.

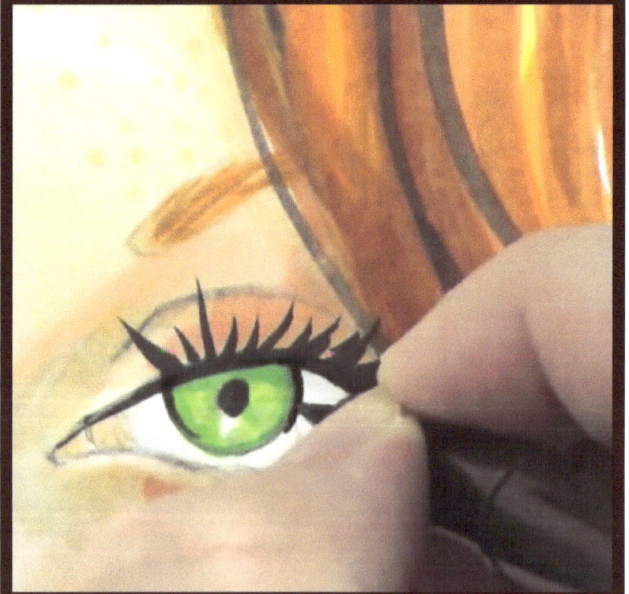

Step 12. Use a brush pen to apply lashes, draw the pupil and outline the irises.

Scot

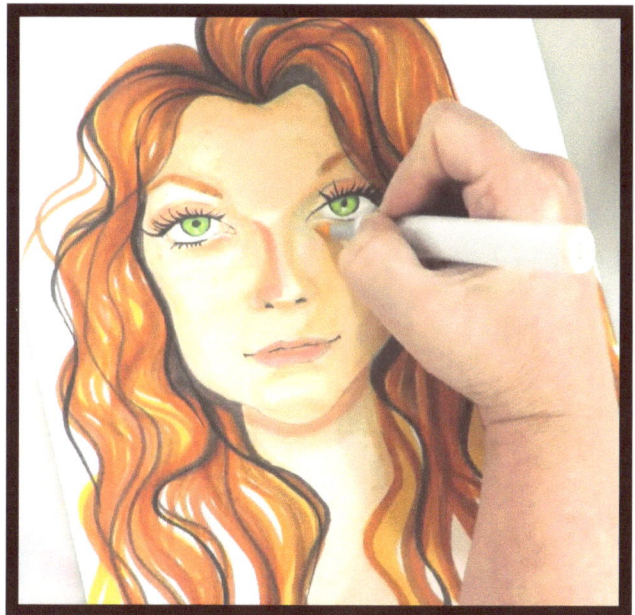

Step 13. Use the lightest skin color and apply it all over the face to blend and smooth.

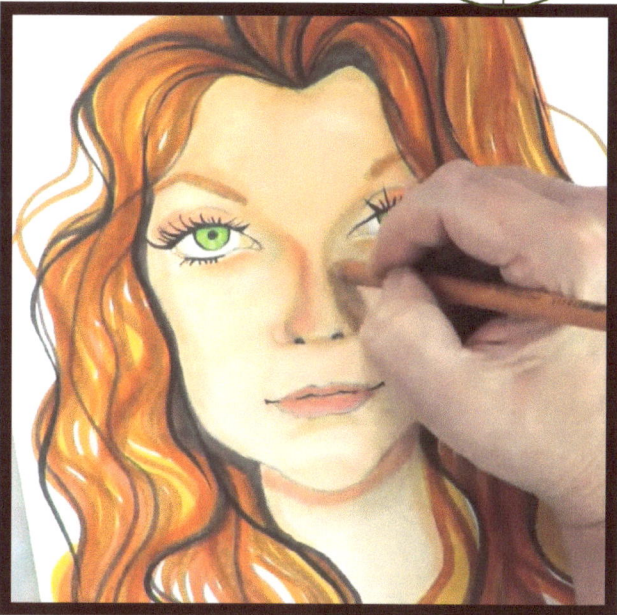

Step 14. Use colored pencils that match the marker colors to add shading or to blend.

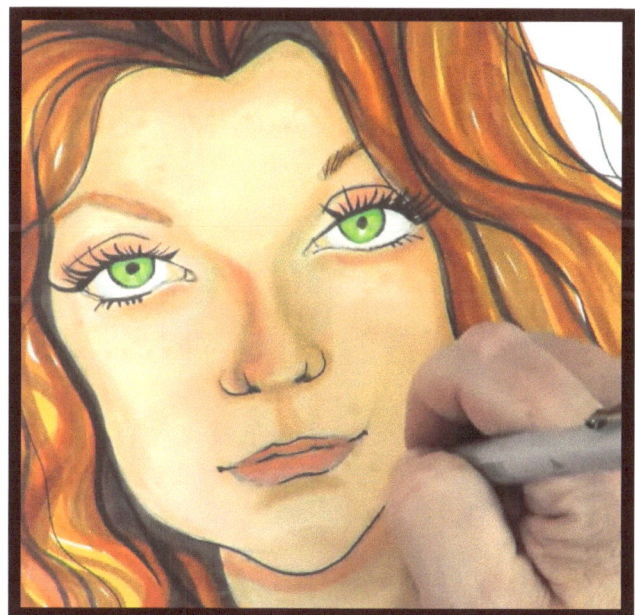

Step 15. Use a fine liner to outline the face and features including the eye lids, tear ducts and eyebrows.

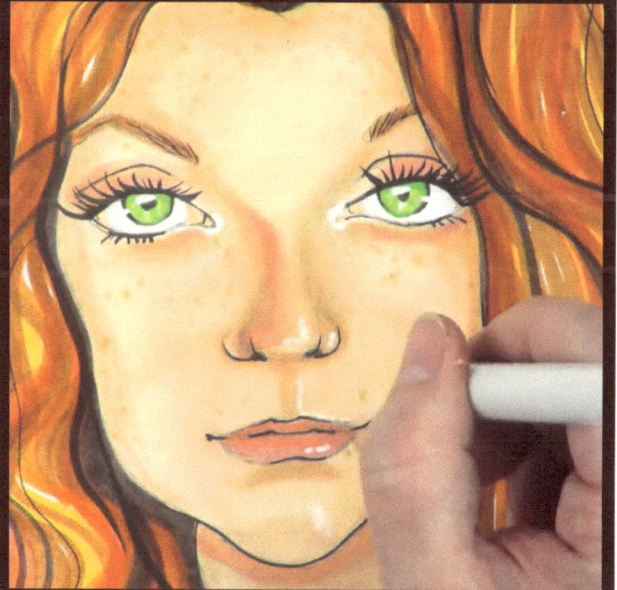

Step 16. Use a white paint pen to add highlights to the eyes, nose, mouth, chin or wherever you want a pop or sparkle!

Student Spotlight

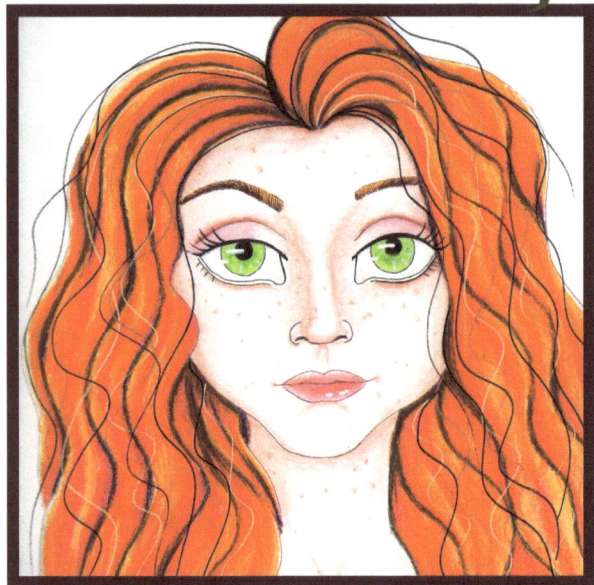

Patricia Veneman. Coloured with Prismacolour pencils and gouache. *"I love working with pencils. It gives you control and is very relaxing."*

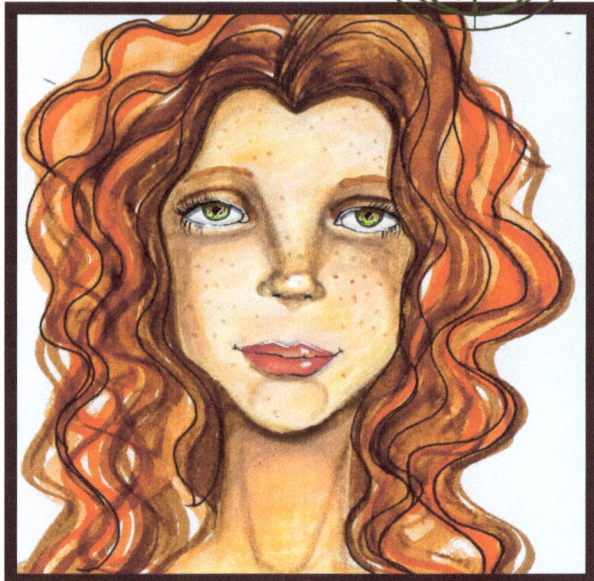

Kate Ivester. Created with Tombows, alcohol markers and white pen. *"I had an amazing time playing with the fair skinned Scottish lass."*

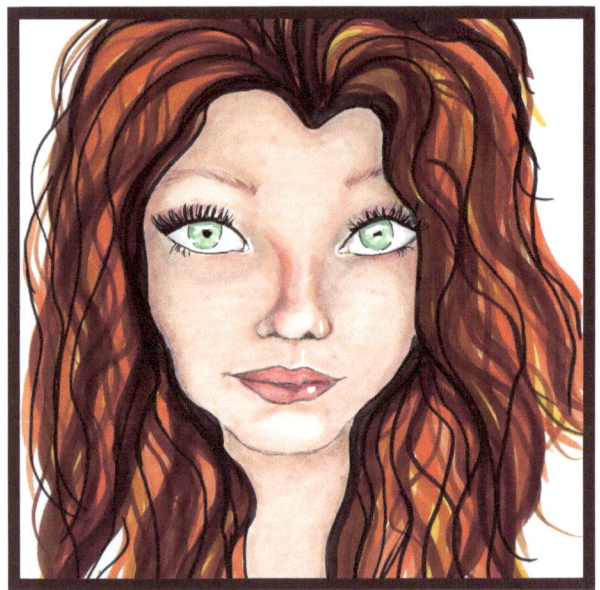

Karen Pulfer. Alcohol markers, colored pencils and pens. *"I chose these because I just started drawing after finding Karen's Awesome Art School on YouTube in May."*

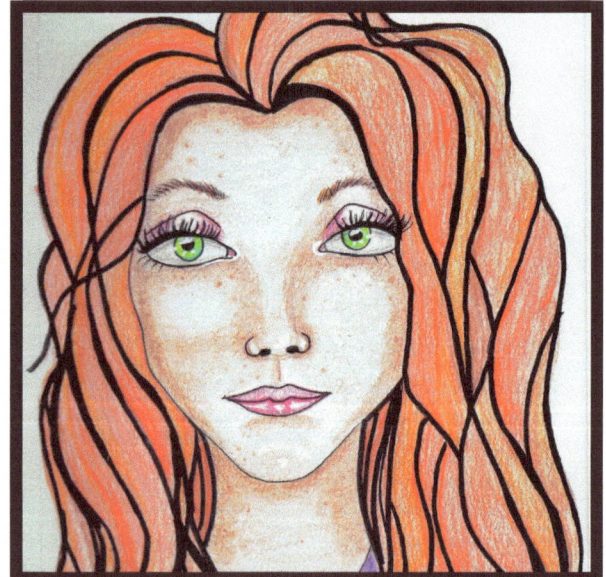

Viki Colonna. Watercolor pencils and a Tombow marker. *"This was my first time using watercolor pencils and I wanted to play around with them."*

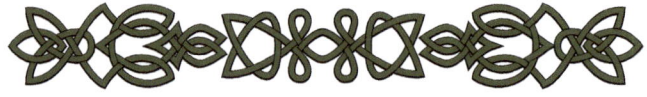

ASIAN AWESOME

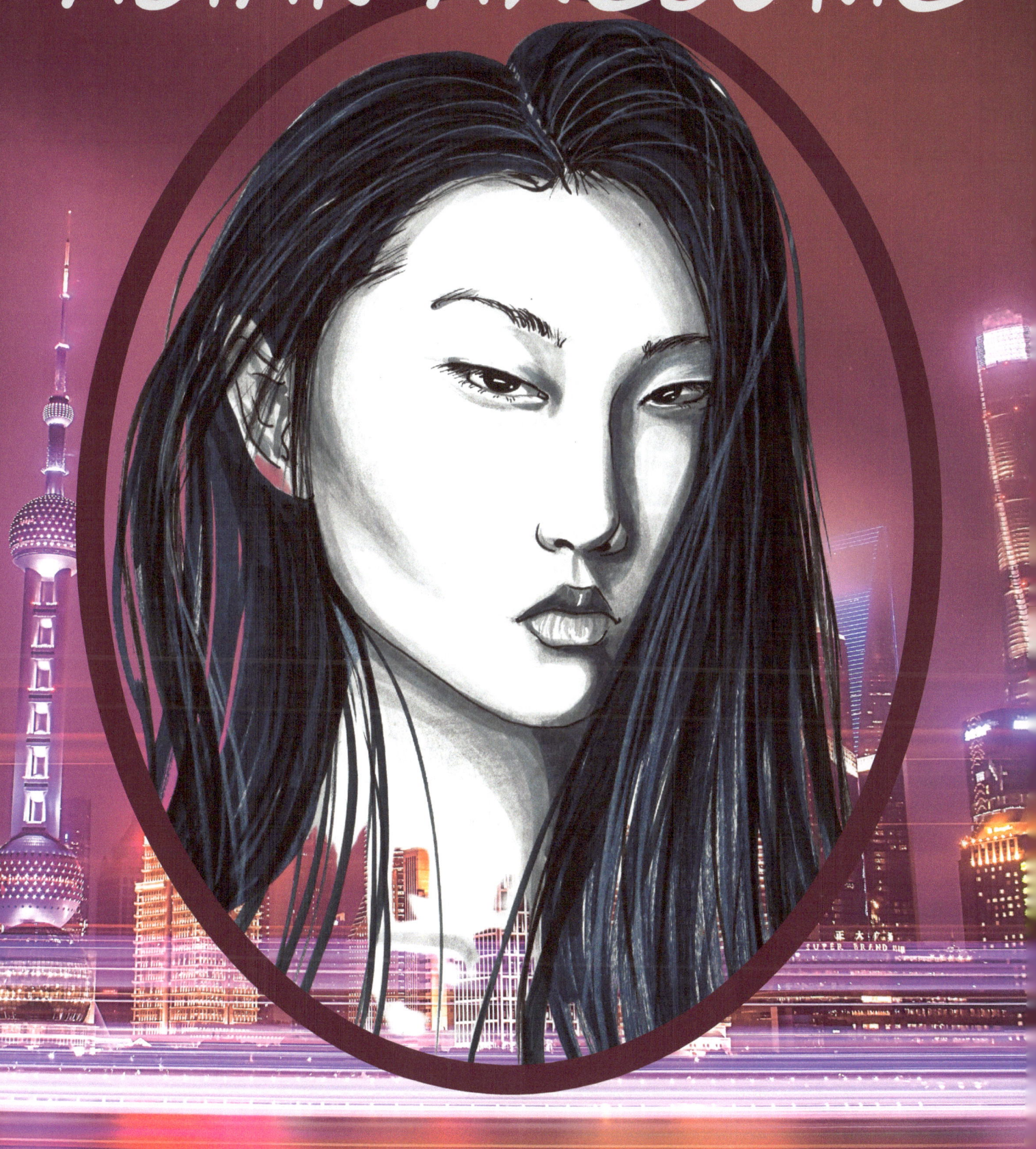

ASIAN

This portrait view, where the face is partially turned, is known as the "three-quarter" view.

It is called this because the face is turned a quarter of the way around so you can see 3/4 of the face!

When drawing this angle, we start with a circle first, rather than an oval.

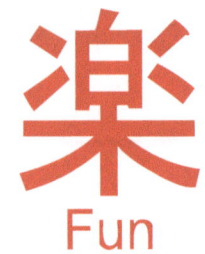
Fun

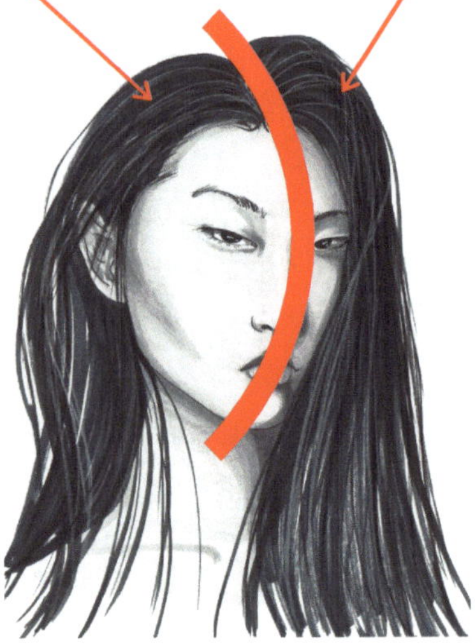

3/4 of the face can be seen

1/4 is turned away

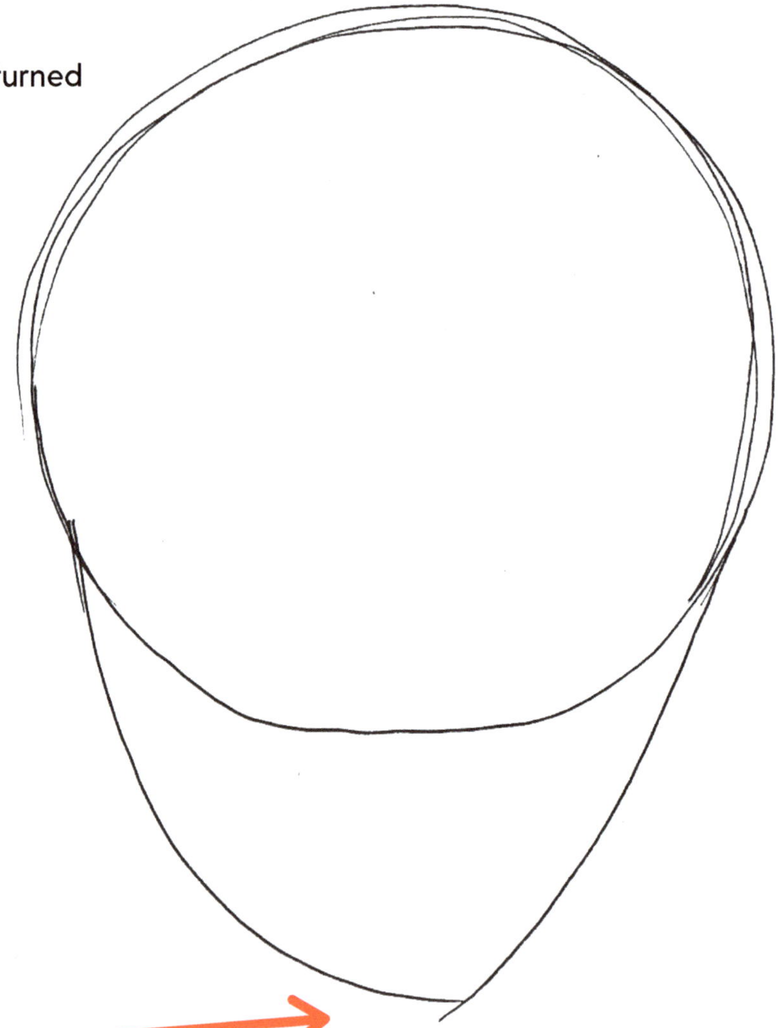

Then make a soft, sweeping "V" shape where the lines come together in a rounded fashion at the bottom.

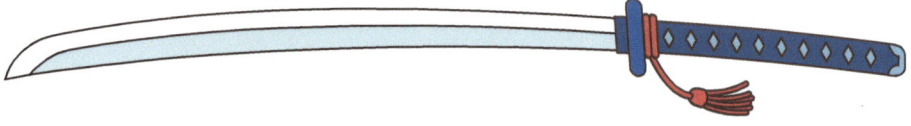

ASIAN

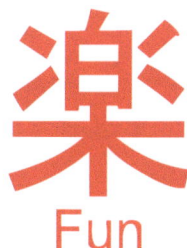
Fun

Because the face is turned, your center (vertical) line must move too! Place it over to the side to reflect the quarter turn.

Make this vertical line curve a bit to reflect the roundness and angle of the face and head.

The eyeline is typically a bit more lowered than the one shown here, but because of the head angle and the hair volume that we will be adding later, it appears here as half way down across the circle.

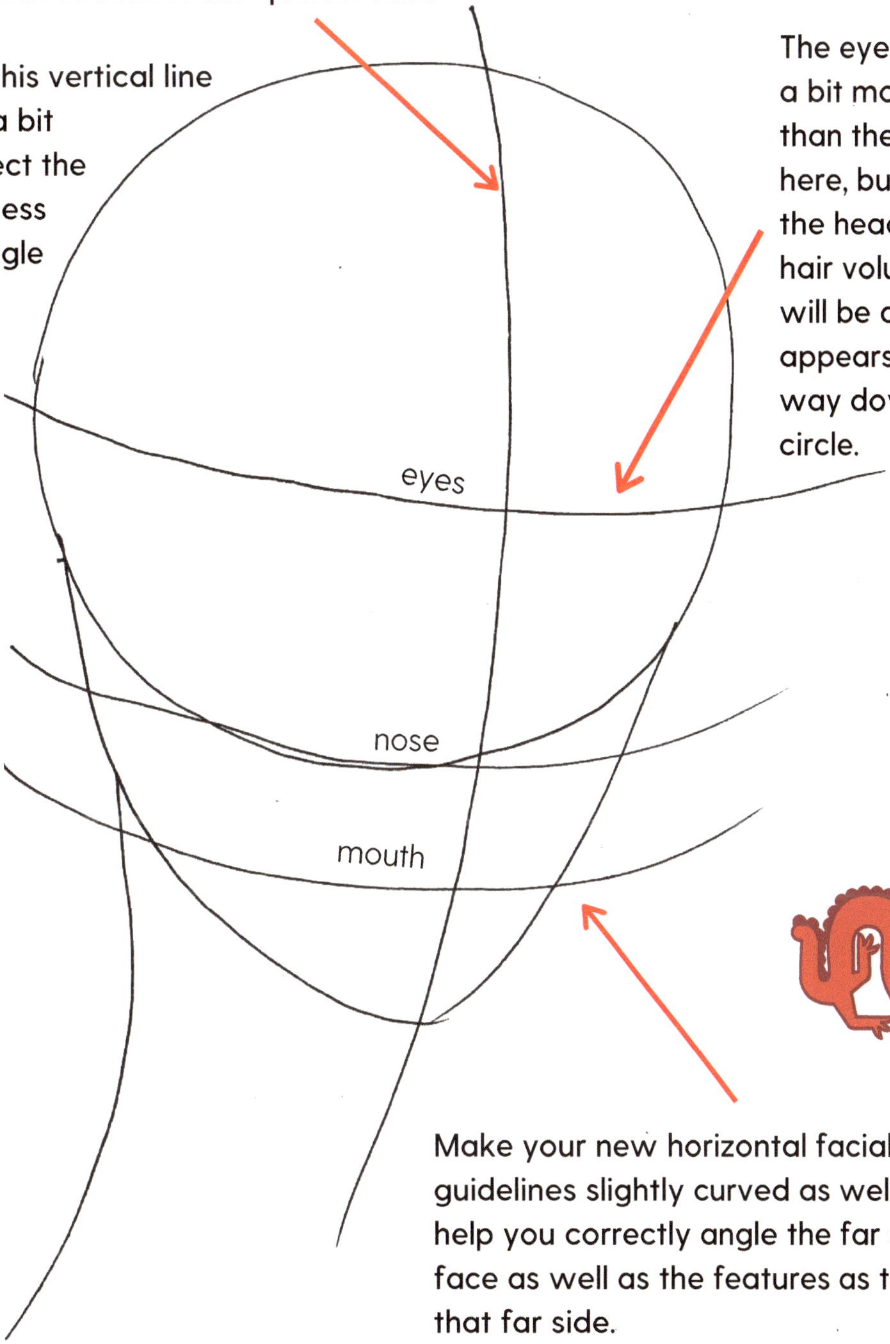

eyes

nose

mouth

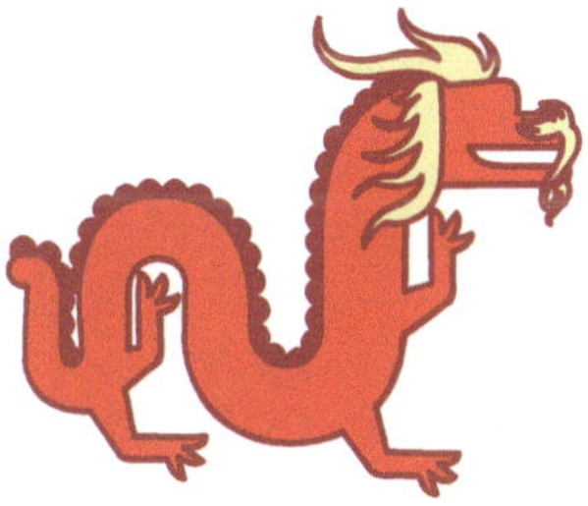

Make your new horizontal facial feature guidelines slightly curved as well. This will help you correctly angle the far side of the face as well as the features as they round that far side.

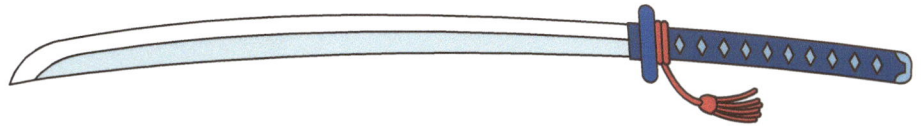

ASIAN

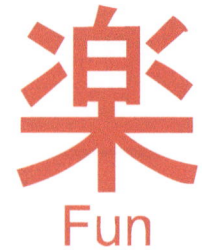
Fun

The ear sits perfectly between the eye and nose line.

The far side eye goes right to the very edge of the circle.

This girl has a beautifully angled jaw line. Make the line between the ear and neck angled straight before swooping around to the chin.

Sketch in the ovals as "placeholders" for the eyes, nose and mouth.

Now you can add the hair outline. Note how much volume there is both above and below the original head circle.

Note how the neck lines come straight out of the face, slightly swooping outward as they go out towards the body.

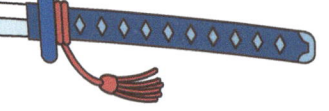

42

ASIAN

楽
Fun

Add the eyebrows (which line up with the eyes).

Erase your guidelines (exciting!!).

Note the subtle curving of the nose bridge. It points up to the right side brow.

Note that the far side eye and mouth both go right up to the side of the face!

Add the irises, ear squiggles and more hair sections.

Get ready to color her in!

I'm using only greyscale markers for this lesson. It's a great way to learn about values, shading and highlights!

ASIAN

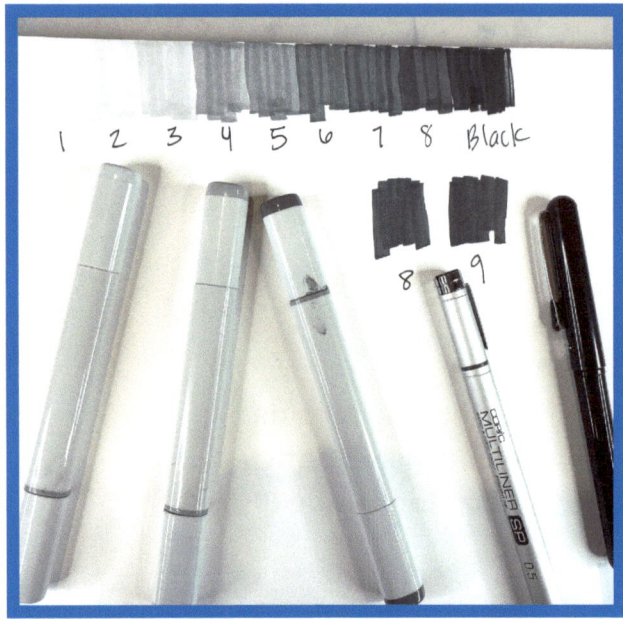

Step 1. Swatch your colors (as always!) and get a game plan for which colors to use.

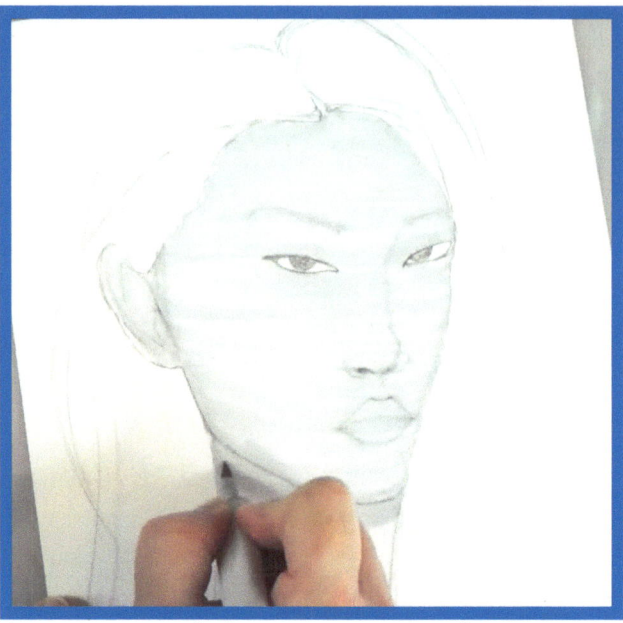

Step 2. Use a light grey to color the entire face except for the whites of the eyes.

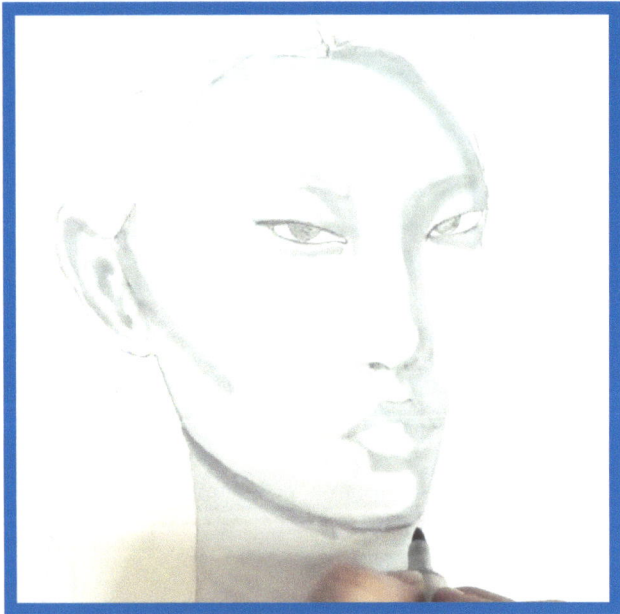

Step 3. Use one shade darker to add shading to the areas shown (right side of the face, under chin, ear and left cheekbone).

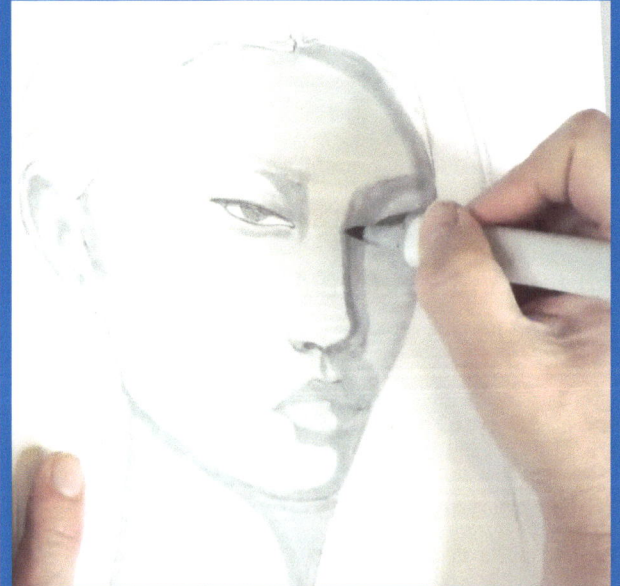

Step 4. Use one shade darker still to add shading to the same areas. This time, do not bring the shading out as far (leave the first shaded areas exposed a little).

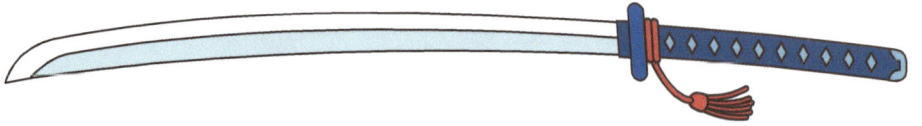

ASIAN 楽

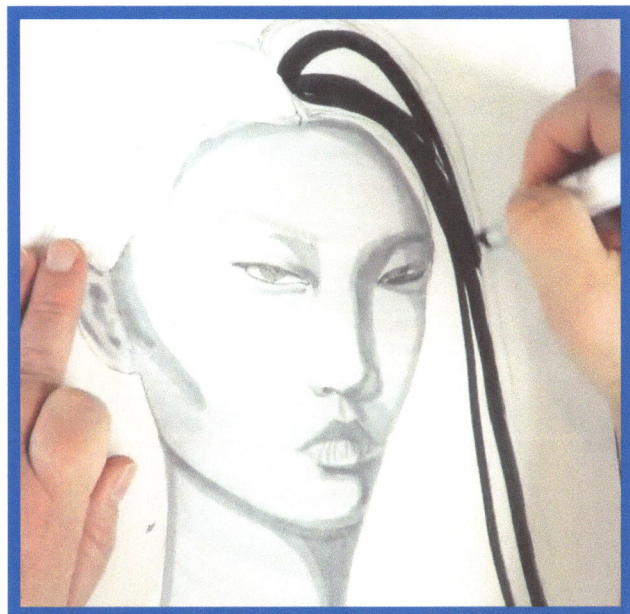

Step 5. Using the wide chisel nib of your marker, draw hair strands from root to tip.

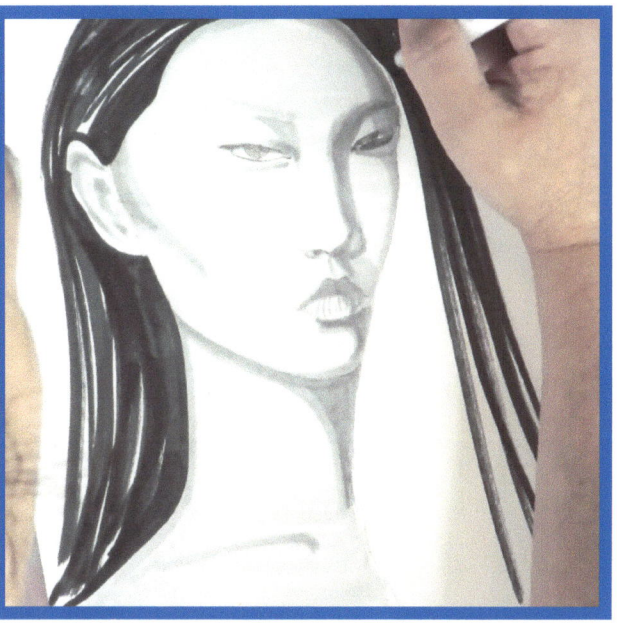

Step 6. Keep going until the entire head is filled, making sure all lines start from the root.

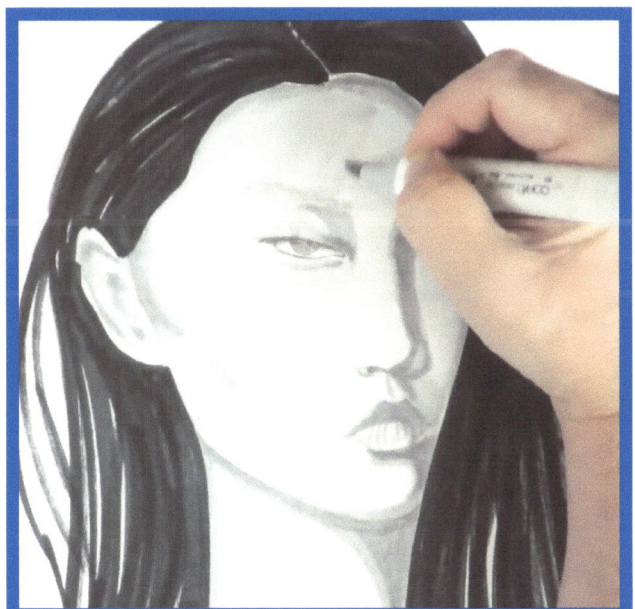

Step 7. Use the lightest grey possible (lighter than the first shade you used) to color in the entire face and neck going in OPPOSITE directions as your first layer. This helps reducing the appearance of streaking.

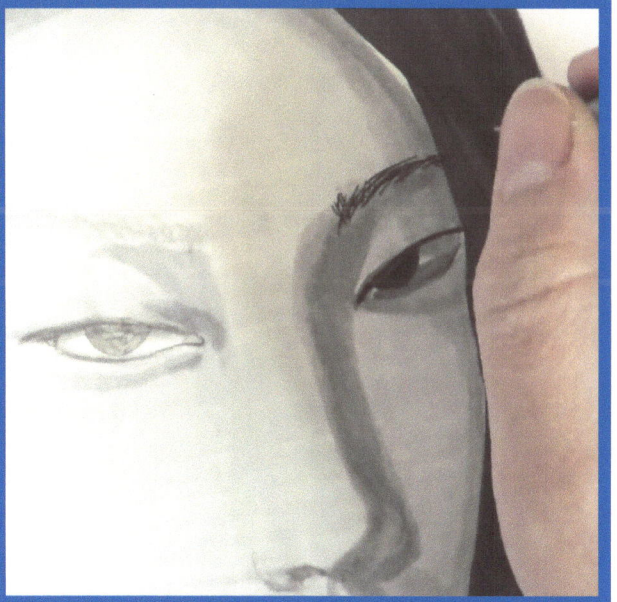

Step 8. Use a black fine liner to draw on the eyebrows and outline the eyes, nostrils, mouth details, chin and ear.

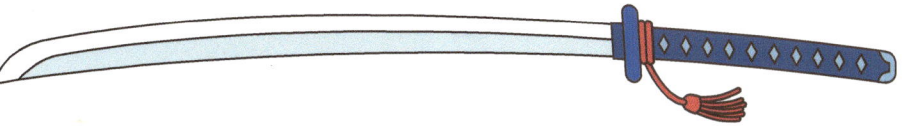

45

ASIAN

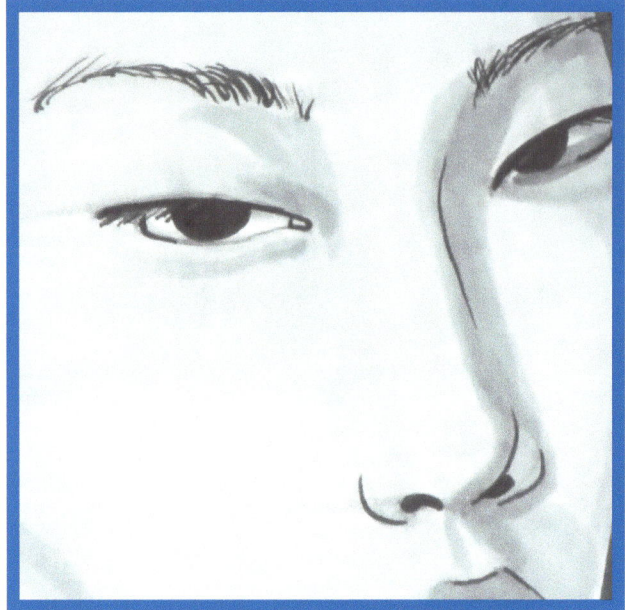

Step 9. Draw short, downturned lashes on the upper lid only. Note fine liner details.

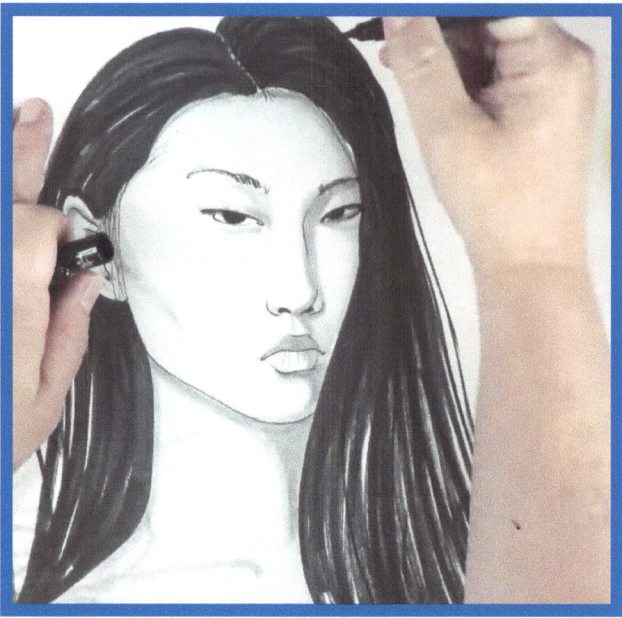

Step 10. Use a brush pen in black to create a few more realistic looking hair strands.

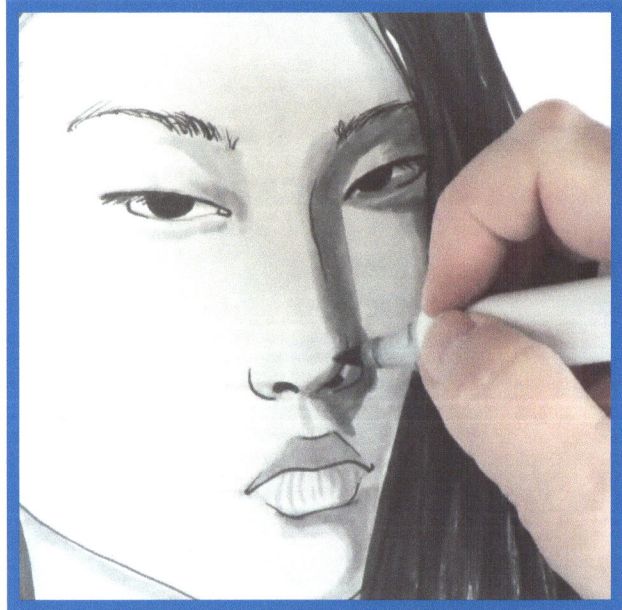

Step 11. Use a medium grey to add even more shading to the same darker areas. Again, leave exposed some of the lighter areas from before so the shades blend together.

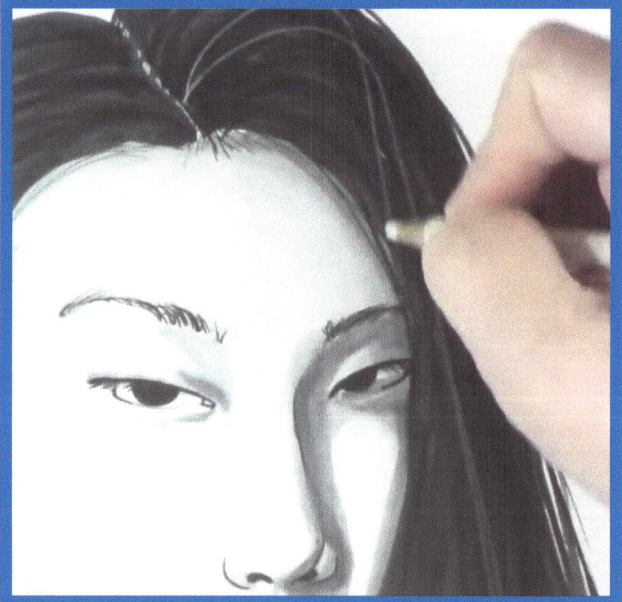

Step 12. Use a white colored pencil to add highlights to the hair. Make only about 5 – 6 strands on each side. Just a few here and there is all you need!

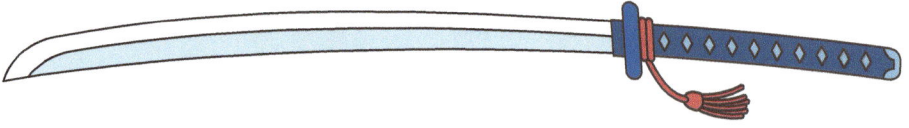

ASIAN

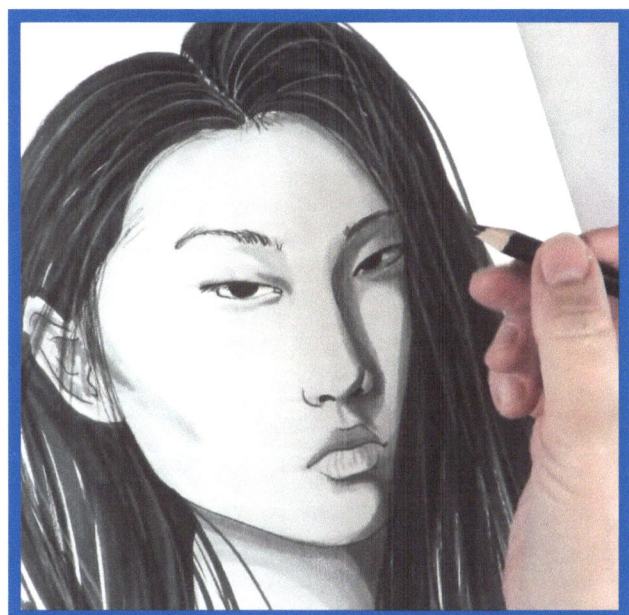

Step 13. You can also use a black colored pencil to create a more realistic hair texture.

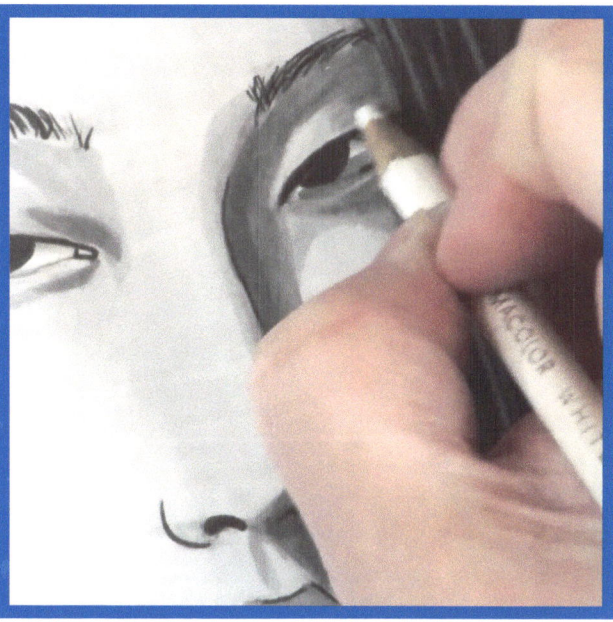

Step 14. Use a white pencil to define the right eyelid.

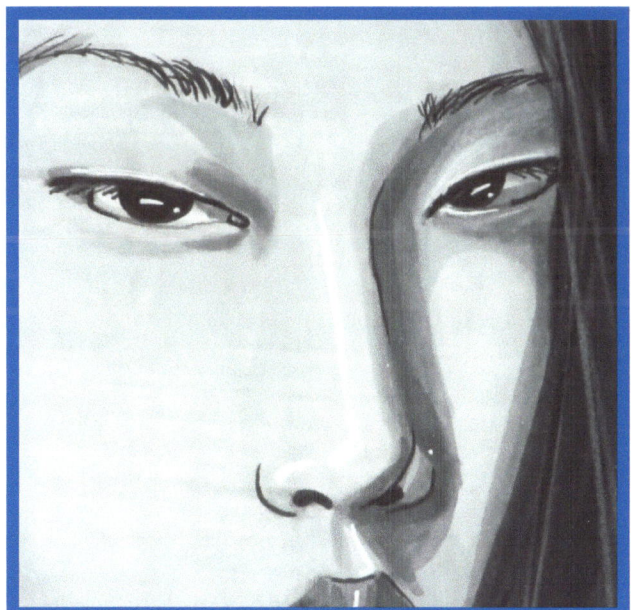

Step 15. Use a white gel or paint pen to add highlights to the eyelids, nose and mouth.

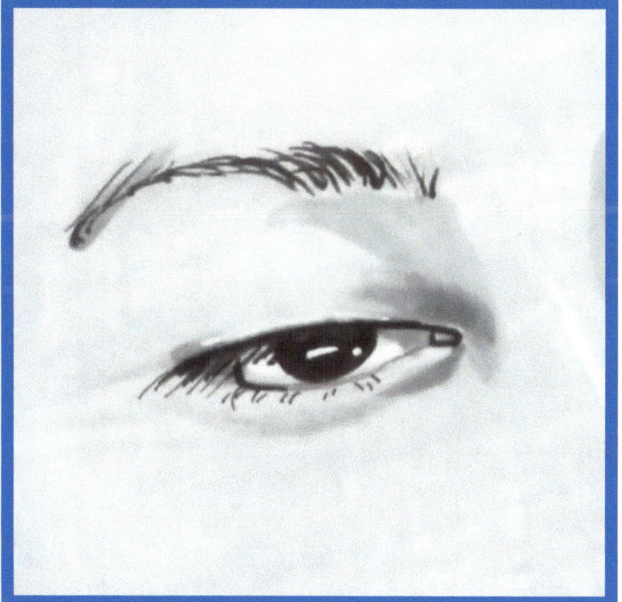

Step 16. Add tiny lashes to the bottom lid and create extra hair whisps at the ear and hairline above.

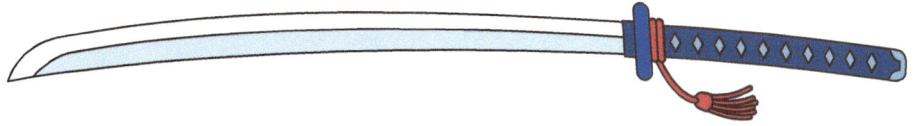

STUDENT SPOTLIGHT

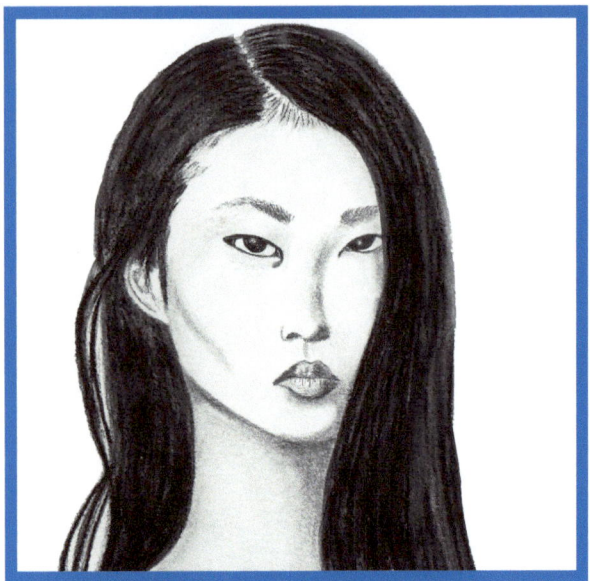

Deb Bratcher. Watercolor paper and black Stabilo pencil, graphite pencils and blender. *"I'm new to the Stabilo, a bold useful pencil!"*

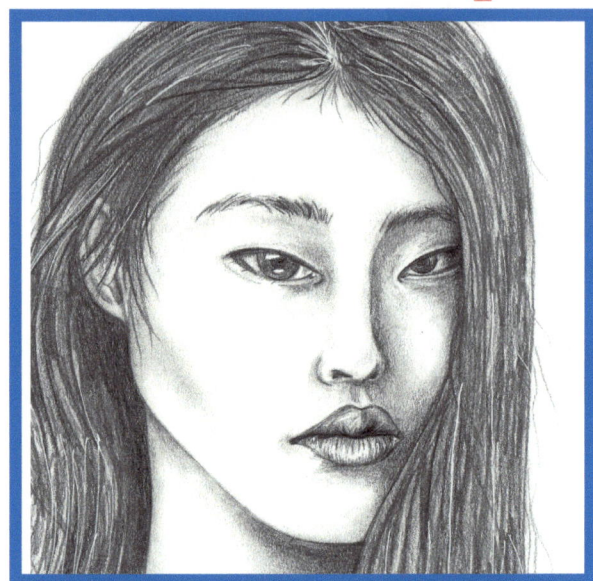

Susan Spinnato. Faber Castell 9000 graphite pencils. *"I absolutely love the dramatic effect of blending graphite."*

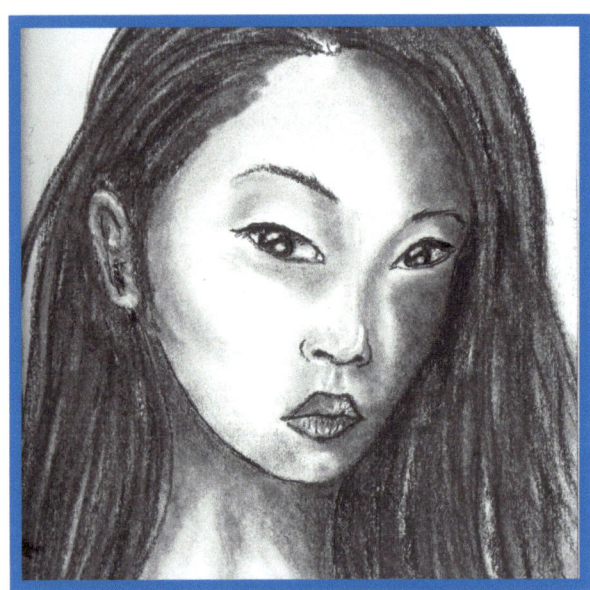

Lilian Hurst. Charcoal and Cotton Buds. *"I've been using different media to do the girls, mainly with Copics as I never using this media in faces, and was a big challenge for me, but the instructions of Karen in the class made them so easy to follow."*

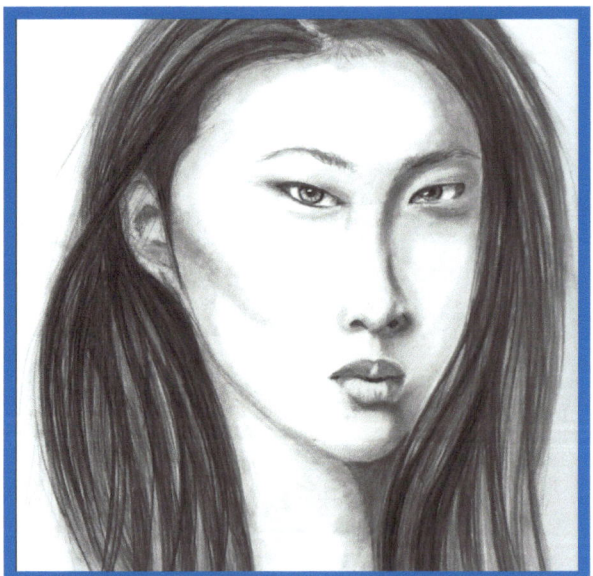

Debbie Starmer. *"I drew this beautiful asian girl with a HB 2B 4B 8B pencil. She challenged me, it took 3 attempts but I loved it."*

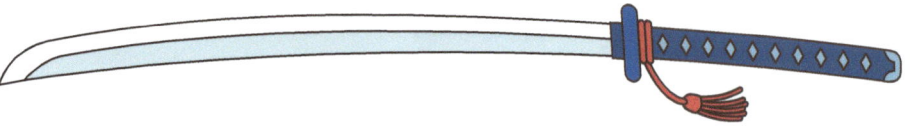

african american

african american

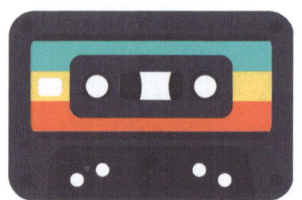

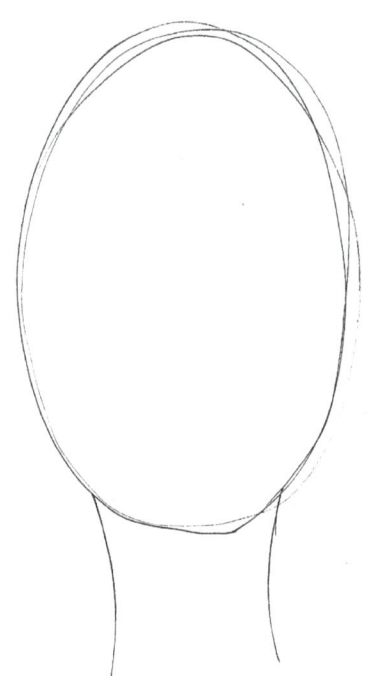

As always, you'll be starting with an oval and a neck. Funny how all humans start out exactly the same way!

Then add the guidelines using the same proportions as we did for the previous forward facing women.

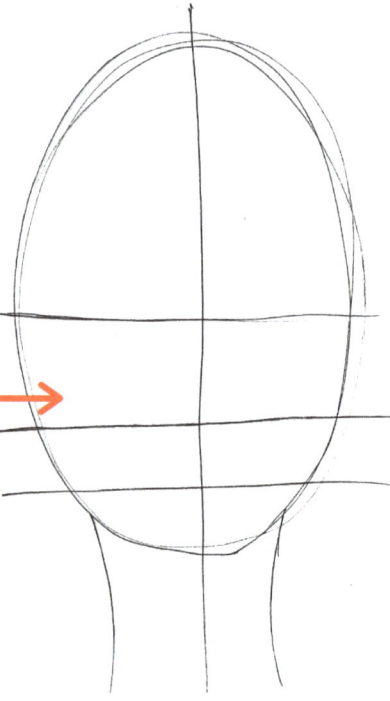

Draw the three eyes across to get the proper proportions. Her eyes are really large so you can make the ovals a bit less squished than we did for the others!

One oval and 2 circles on either side will get you ready to refine her nose quickly and easily.

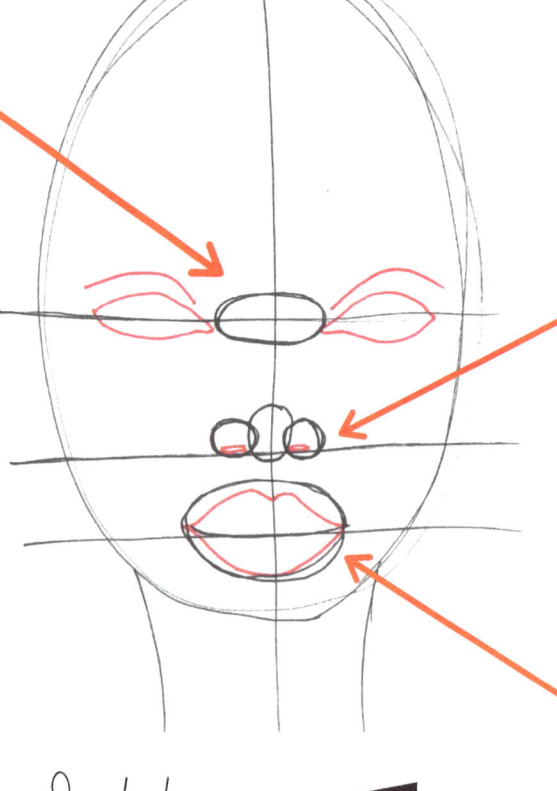

Create a large oval and get ready to define the lips within!

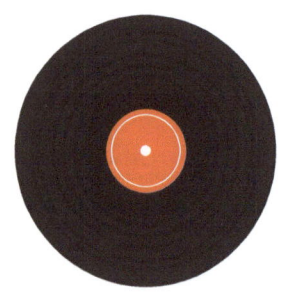

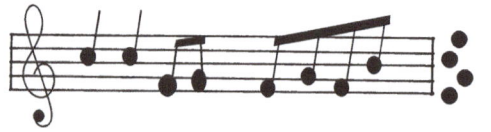

50

african american

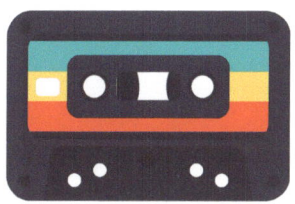

Draw the outline of the hair.

Remember: hair goes OVER the head oval as well as INTO it and across the forehead!

head oval

Erase the middle eye (placeholder).

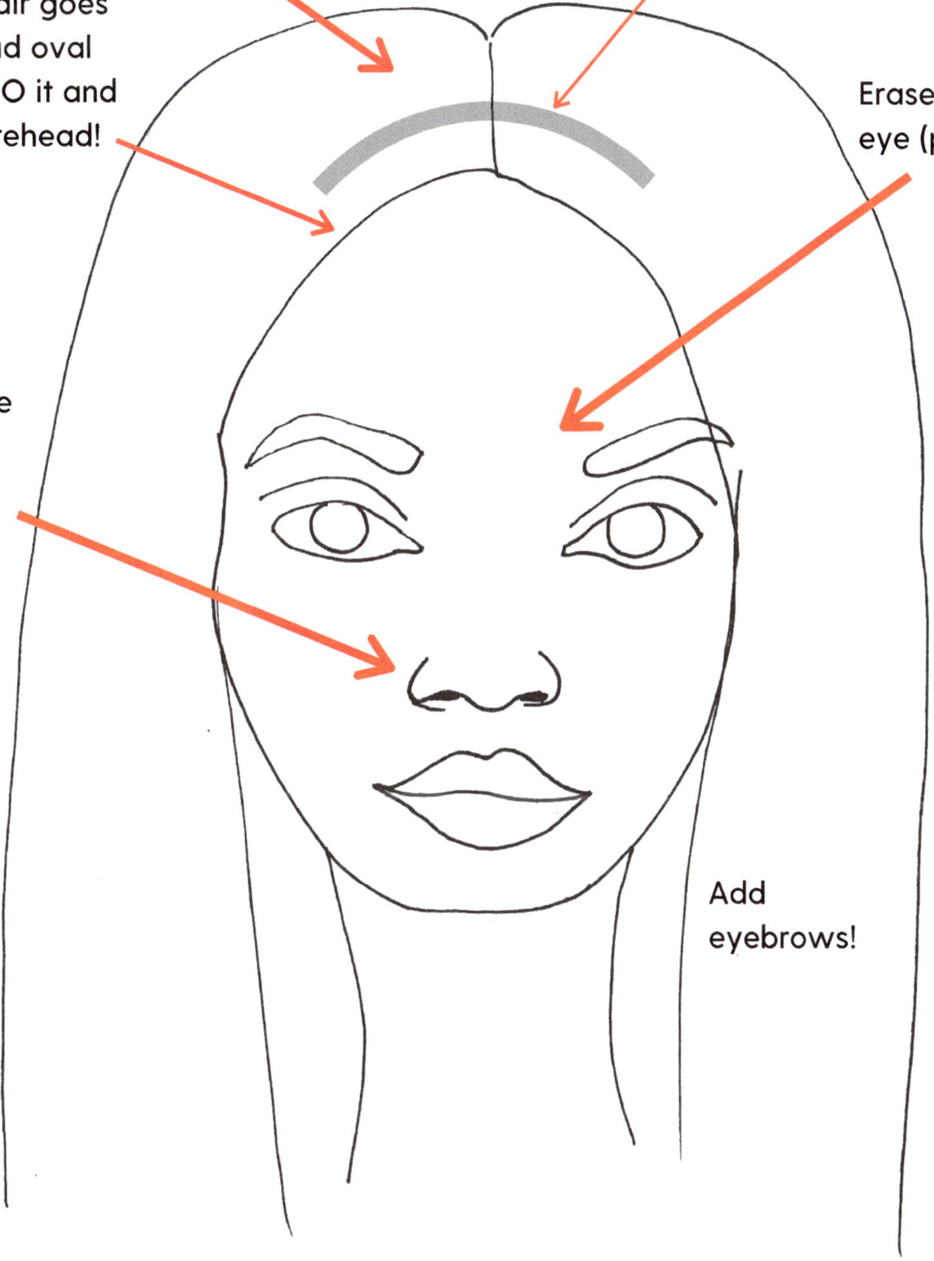

Erase the nose guidelines - leave just the outer nostril "parenthesis" shapes on either side.

Add eyebrows!

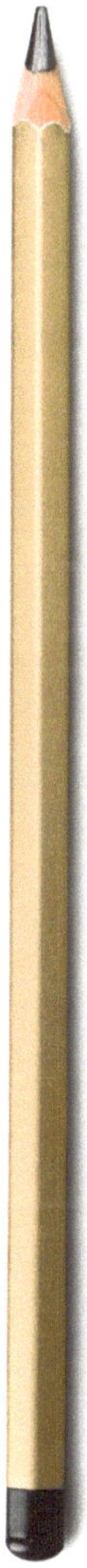

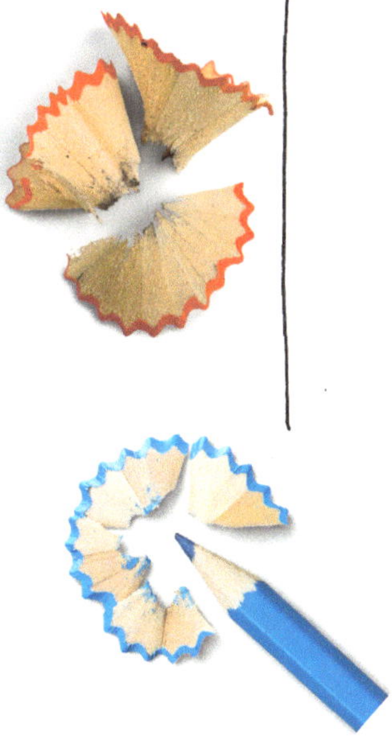

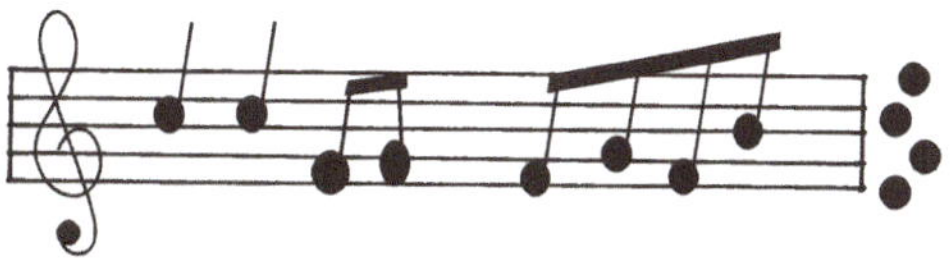

51

african american

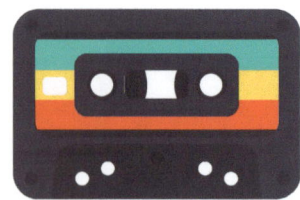

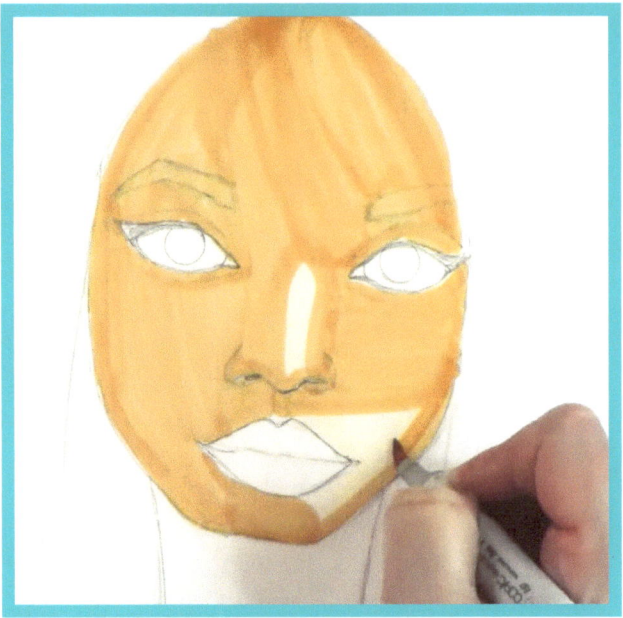

Step 1. Draw the "wings" of the eye make-up. Then color entire face with light brown.

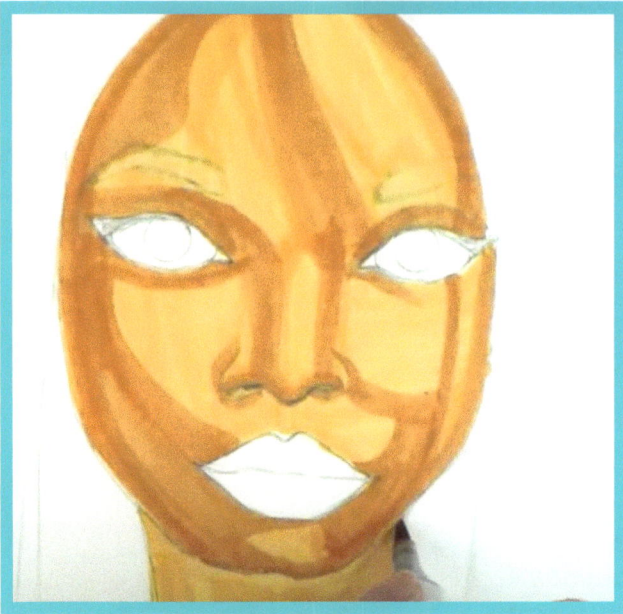

Step 2. Use a deeper shade on the areas as shown. Looks crazy, it's okay!

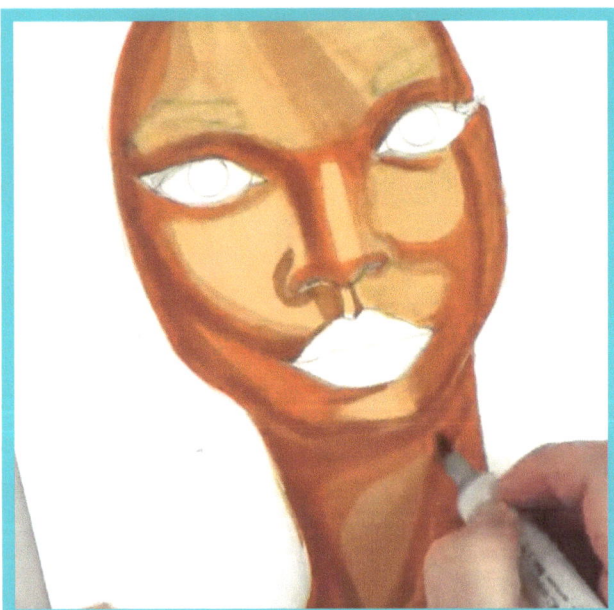

Step 3. Go deeper still and cover areas shown. This is the "ugly" phase, don't panic!! It's perfectly normal and the only way to get passed it is to keep going! Let's go!

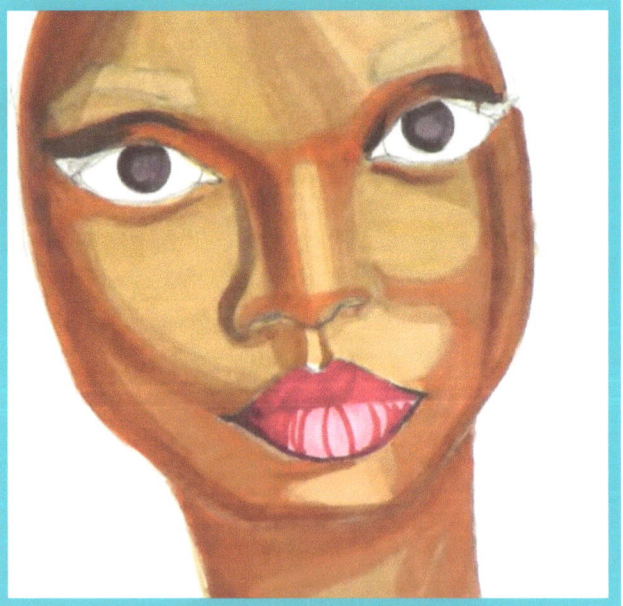

Step 4. Color irises brown and add dark brown to eyelids and along left side of nose. Then color lips a light pink base with a darker shade on top. Make curved strips on bottom.

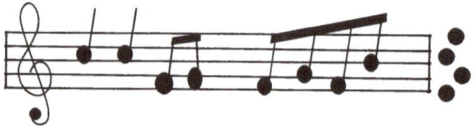

african american

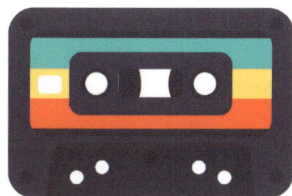

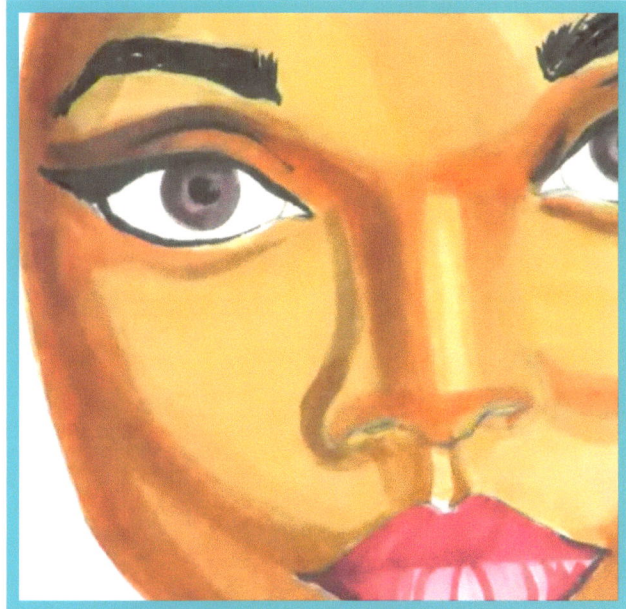

Step 5. Use a black brush pen to create eyebrows and outline eyes and pupils.

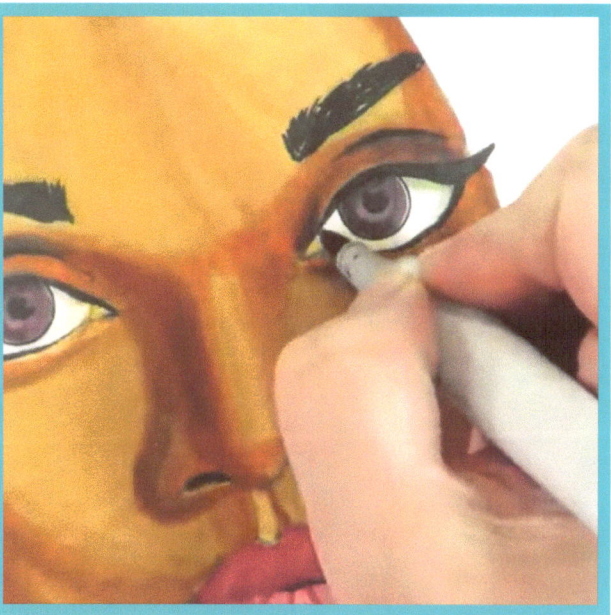

Step 6. Use a light grey to color in the perimeter of the whites of the eyes.

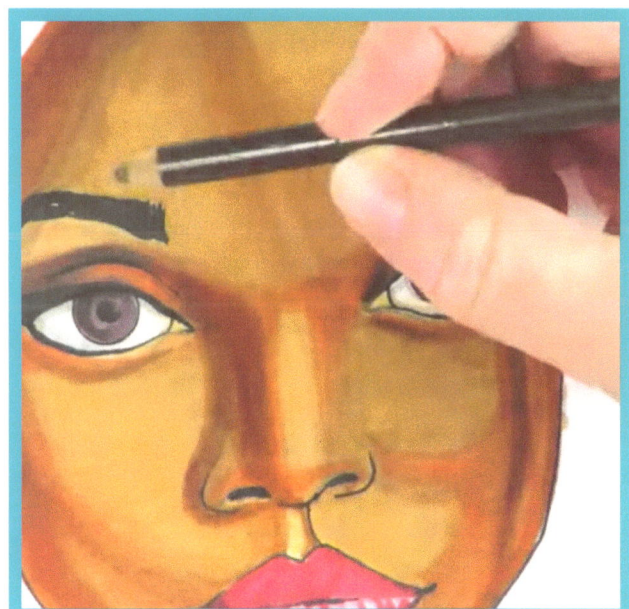

Step 7. Use colored pencils in similar skin tones to deepen shading or eye make-up as desired! You can also use colored pencils to smooth transitions between shaded and colored regions.

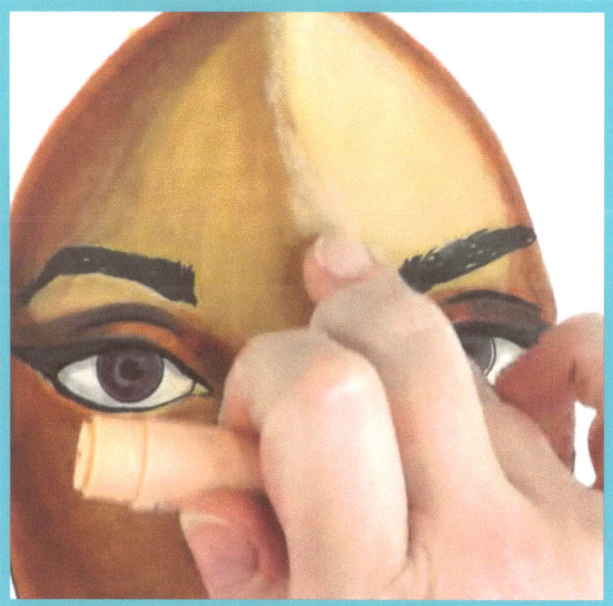

Step 8. Try experimenting with art crayons like Gelatos (by Faber-Castell) to see if that helps you achieve more shading or highlights. I quite liked using them for the lighter areas!

african american

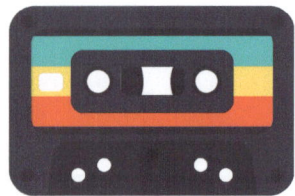

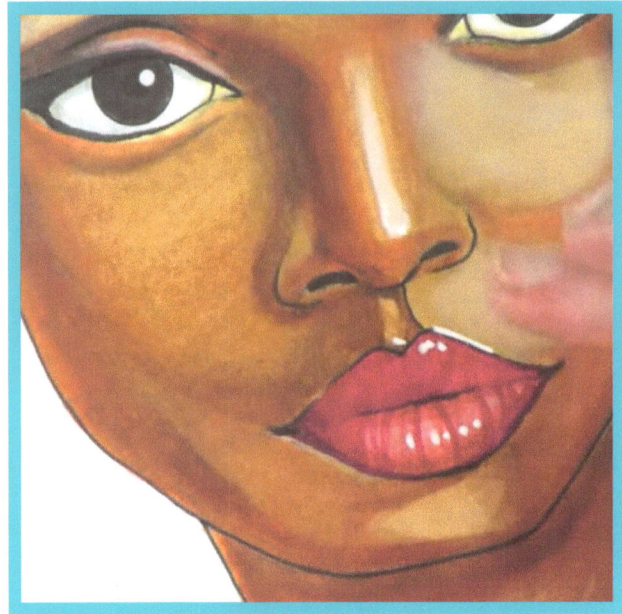

Step 9. Use a white paint pen to add highlights to the eyes, nose and mouth!

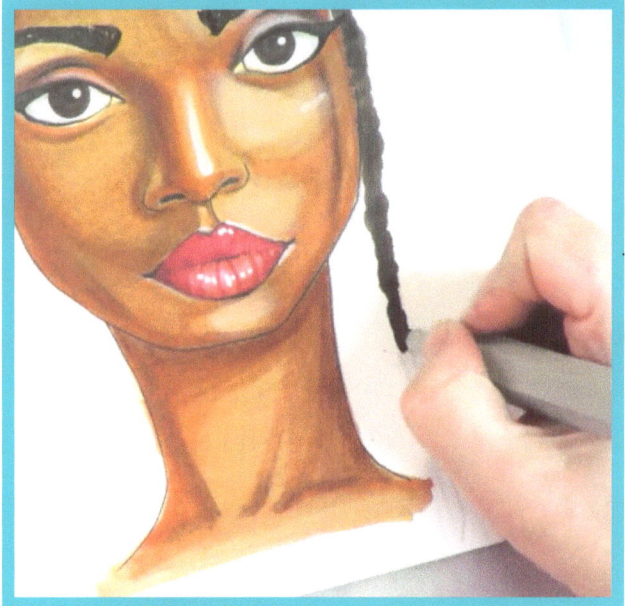

Step 10. Use a dark brown marker to make small circular motions to create long strands.

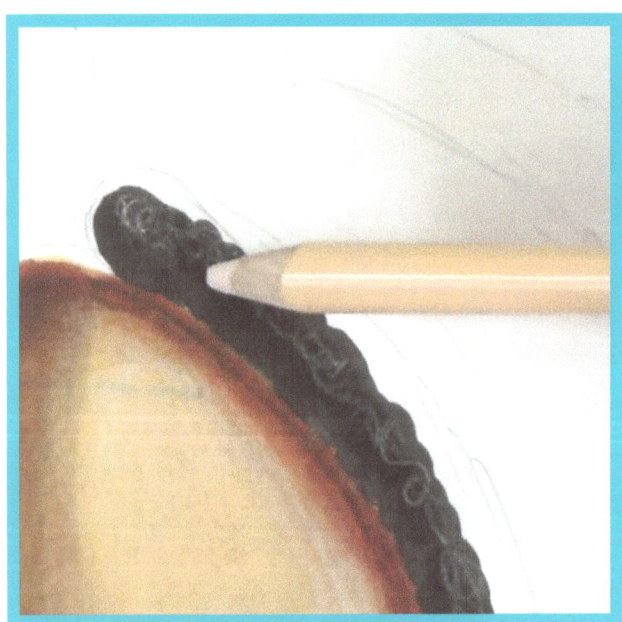

Step 11. Use a light colored pencil to lightly make squiggles on just the TOP portion of the strands. Add dots of black on the UNDERSIDE part of the strands.

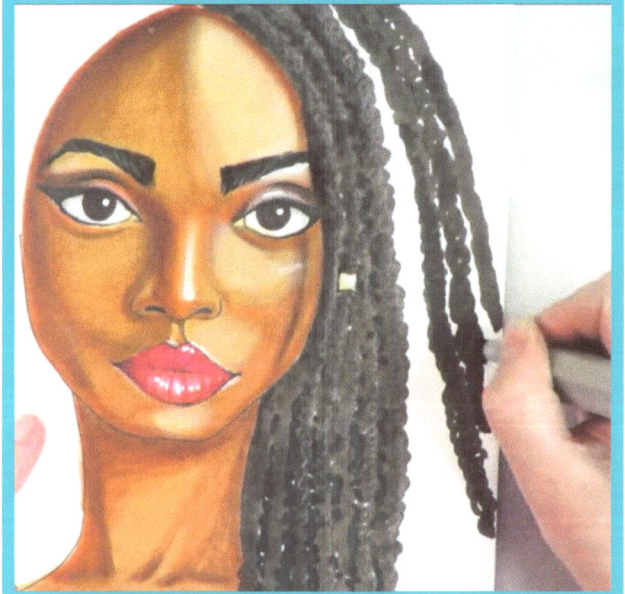

Step 12. Repeat over and over until the entire head is covered in beautiful dreads! First one side, and then the other. You can sketch them in pencil first or just go for it like I did!!

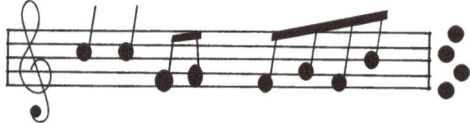

african american

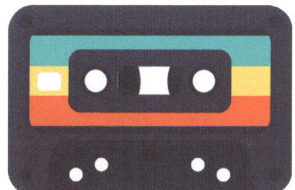

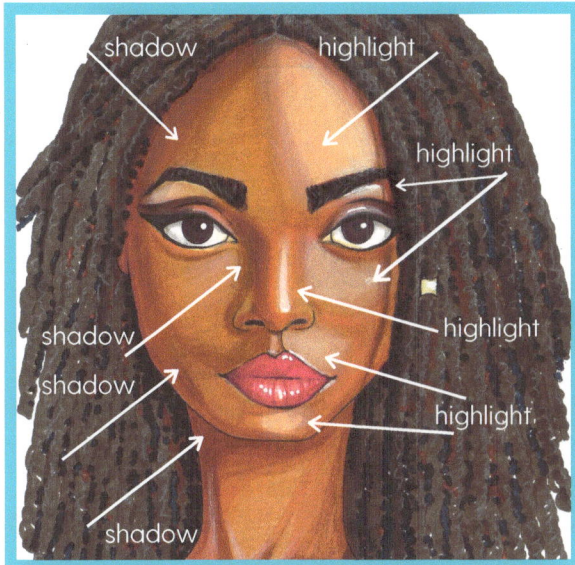

Coloring Tip 1. Don't guess where to put shading and highlights. Look at the reference! That will tell you exactly where they go!

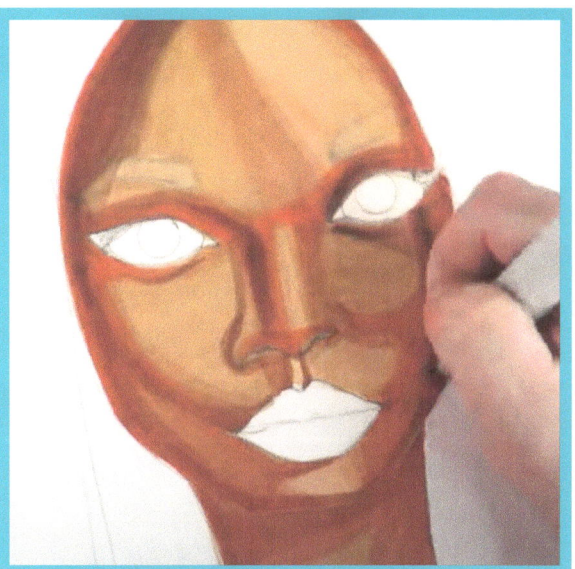

Coloring Tip 2. If the skin is looking too choppy, sweep a light shade over the ENTIRE face once or twice to help blend them all together better!

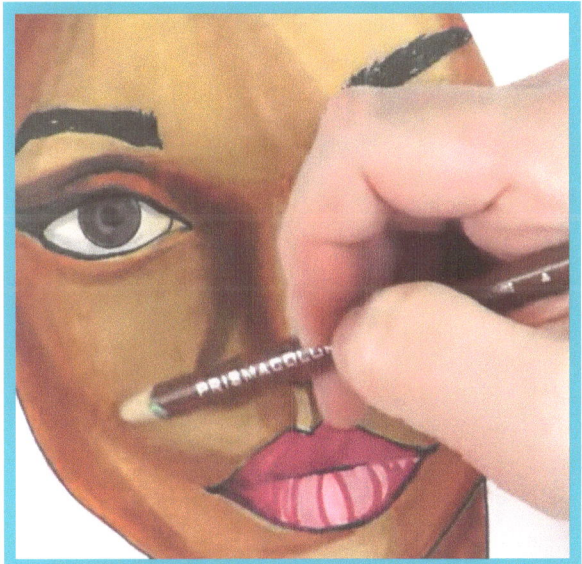

Coloring Tip 3. Use both light and dark colored pencils to help fix your marker mistakes. You can also add a glow to lighter areas by using white and even deepen your darker shadows by using your darker skin tone colors for added drama!

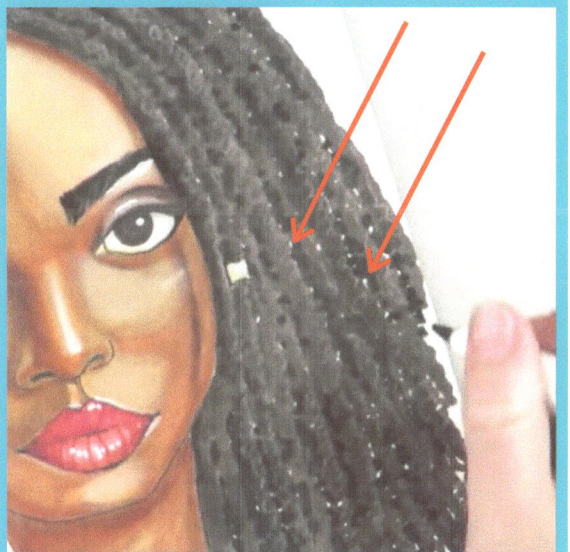

Coloring Tip 4. Use a secondary brown (in addition to the first brown and black marker) and apply it sparingly around the different hair strands where the white of the paper peeks through. This will add more dimension and a touch of "realness" to those gorgeous locks!

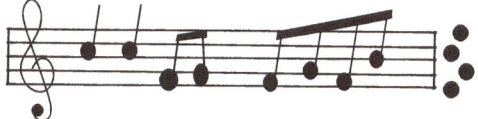

student spotlight

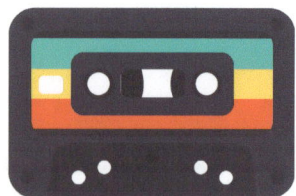

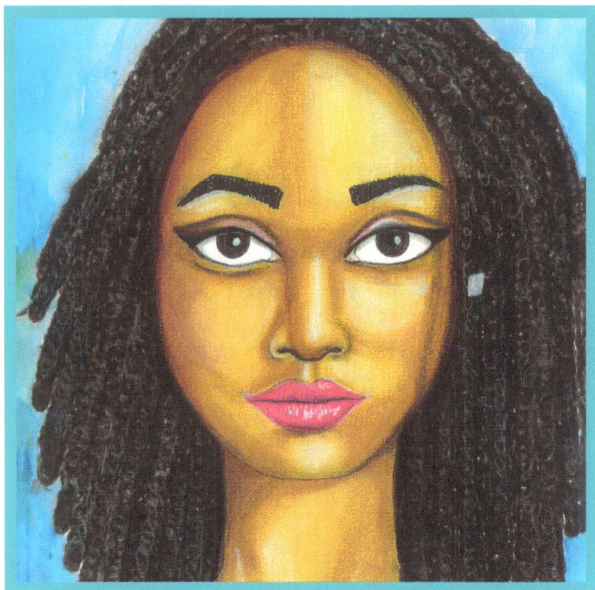

Junirose De Armas. Watercolors, Ecoline markers, Crayola markers, Gelatos, paint pens. *"They go easily with each other."*

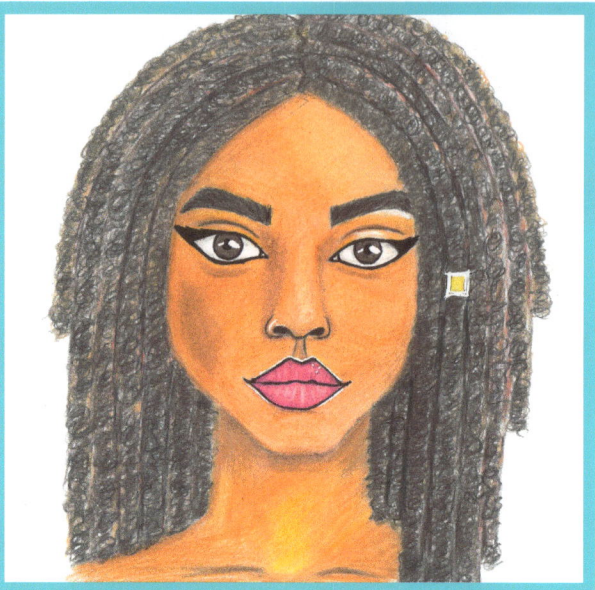

Anette Severinsson. I used Arteza colored pencils, white and black Posca. *"I love how this pencils works together in beautiful colors."*

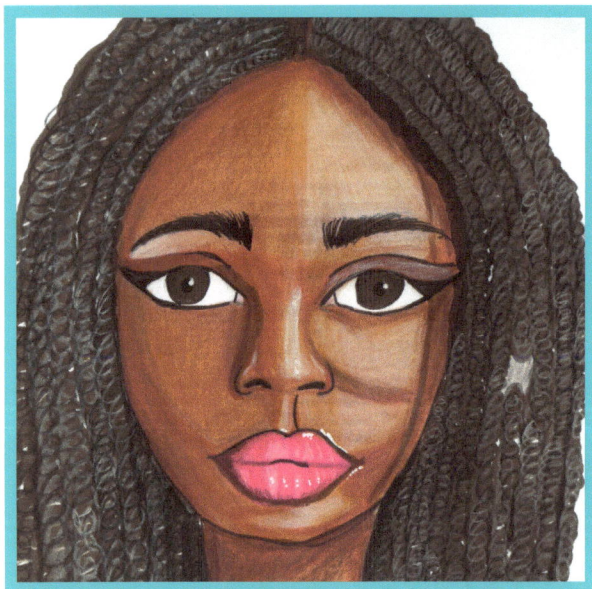

Donna Holmes. Spectrum Noir markers, coloured pencils and a touch of Uniball Signo pen. *"I used these because I have not used markers to make darker skin tones and I wanted to see how well I could achieve it."*

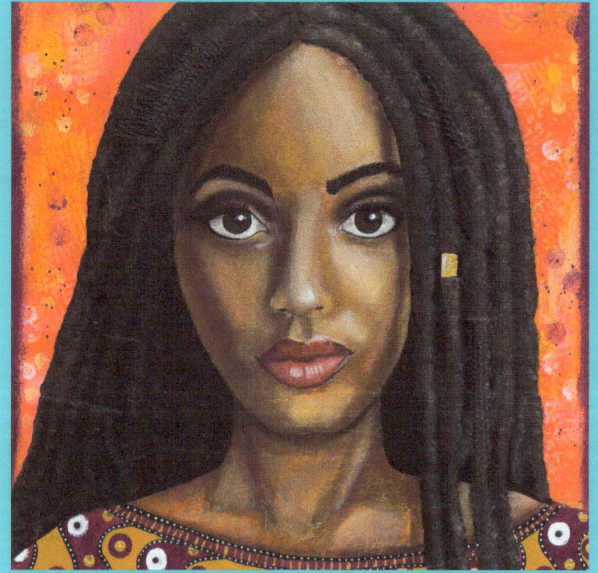

Cindy Nijssen. Mixed media painting on wood with collage, acrylic paint, stamp and stencils. *"I love to use acrylic paint on wood because it is great to blend the paint that way and you can go crazy with the background!"*

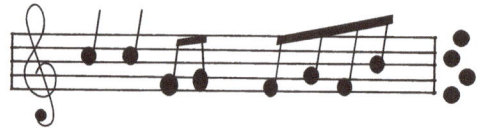

Middle Eastern Beauty

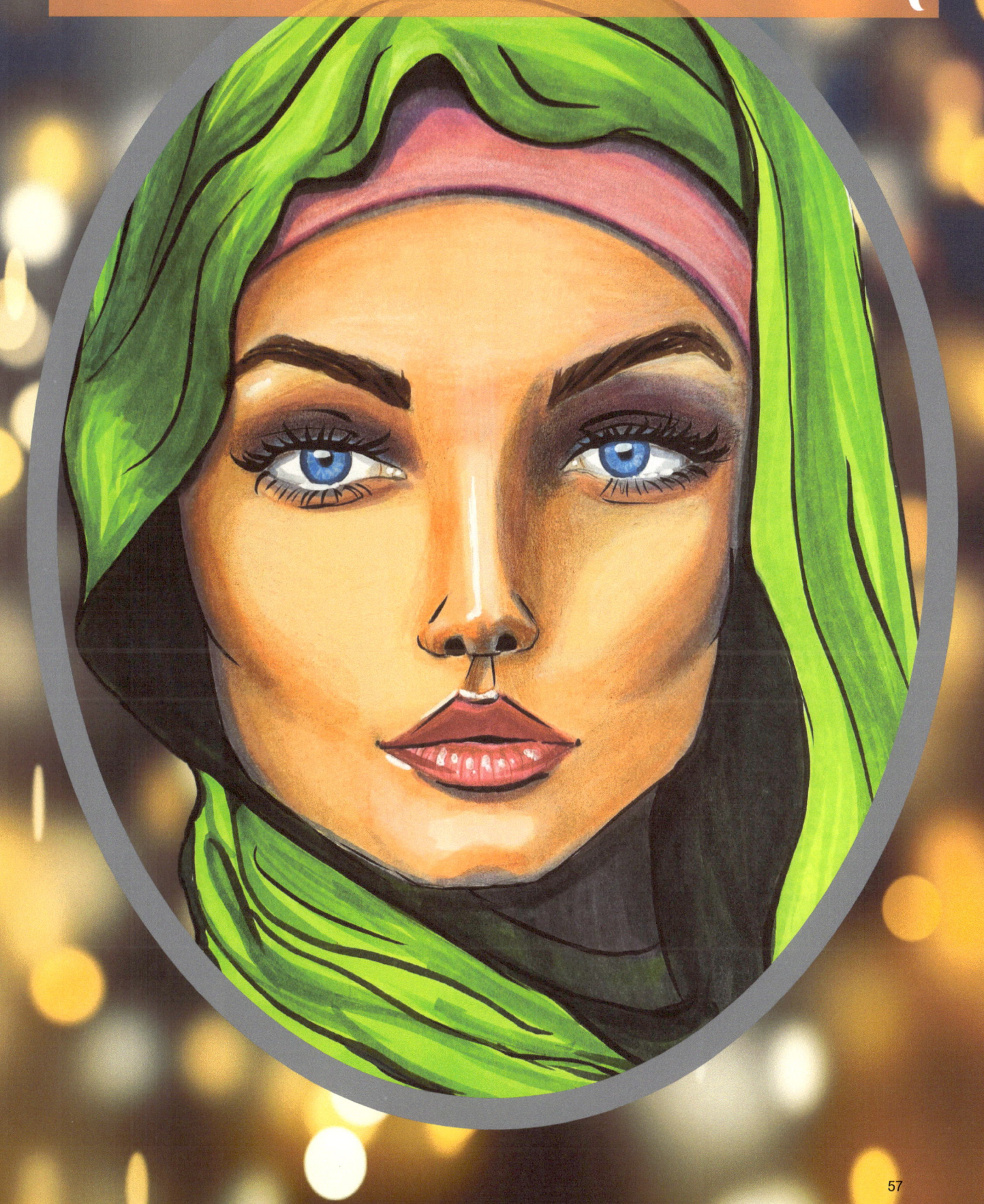

Middle Eastern

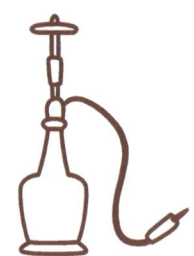

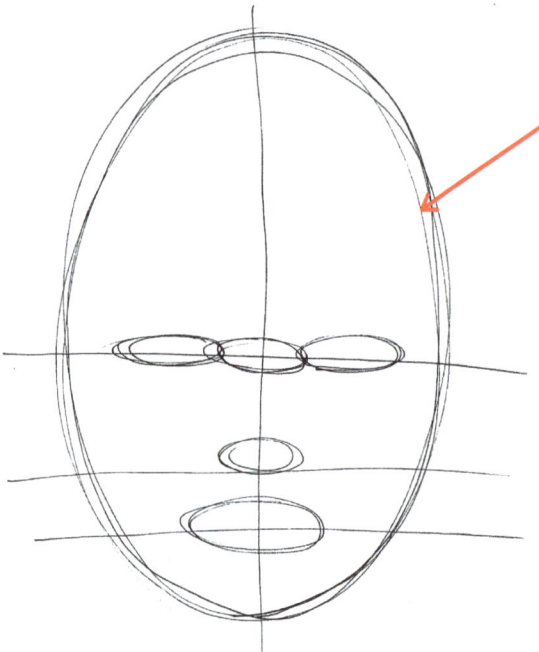

Just as we began with an oval and the facial feature placeholders in the previous lessons, we begin the same way for this gorgeous middle eastern woman.

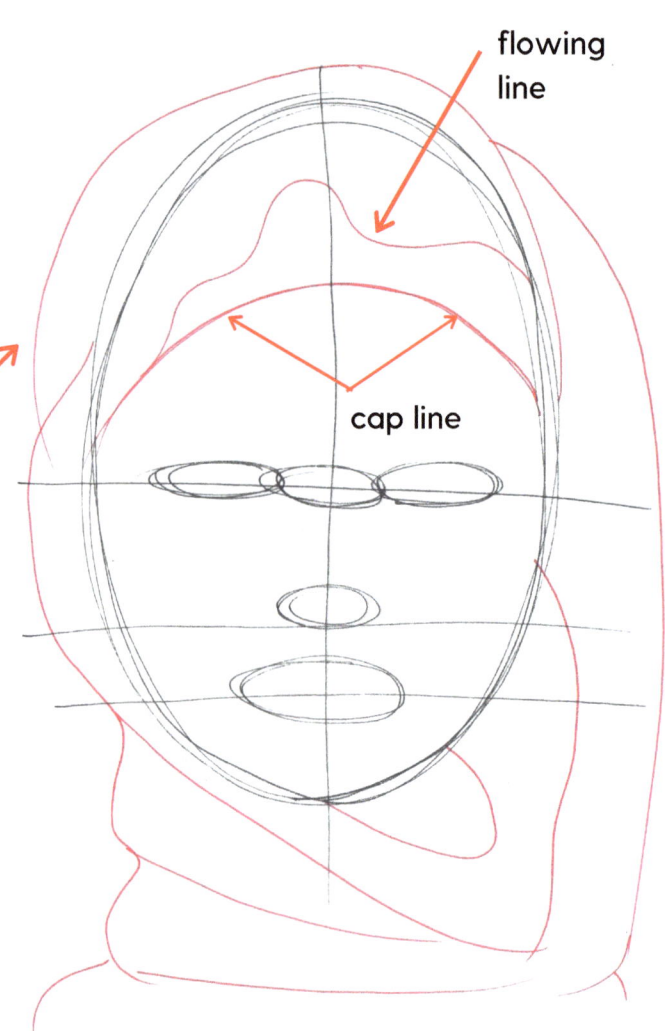

flowing line

cap line

The head scarf is drawn in the same way that we would draw hair. Make sure to draw the top of the scarf well off of the original head oval. Also make sure that the cap (rendered in pink in the reference drawing) comes down lower across the forehead.

The flowing portion of the top of the scarf can be depicted as a loose, flowing line below the head oval but above the pink cap.

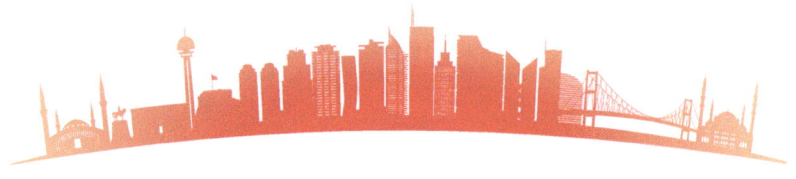

Middle Eastern

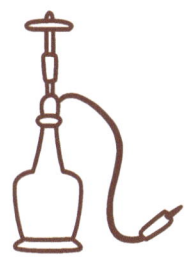

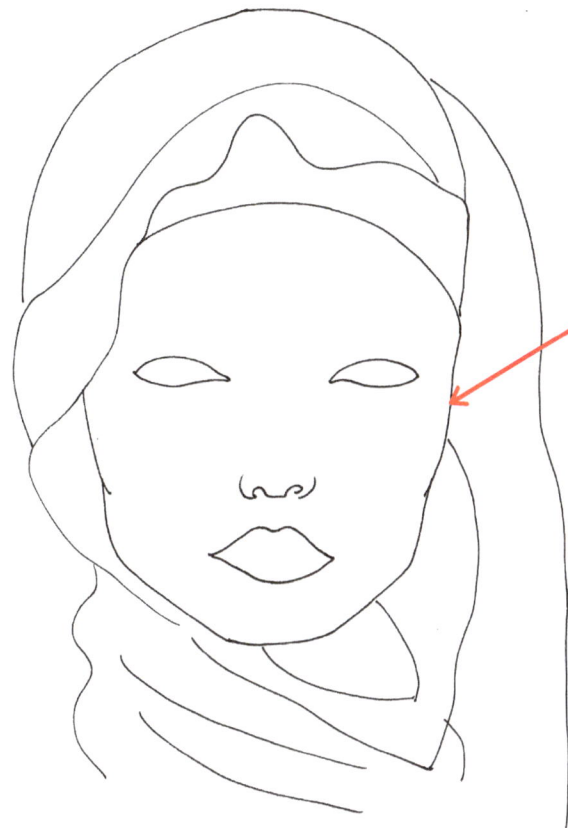

Take a moment to notice her gorgeous face shape. Her cheekbones are so defined that they cut in a little on either side. You can create this look by picking up your pencil at these points and starting a new line below the bone.

Also notice how squared off her chin is. Beautiful!

Once the features have been more properly defined (and note how different her nose is from the last lesson!) you can erase the guidelines.

Then add the eyebrows, irises, eyelids, nose filtrum (or "lip-dip" as I like to call it!) and mouth line.

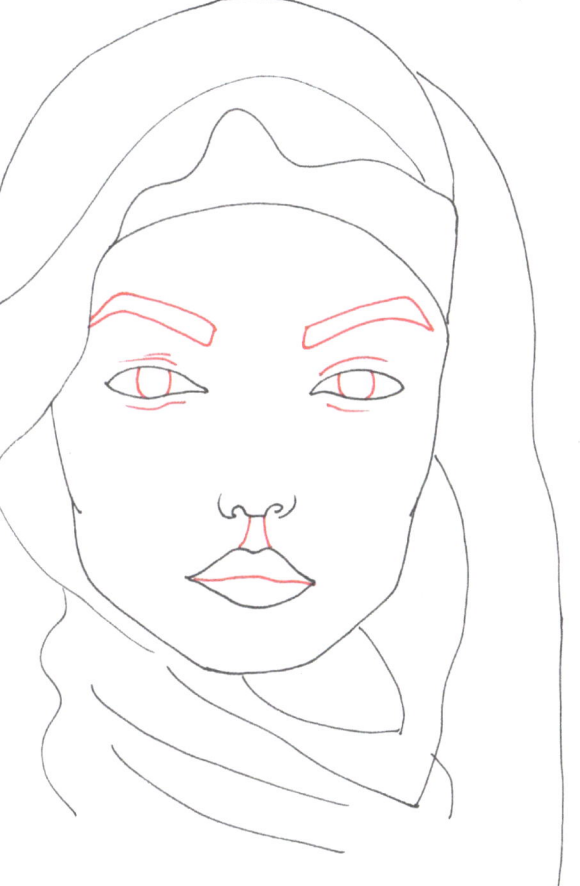

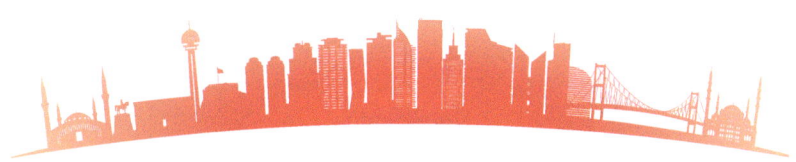

Middle Eastern

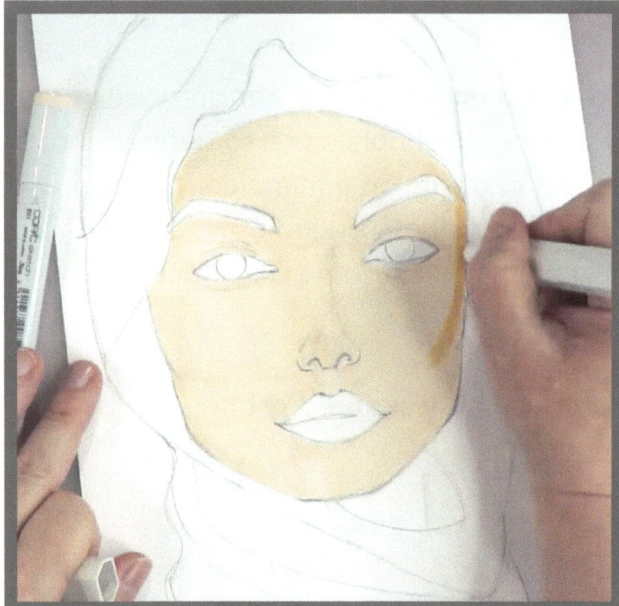

Step 1. Color the face all over in a light skin tone. Work quickly to minimize streaking.

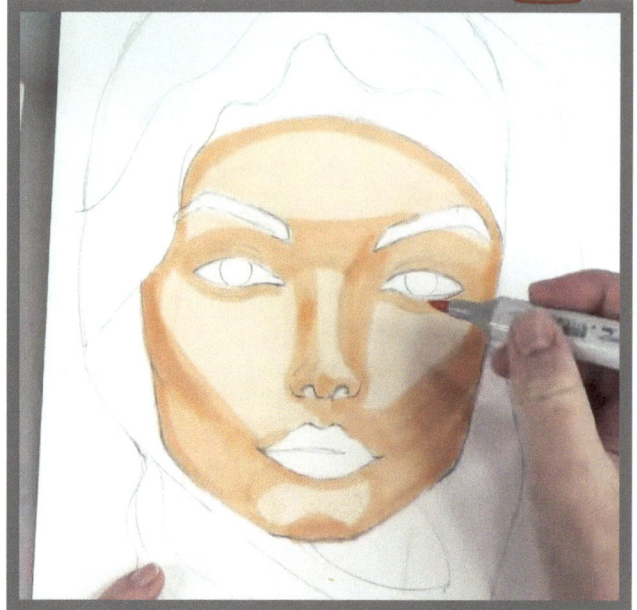

Step 2. With a slightly darker shade, add color to the areas shown. Leave the chin, forehead, cheeks and nose bridge open.

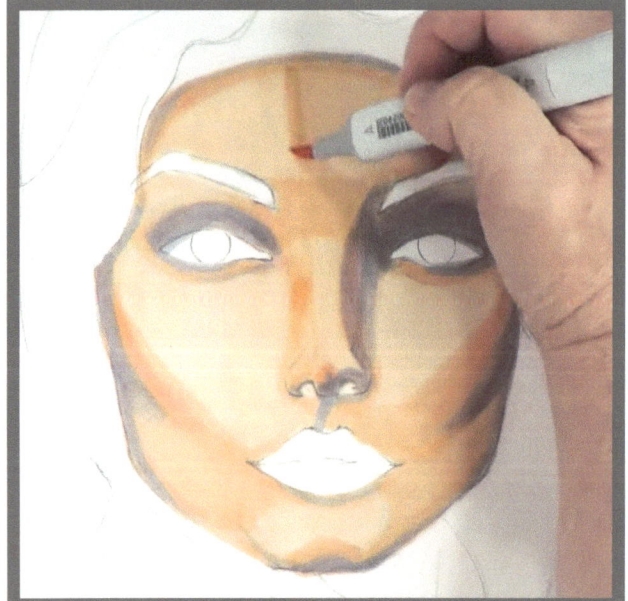

Step 3. With a medium grey (or lavender) shade, add shading around the eyes, along cheeks and under mouth and chin. Then repeat skin tone all over.

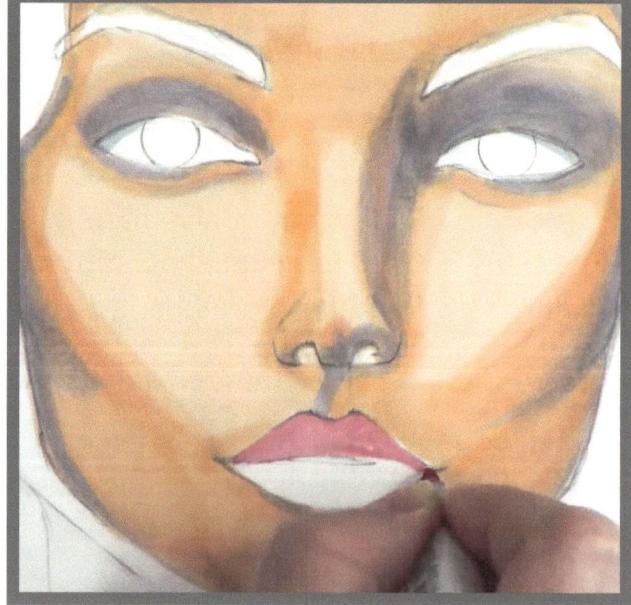

Step 4. Color lips with a medium shade of pink.

Middle Eastern

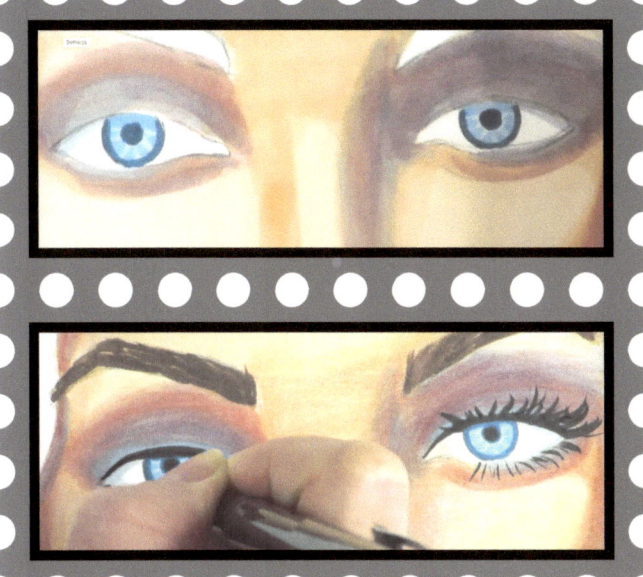

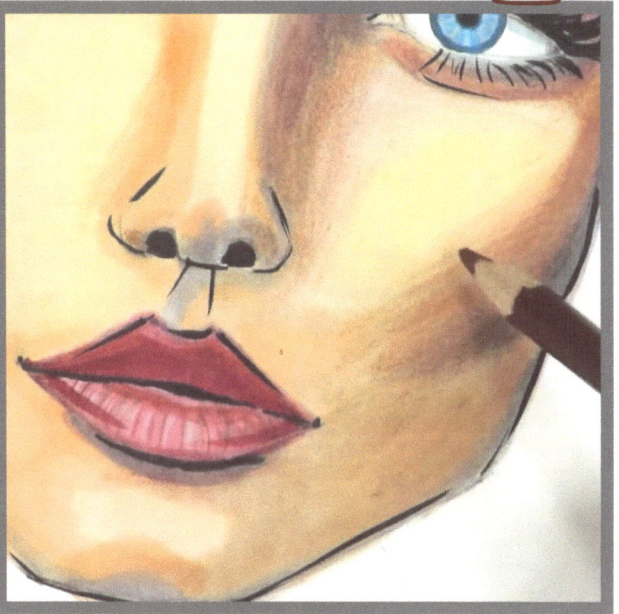

Step 5. Color irises with blue/grey color. Add lashes and eyebrows. I use the same brush pen for drawing lashes and outlining the face.

Step 6. Use colored pencils to add more shading to the darkest areas (remember to look at the reference to see where to go!).

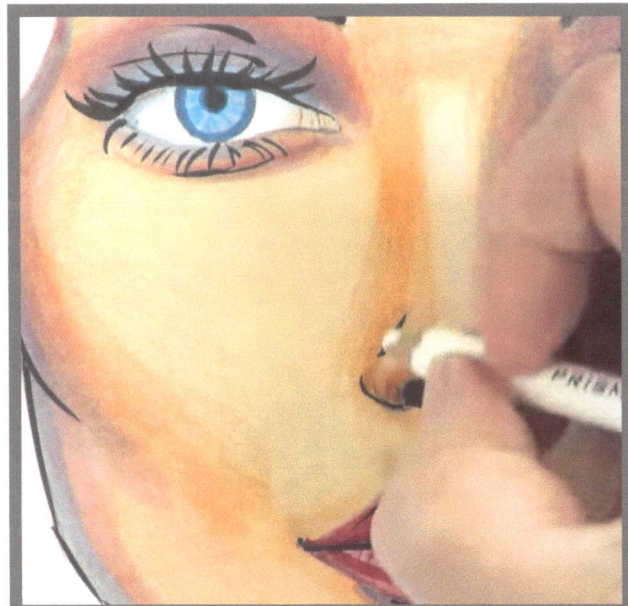

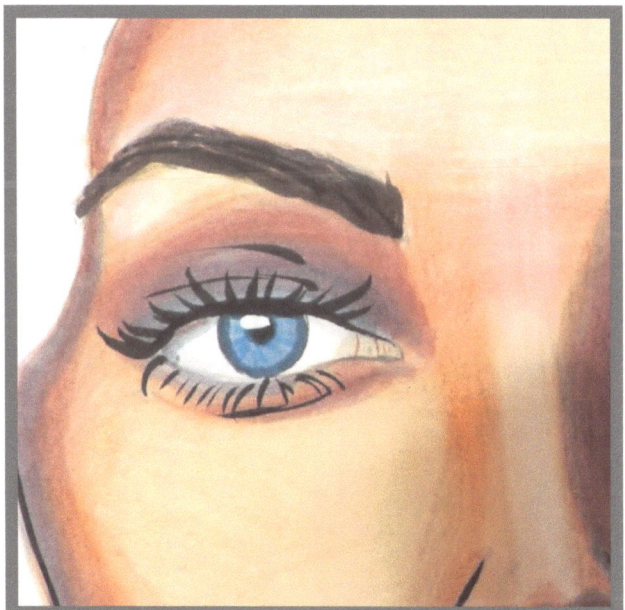

Step 7. Use white colored pencil to create the "glow" in the highlighted areas (nose-bridge, cheeks, chin and forehead).

Step 8. Use a white paint marker to create stunning highlights! The eyes are the first to get a twinkle. Turn the page to learn the other best places to put highlights on faces!

Middle Eastern

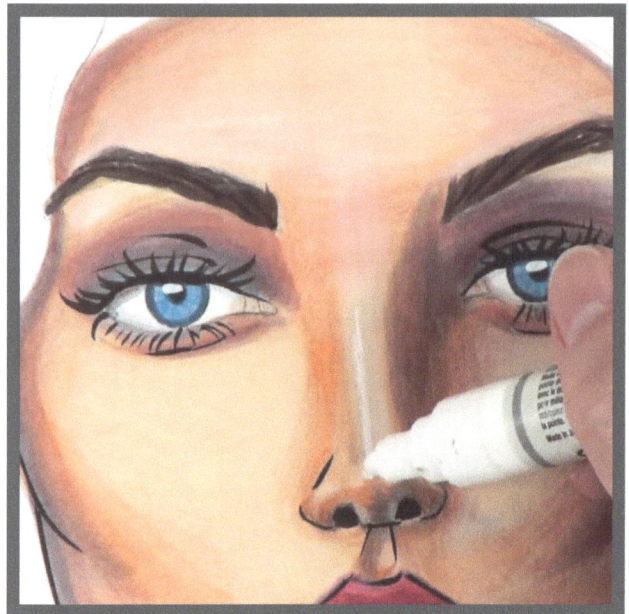

Step 9. Draw a line down the nose bridge and then blend it slightly with your figure to create a stunning highlight effect!

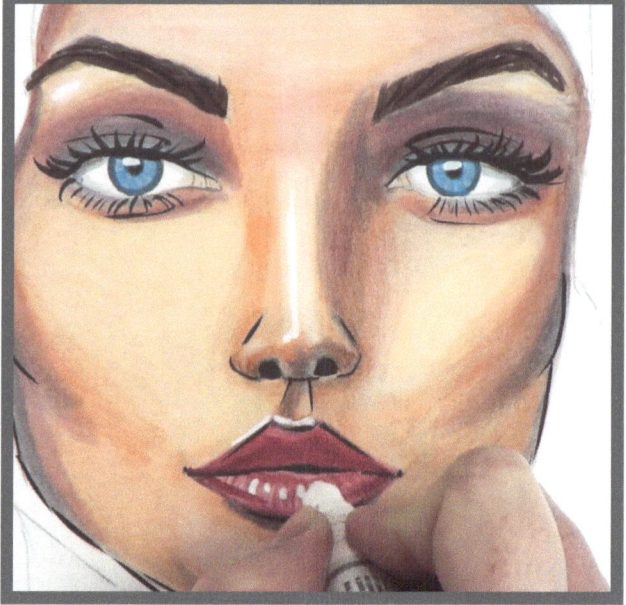

Step 10. Lastly, line the top of the lips and then put some white dots along the lower lips. Dab with your finger and done!

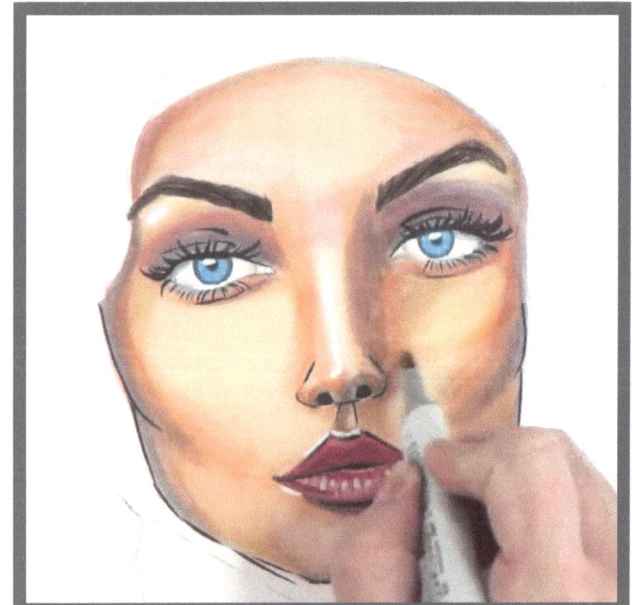

Step 11. Use a mid tone skin tone to go over any last areas one more time. This blends all the previous layers together for a final finish.

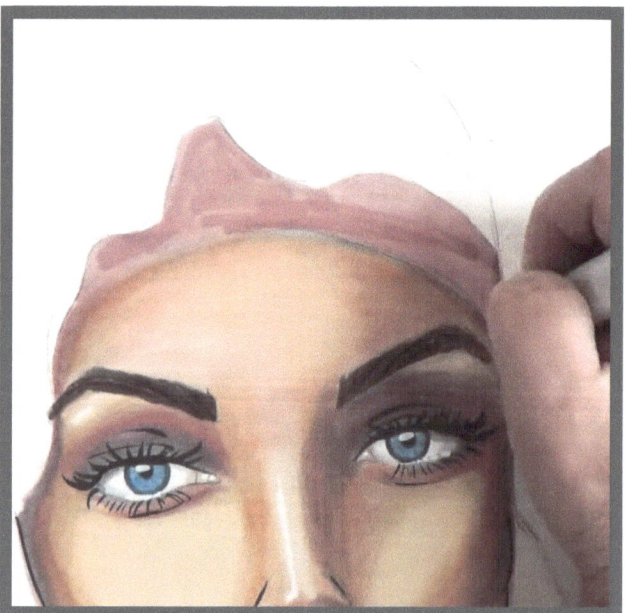

Step 12. Moving on to the headpiece. First, color the cap in with a lovely pink color. You can go over it with a second coat if desired.

62

Middle Eastern

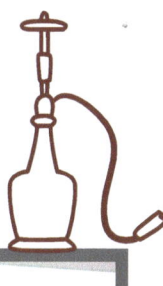

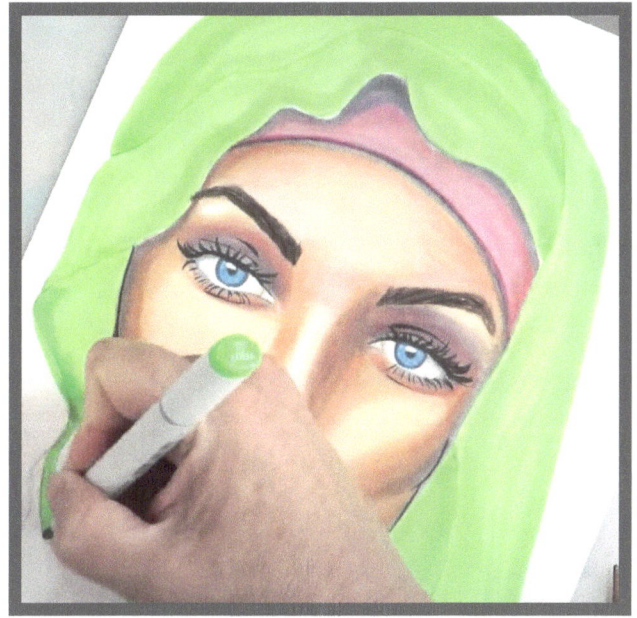

Step 13. Color the entire shawl with a bright green.

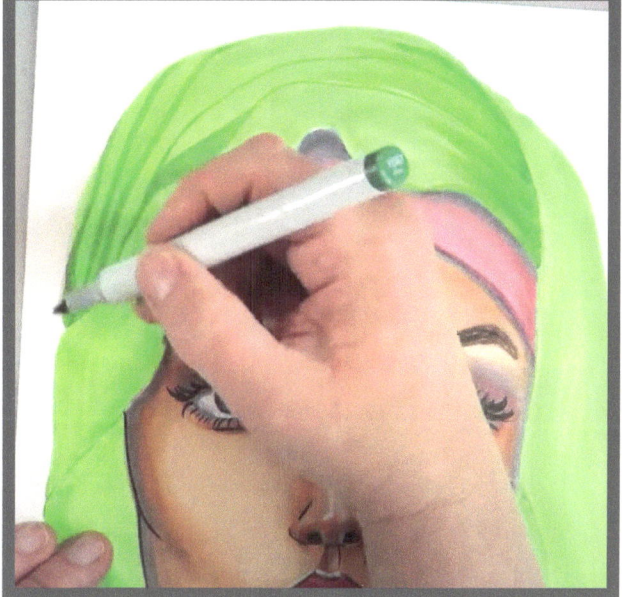

Step 14. With a darker shade, color in the areas where there are shadows. Look at the reference drawing to see where to apply.

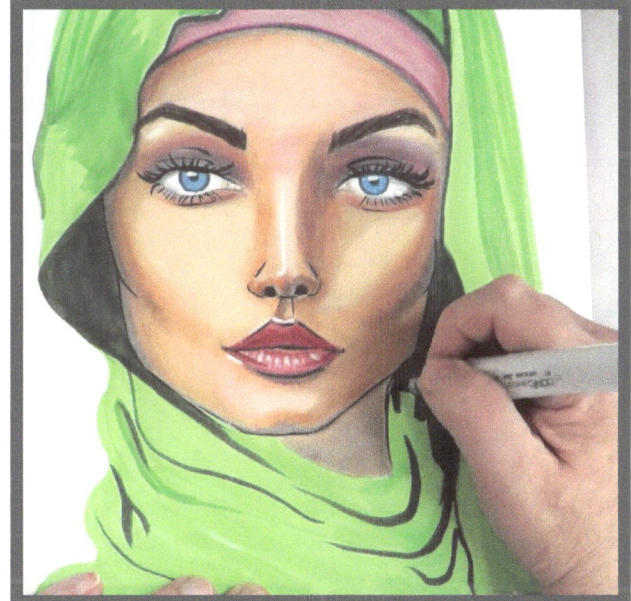

Step 15. Use dark grey to color the inside areas of her headpiece and along the darkest creases and folds. Again, refer to the reference so you know where to go.

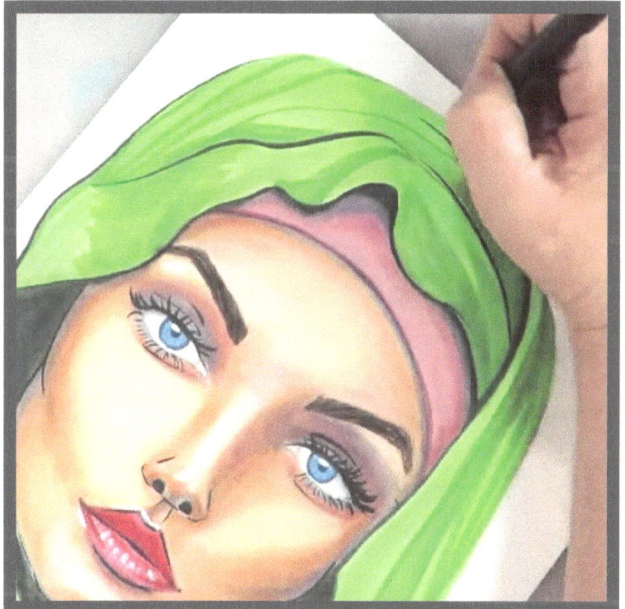

Step 16. Use a black pen to outline the entire headpiece and face if you haven't done so already. Congratulate yourself on a job well done!

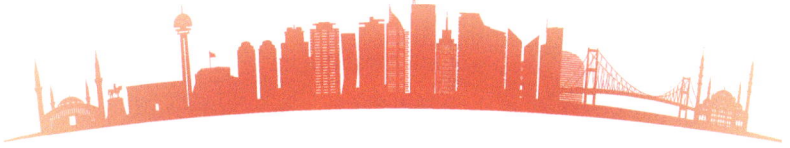

Student Work

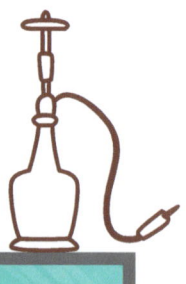

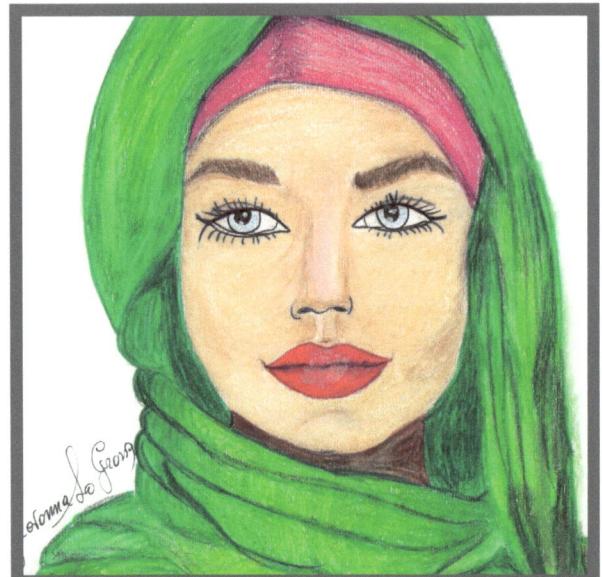

Giovanna Lo Grasso. Giotto watercolor pencils *"I used these materials because being a beginner I think they are easy to use to get good shades and bright colors."*

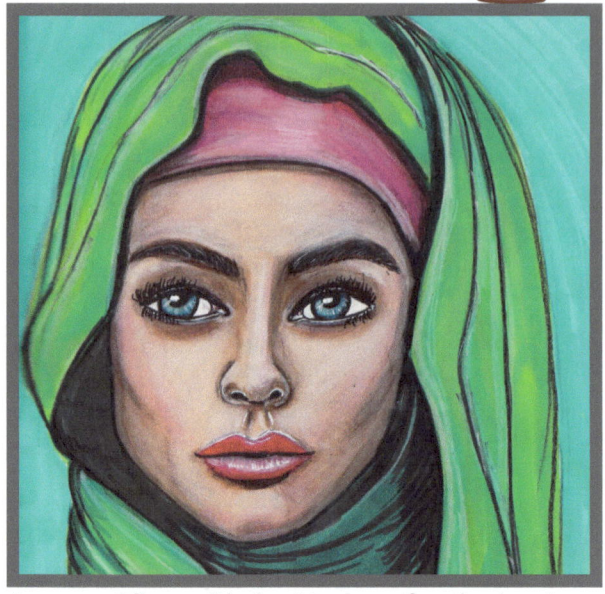

Joanne Oliver. Ohuhu Markers for the basic shading and colouring, pencils of similar colour to blend and pastel for the final high lights...*"White pen too for that sparkle!"*

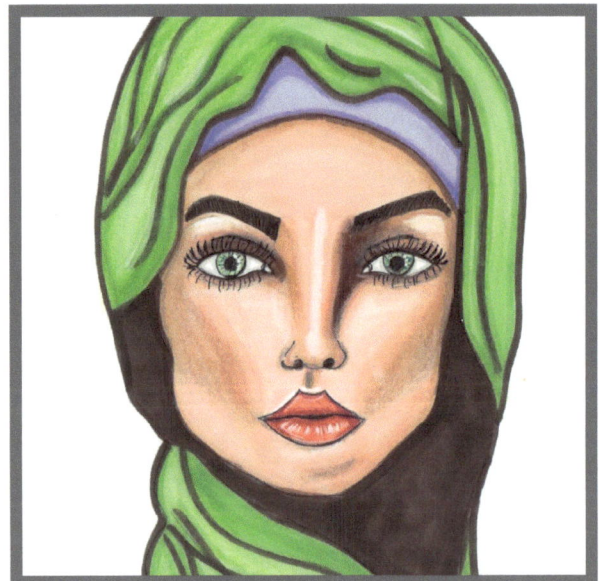

Jayne Charlton. Alcohol markers and colored pencils, fineliners and Posca Pen. *"I chose these materials because they are high quality at affordable prices and do exactly what I want then to."*

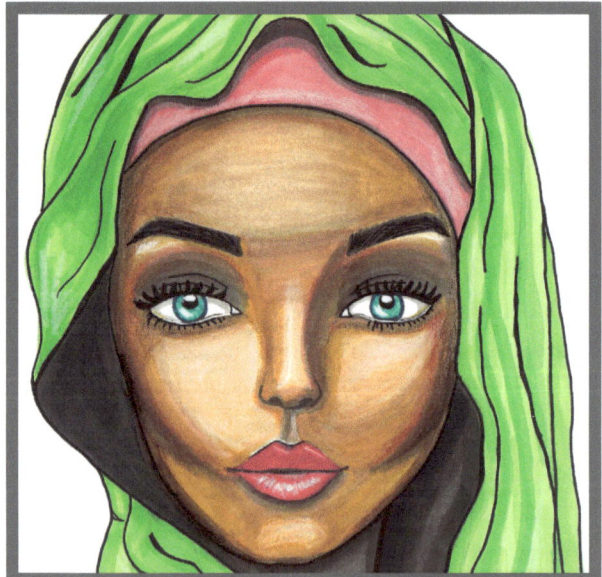

Sandie Gills. Alcohol Markers (Spectrum Noir and Copics) and Arteza colored pencils. *"I found that the pencils on top of the markers blended really well, helping to erode any harsh lines."*

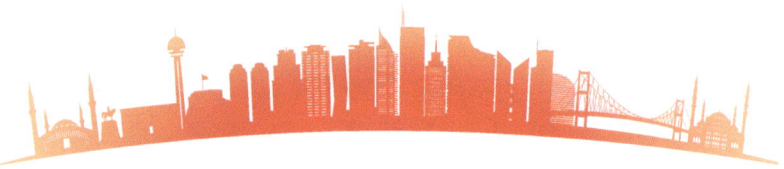

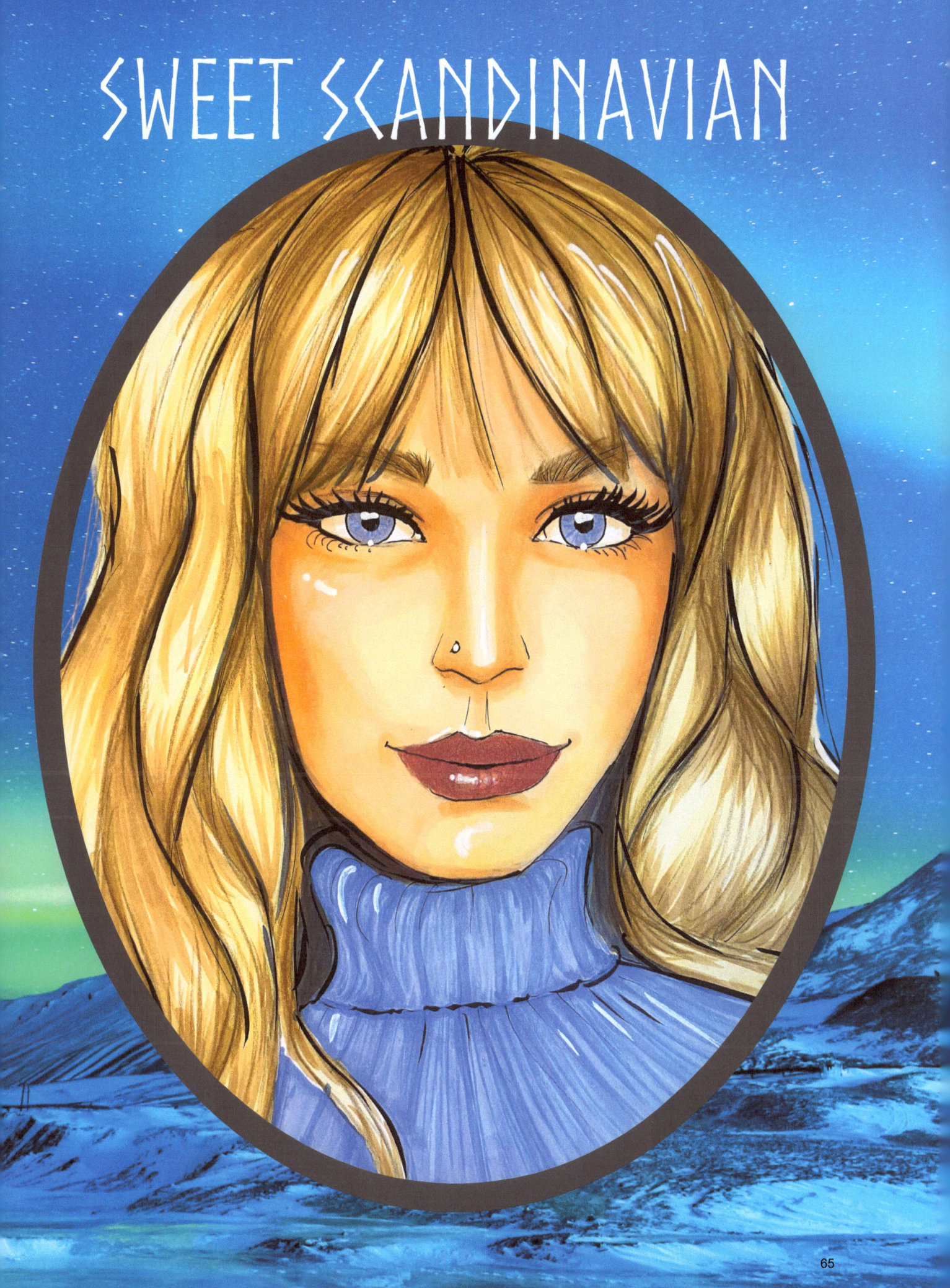

SCANDINAVIAN

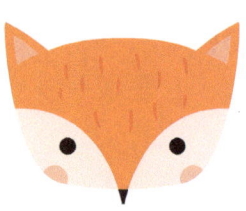

I hope by now this part is a piece of cake!! In go those guidelines and the ovals too!

She has a full mouth, so make sure that the oval is rather large.

As always, hair has much more volume than you'd think. Make sure you make those long flowing locks all start up at the top. Notice her part is in the middle. Her bangs start at the top too and go almost down to the eyeline.

Divide the hair into some simple sections. Don't overcomplicate it. Just start at the middle part and make continuous wavy lines all the way down to the bottom.

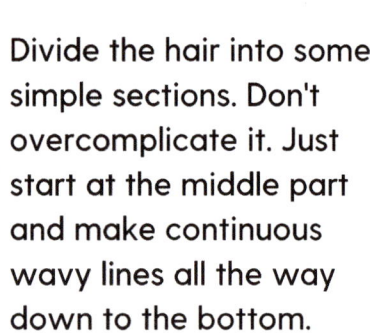

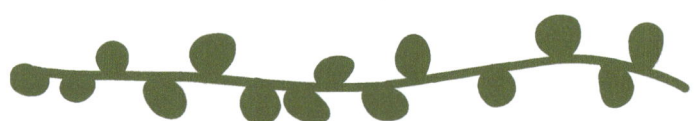

SCANDINAVIAN

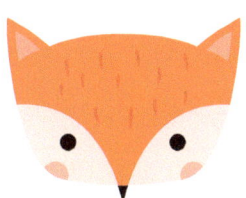

Before adding color, make sure the hair is clearly divided into sections.

You don't need too many, but the ones you have should be clear to you.

This makes coloring so much easier!

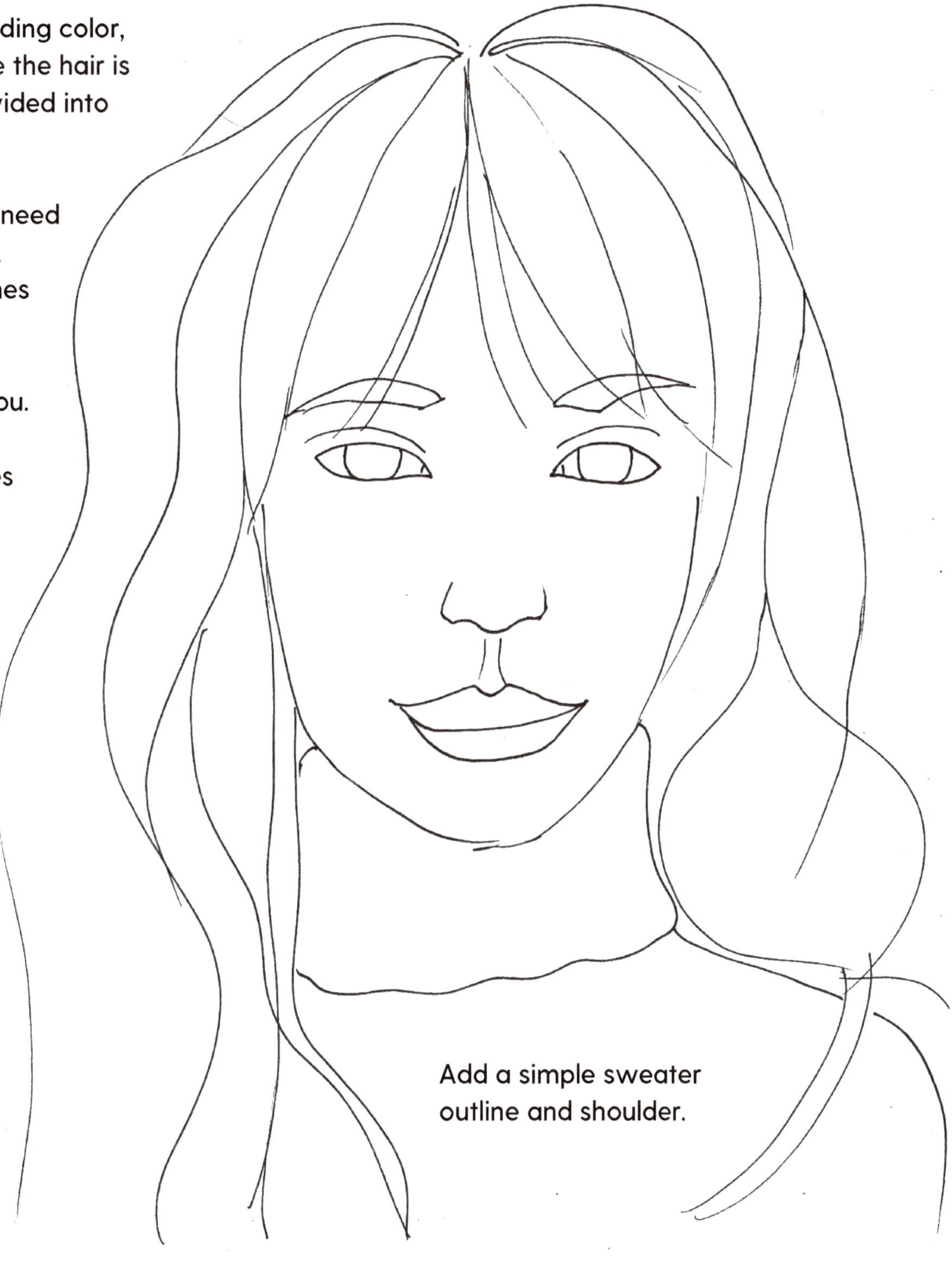

Add a simple sweater outline and shoulder.

SCANDINAVIAN

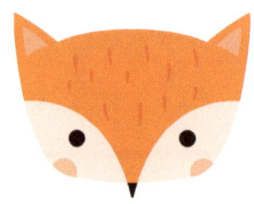

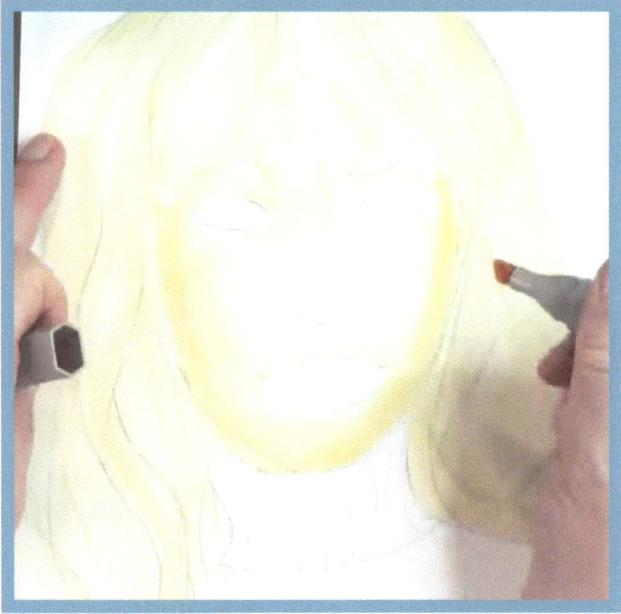

Step 1. Color the entire face and hair a pale yellow (skin) color.

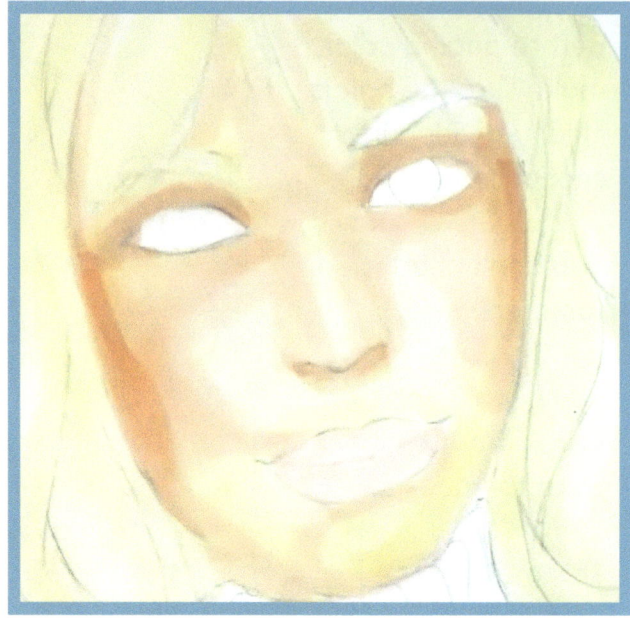

Step 2. Add a pink shade to cheeks, eyes, forehead, sides and under nose and mouth.

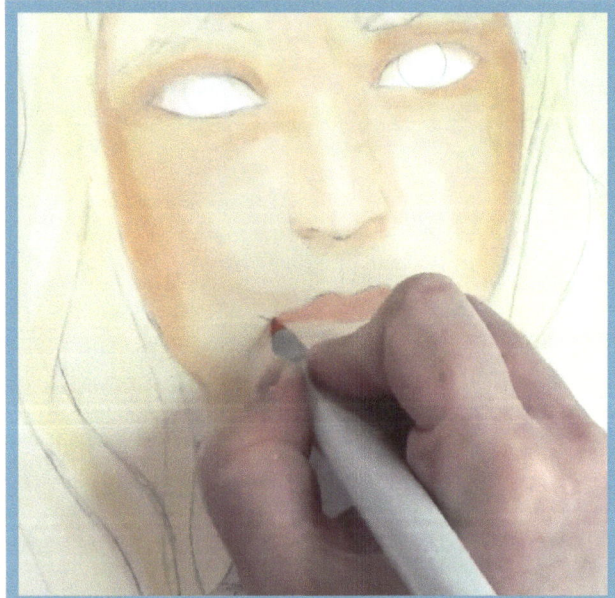

Step 3. To smoothe and blend the skin colors, use a super light marker (skin) color and go over the entire face once or twice, switching directions each layer. Apply pink to the lips.

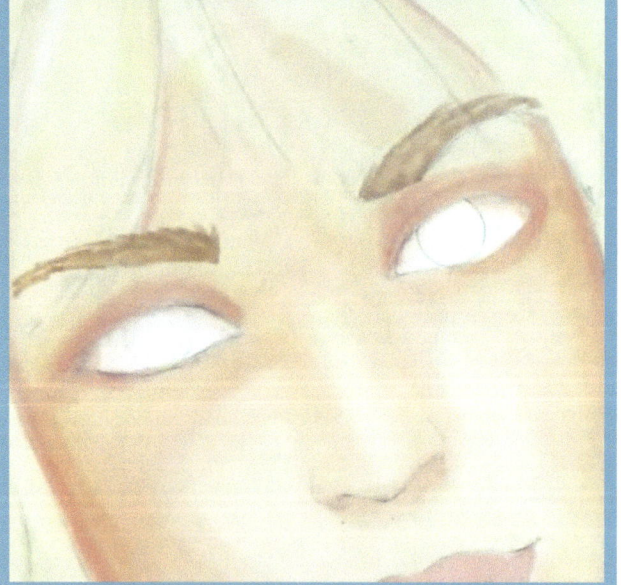

Step 4. Color in the eyebrows with a light brown and then use a light pink on the eyelids and on the sides of the face and under the chin.

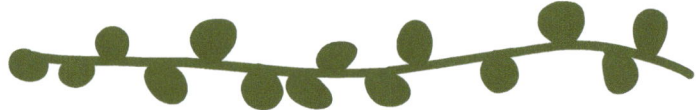

SCANDINAVIAN

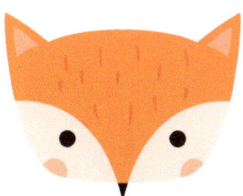

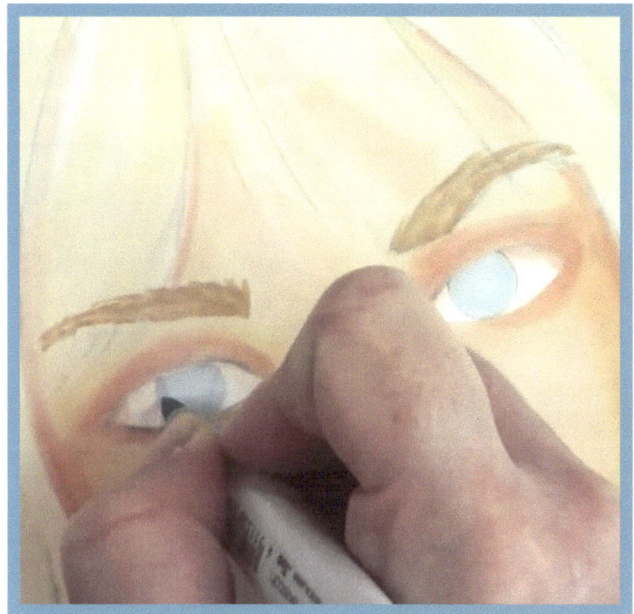

Step 5. Color the eyes a light blue.

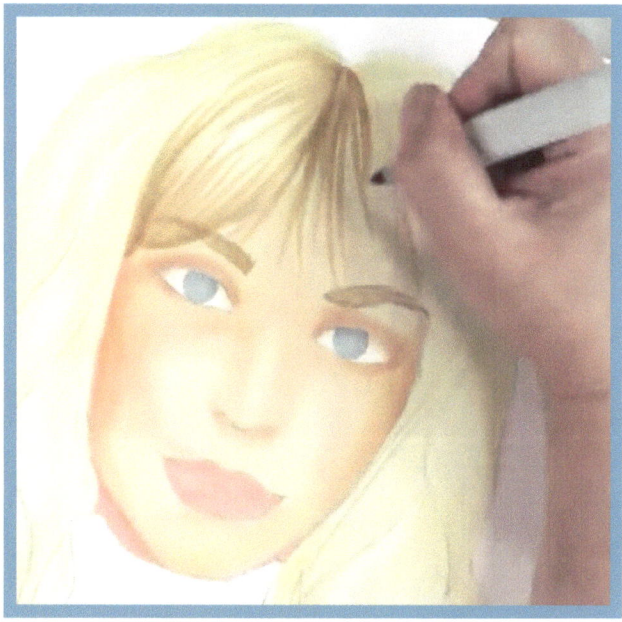

Step 6. Apply a light brown to the roots and tips of each of the drawn sections.

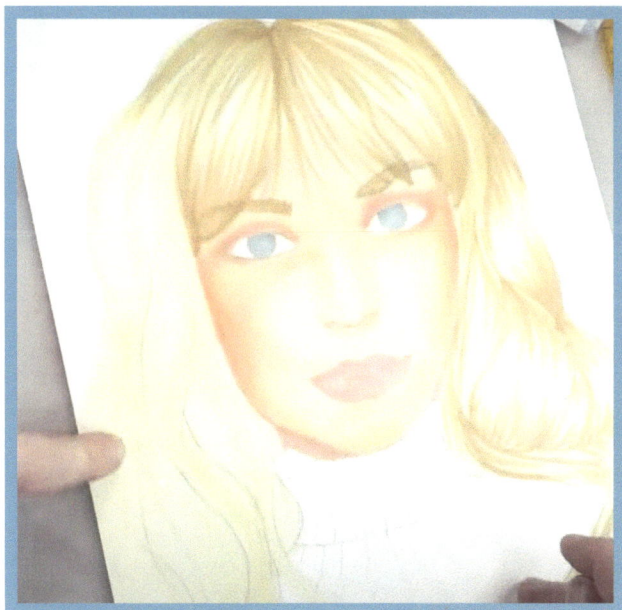

Step 7. Do the same "root and tip" coloring for each section of hair. Slowly work your way around the entire head.

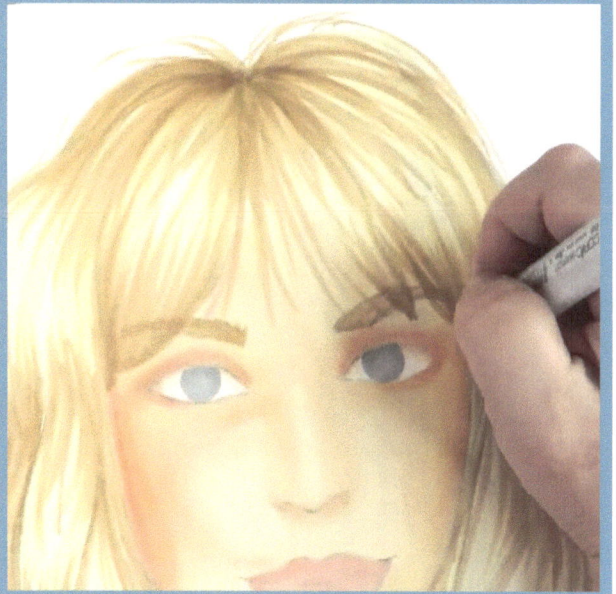

Step 8. Once the whole head is done with the lightest brown, use a slightly deeper shade and go back over the roots and tips again. This time leave more of the first brown exposed in each section.

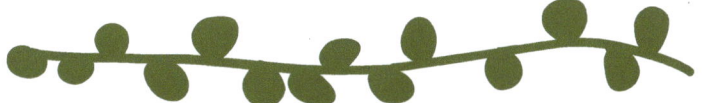

SCANDINAVIAN

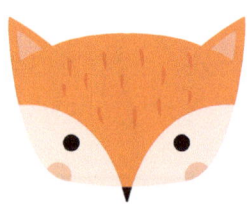

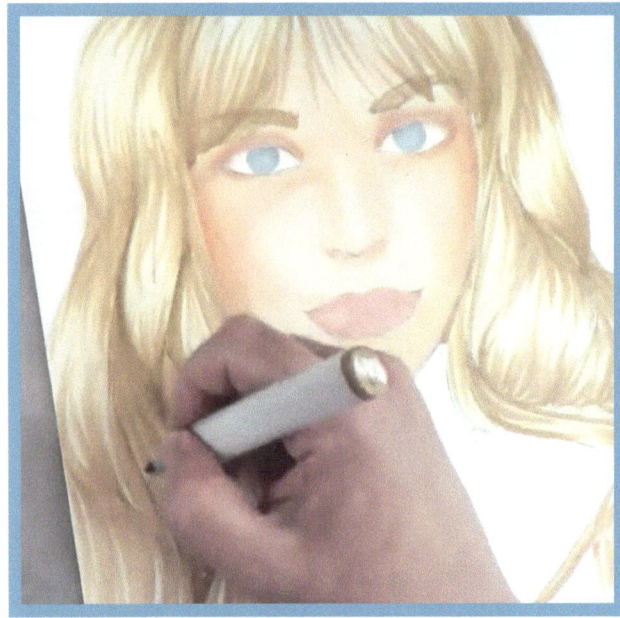

Step 9. Keep working with the darker shade until all sections are done.

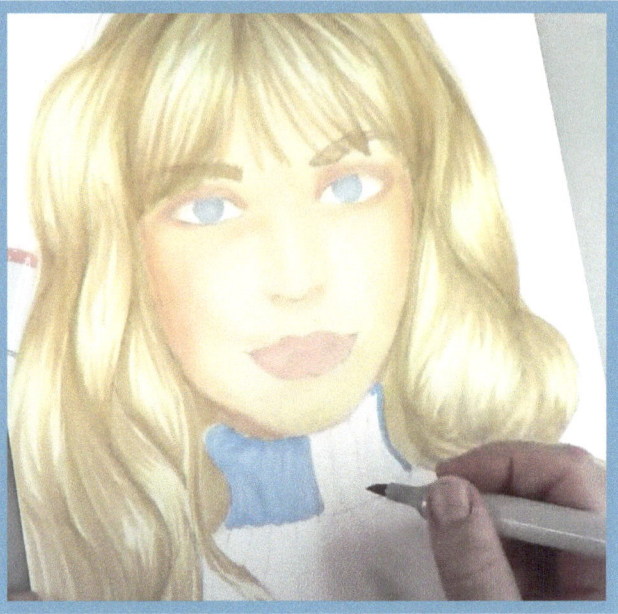

Step 10. When you're happy with the hair, move on to the sweater. Use blue if you like!

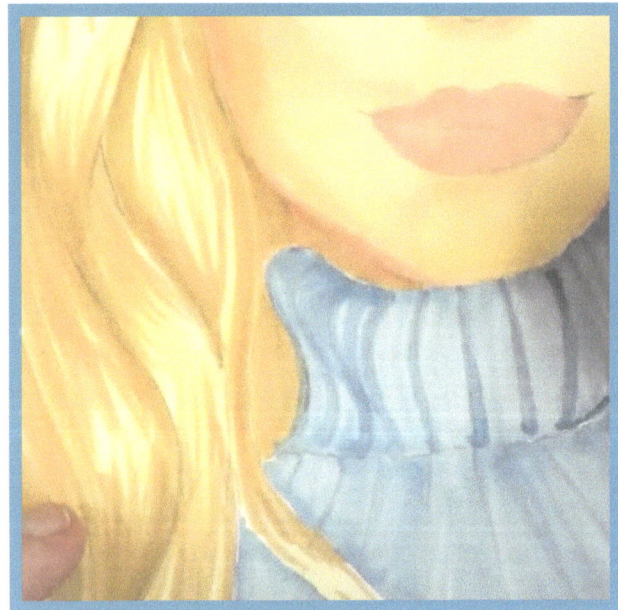

Step 11. Use a darker shade of blue to add stripes in the sweater.

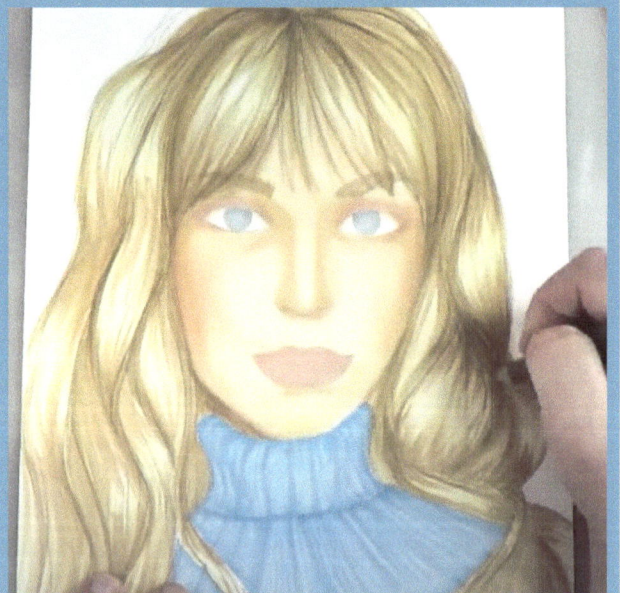

Step 12. Use colored pencils that match your markers to add emphasis and texture to all the parts you like! I love using it on the hair to define the sections, on the sweater to add texture and on the irises for fun!

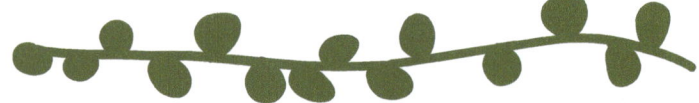

SCANDINAVIAN

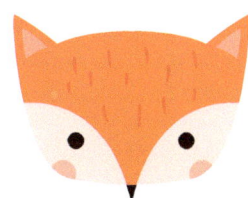

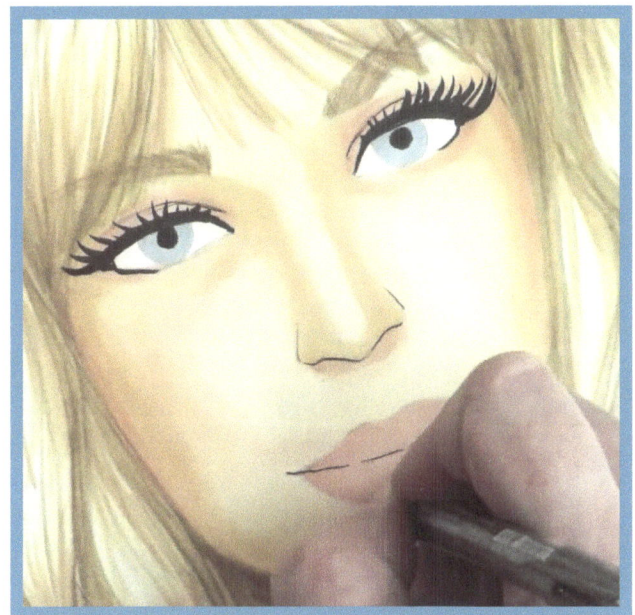

Step 13. Use a brush pen to create the lashes and pupils. Outline nose and mouth.

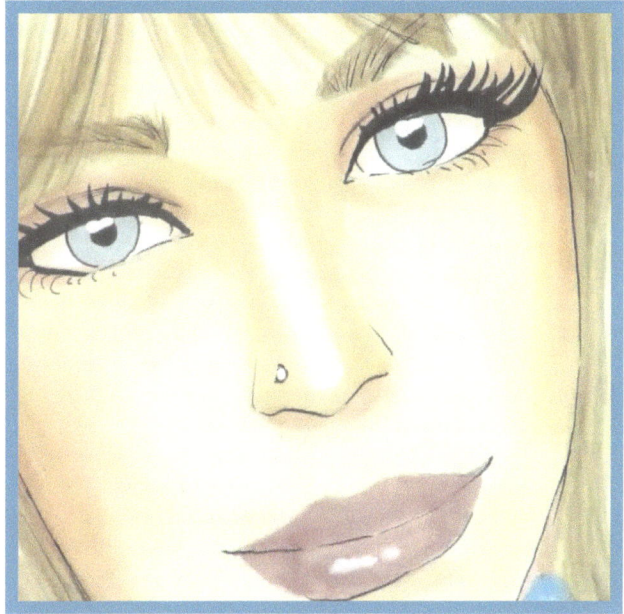

Step 14. Add white paint pen to the eyes, nose ring, nose bridge, bottom lip and chin.

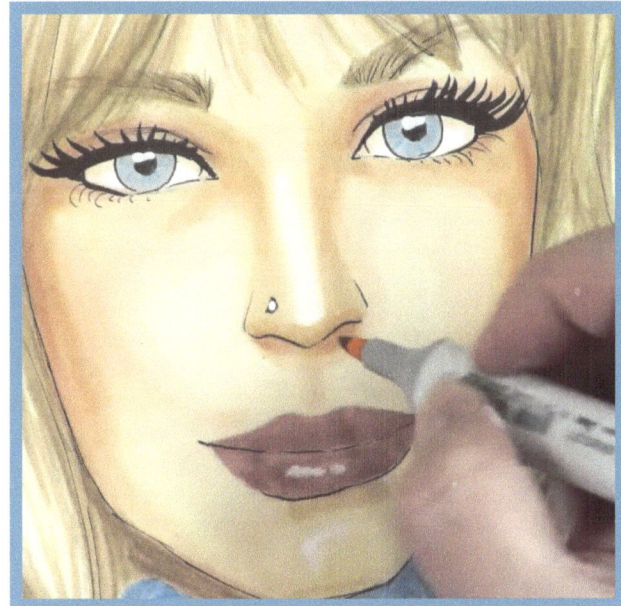

Step 15. Add any additional shading. Here I am darkening the shadow under her nose and around the eyes/cheeks with a pink skin tone.

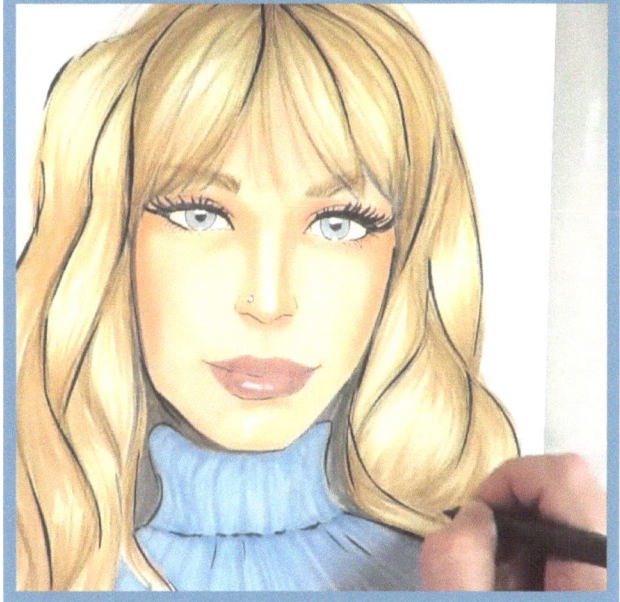

Step 16. This last step is completely optional. I like to outline everything, but you can absolutely stop before and she would be completely finished! Beautifully done!

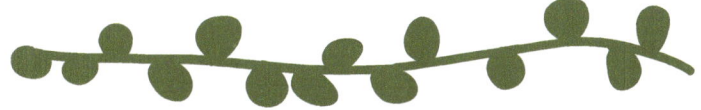

STUDENT SPOTLIGHT

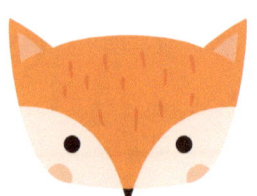

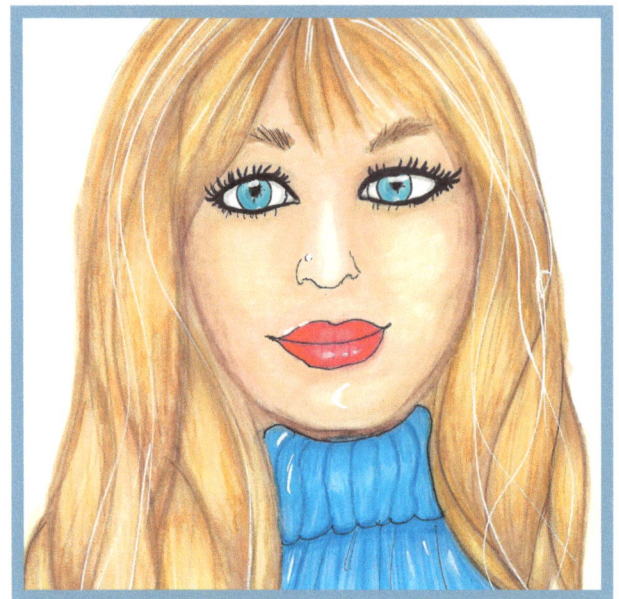

Veronica Schlett. Mixed media. *"I used Copics to improve my coloring and then used the color pencils to help blend the color better."*

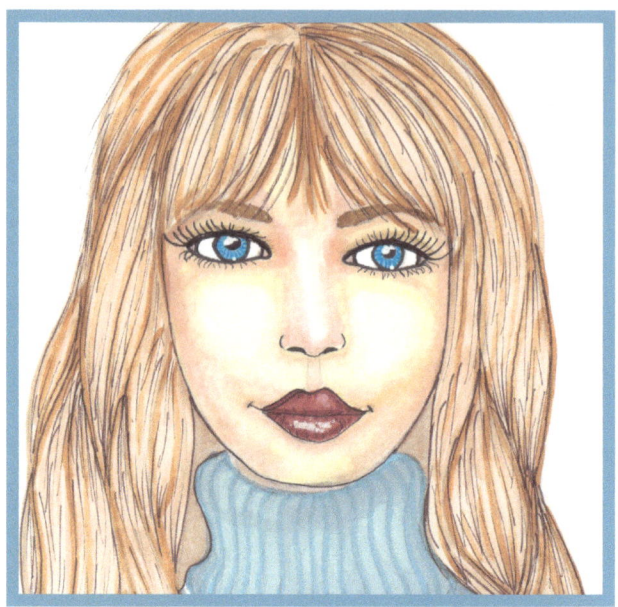

Roxenne Kendall. Alcohol markers on cardstock.

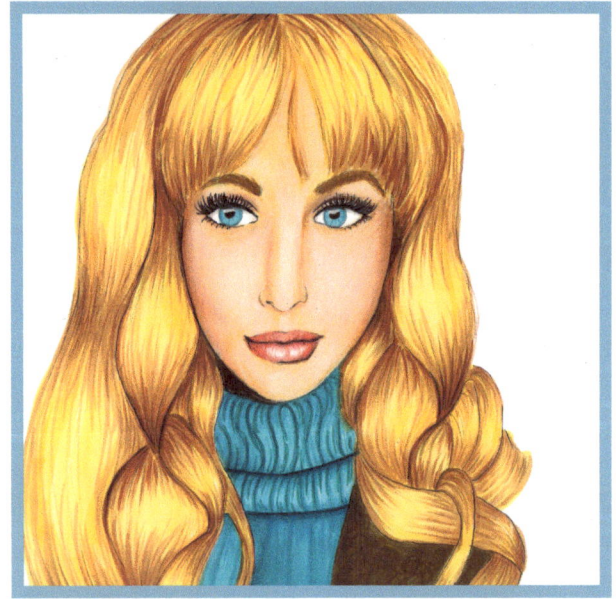

Deborah Palmer. Alcohol markers and colored pencil and pens. *"I used these materials to get the brightness of the coloring in this subject."*

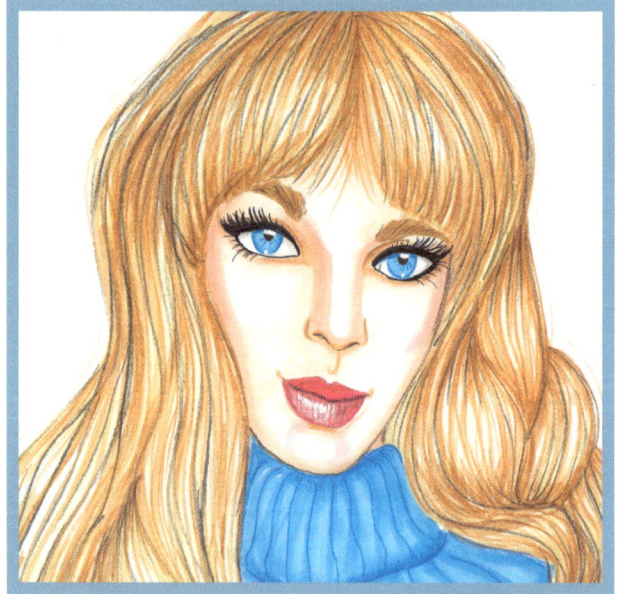

Sharon Nilsen. Mixed media. *"I have always used colored pencils alone in the past, and now I have learned to love using alcohol markers in tandem with the pencils for a smoother finish, particularly on faces and skin tones."*

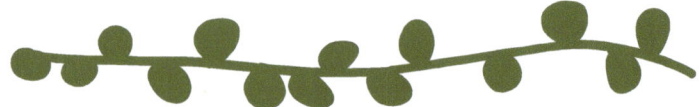

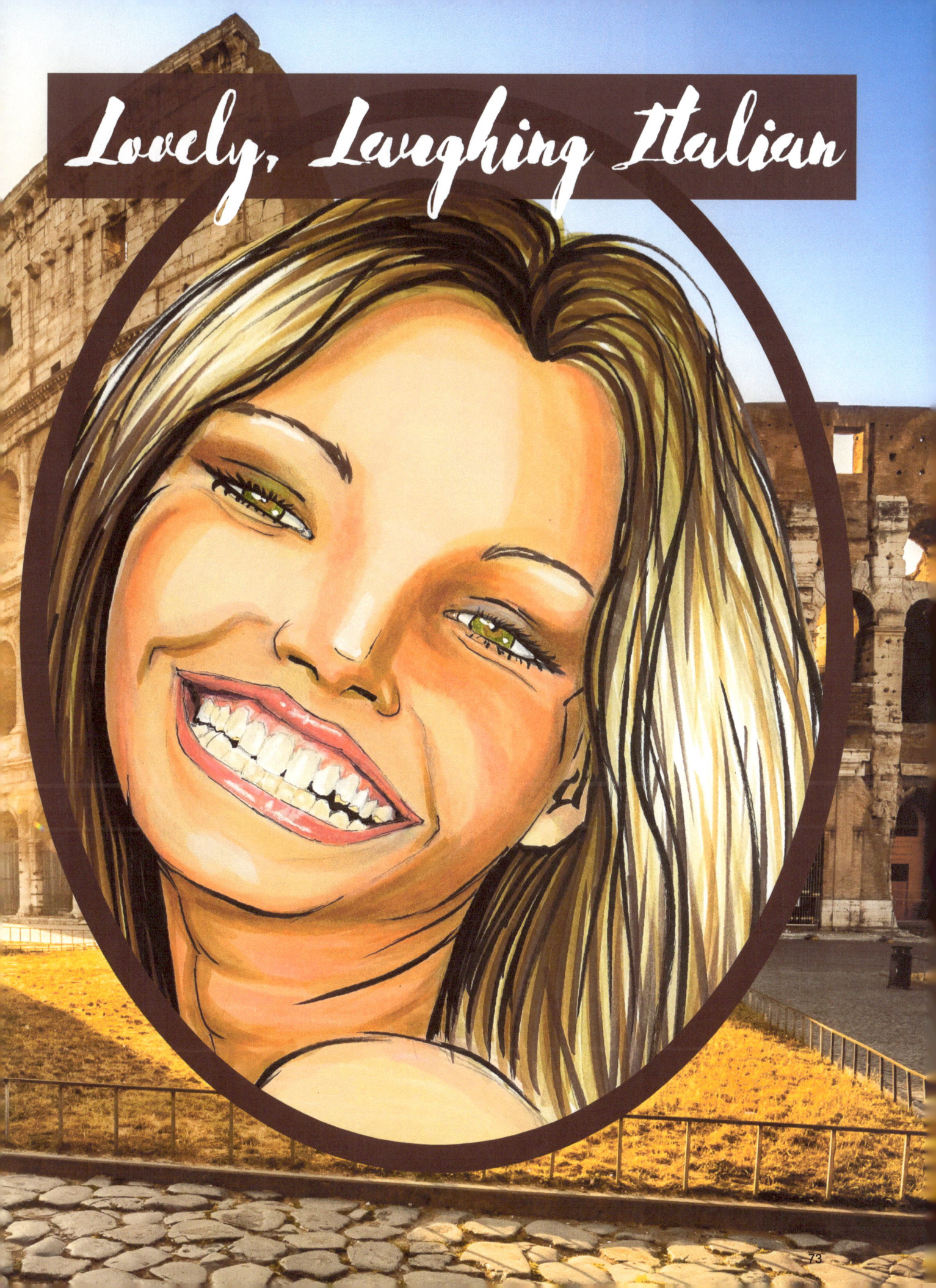

Italian

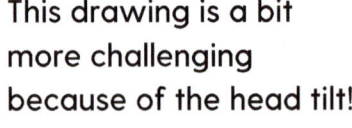

This drawing is a bit more challenging because of the head tilt!

Use the red arrow line to help you orient your oval in this new way.

Your guidelines stay the same and move with the oval.

As always, draw a vertical and horizontal line both down and across the center of the head oval.

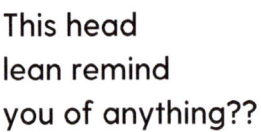

This head lean remind you of anything??

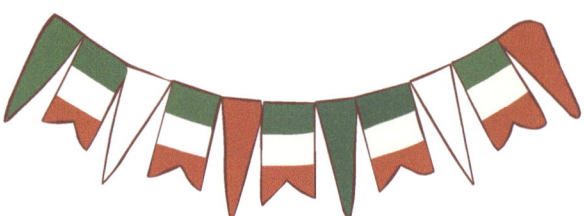

Italian

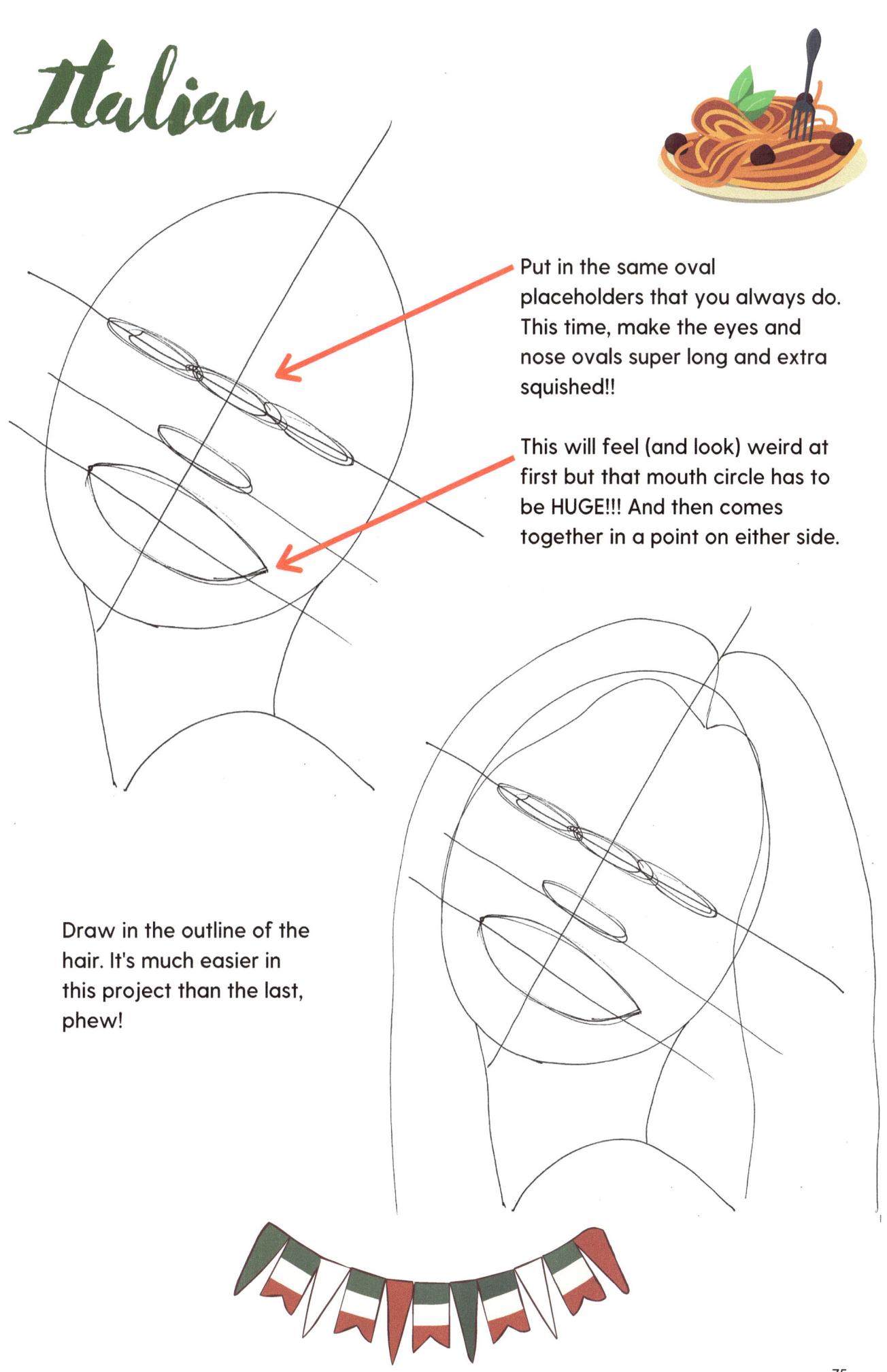

Put in the same oval placeholders that you always do. This time, make the eyes and nose ovals super long and extra squished!!

This will feel (and look) weird at first but that mouth circle has to be HUGE!!! And then comes together in a point on either side.

Draw in the outline of the hair. It's much easier in this project than the last, phew!

Italian

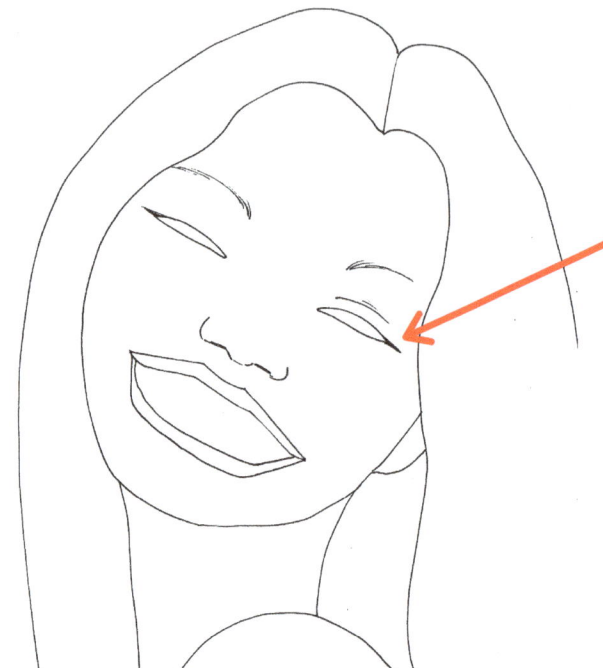

Next, define the features. Her eyes are SUPER thin slits and end in little "V"s because of her cat eye make-up.

Draw thin eyebrows over the eyes.

Draw the lips very thin and the nose wide but thin.

People frequently ask me to how to draw wrinkles and face (expression) lines. The truth is, you draw them just as you see them, and just as they appear!

Don't feel funny about drawing those lines. Without them, she would look "off".

Go ahead and add them with confidence!

Add the gum lines too. They help put the teeth in the right place.

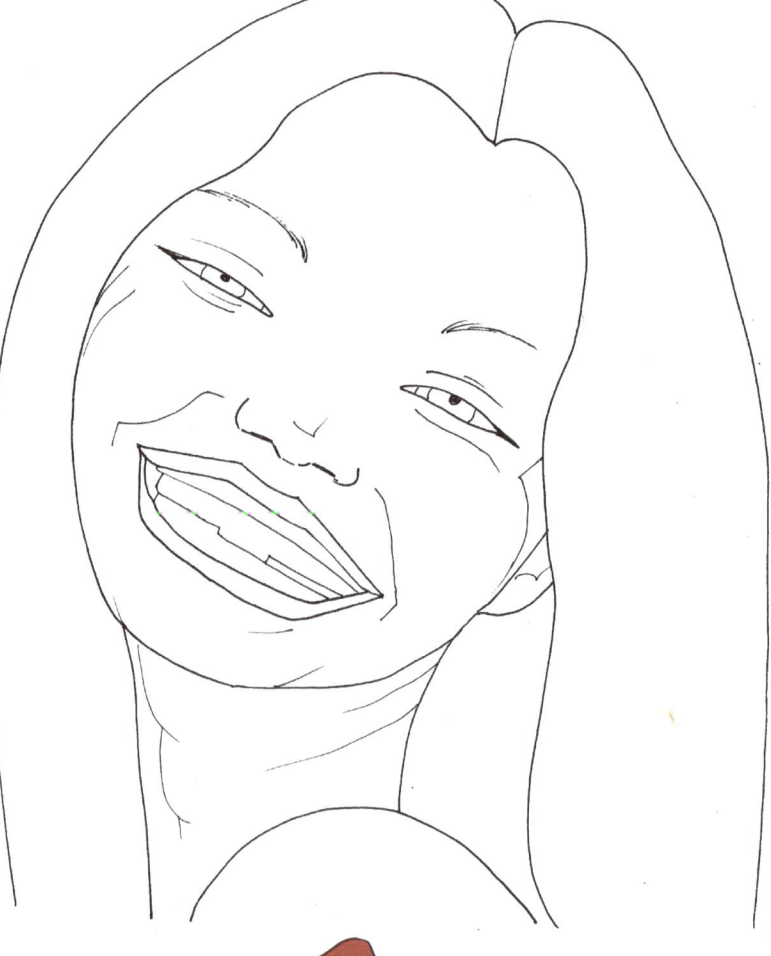

Italian

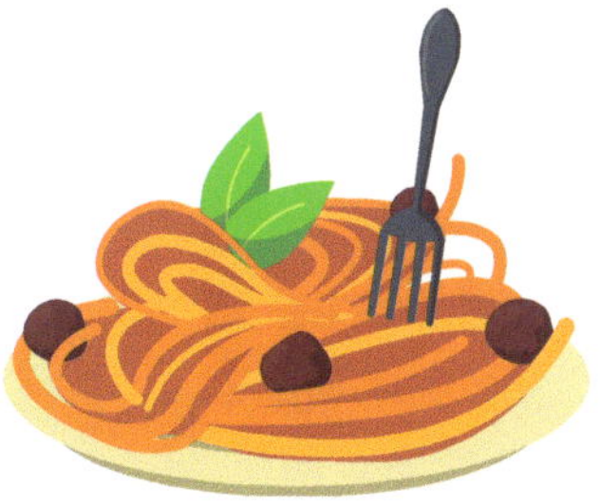

Teeth are funny things to draw! But in order for them to look realistic you have to just draw them like you see them, there's simply no way around it.

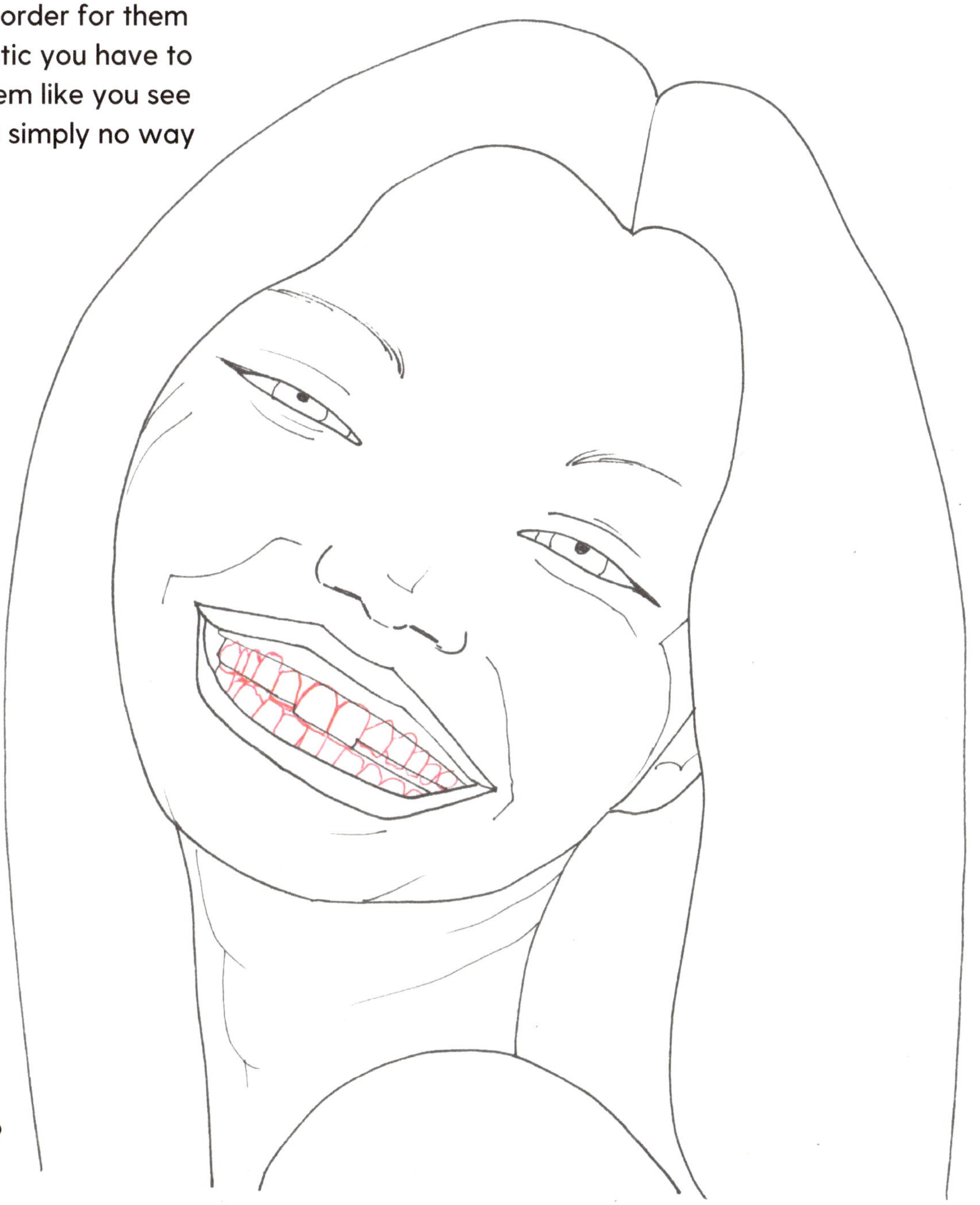

Note how they get smaller as they go towards the back of the mouth.

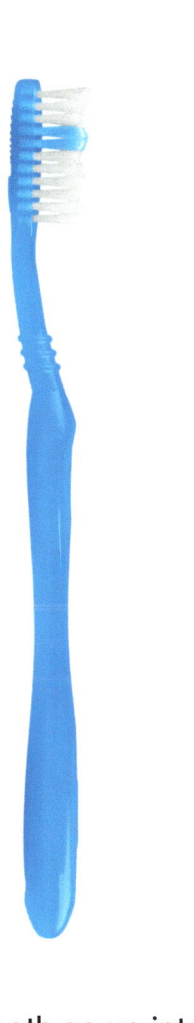

Teeth go up into the gum line so make sure the tops of them aren't perfectly straight.

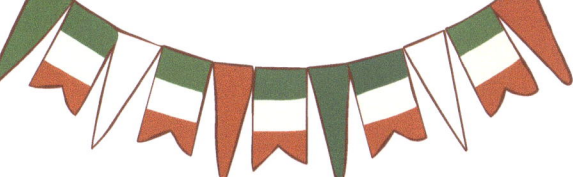

Italian

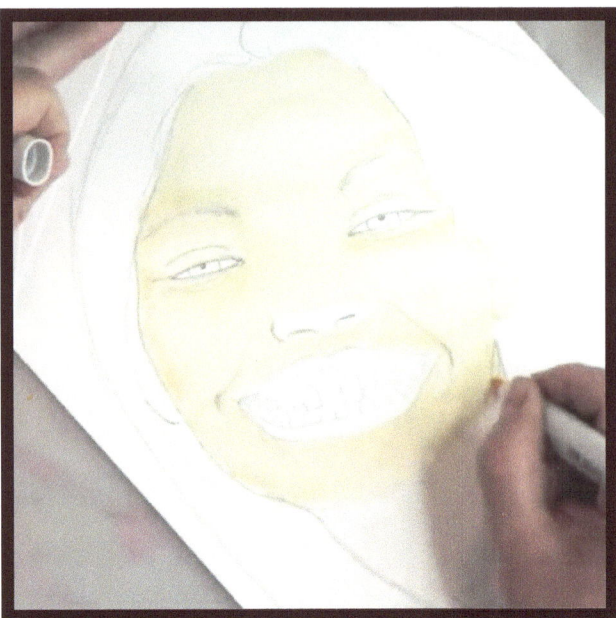

Step 1. Use a light yellow skin shade to color over her entire face and neck area.

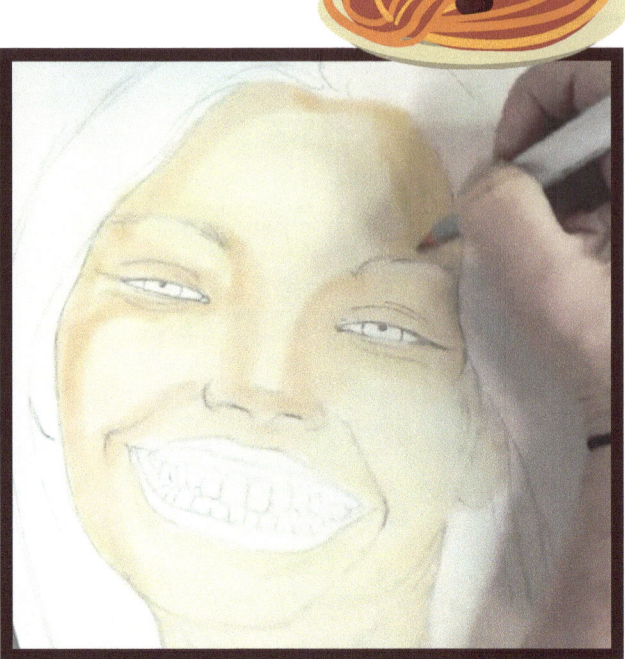

Step 2. Add a pink shade to the hairline, sides of nose, eyes, laugh lines and under chin.

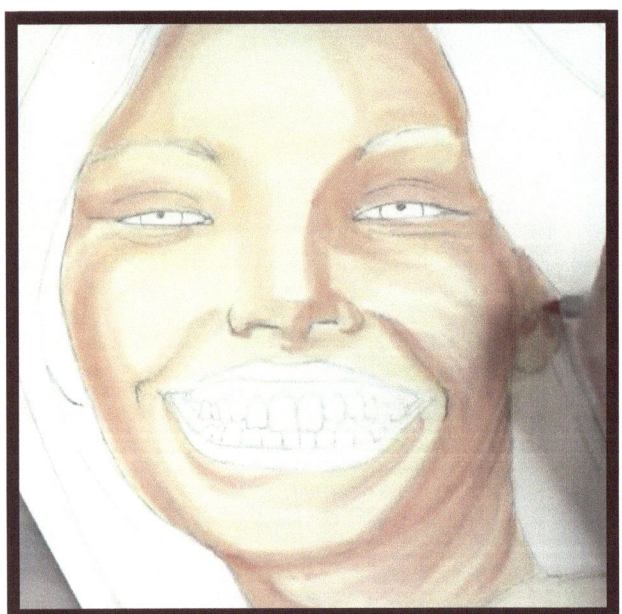

Step 3. Add an even darker shade this time. Make sure there is more shading on the right side than the left.

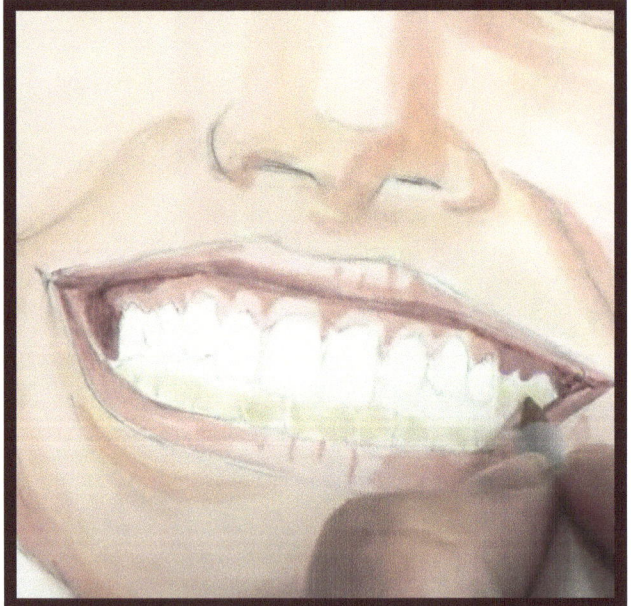

Step 4. Use the same light pink skin shade to color in the lips and gums. Use an off white to color the bottom row of teeth and back molars. Switch to a darker pink and color back gums.

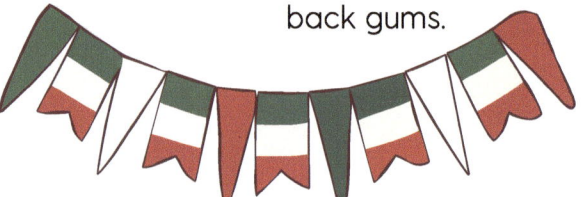

Italian

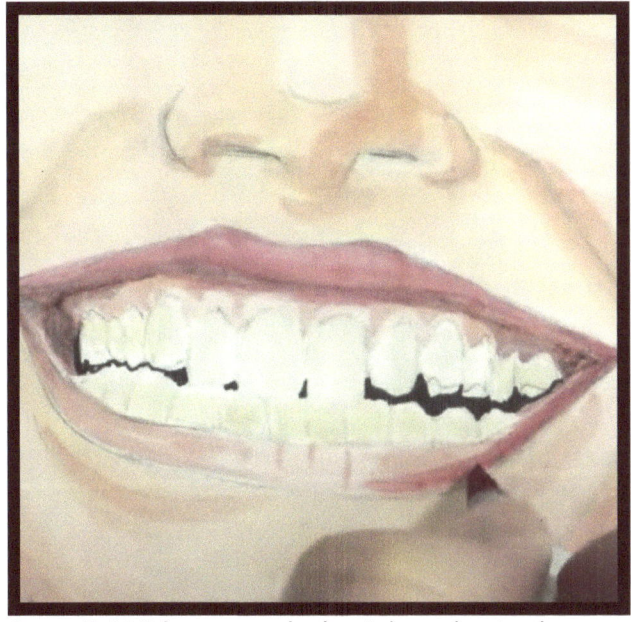

Step 5. With same dark pink, color in the lips and along the upper gum line.

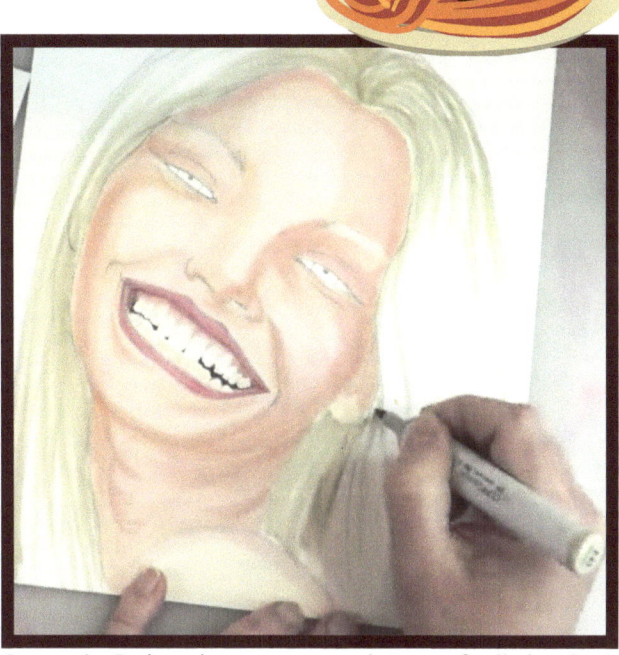

Step 6. Color the roots and tips of all the hair with a light brown or golden color.

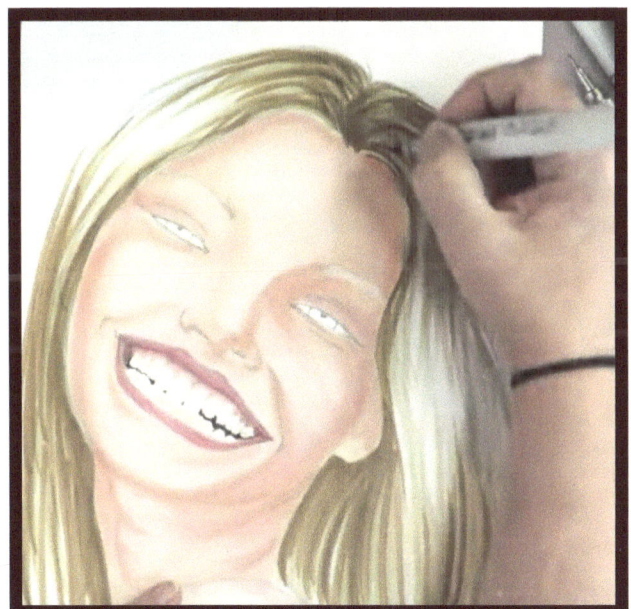

Step 7. Add a darker shade to the hair, again coloring only the roots and tips. Leave a large middle section untouched. This creates the illusion of a highlighted section!

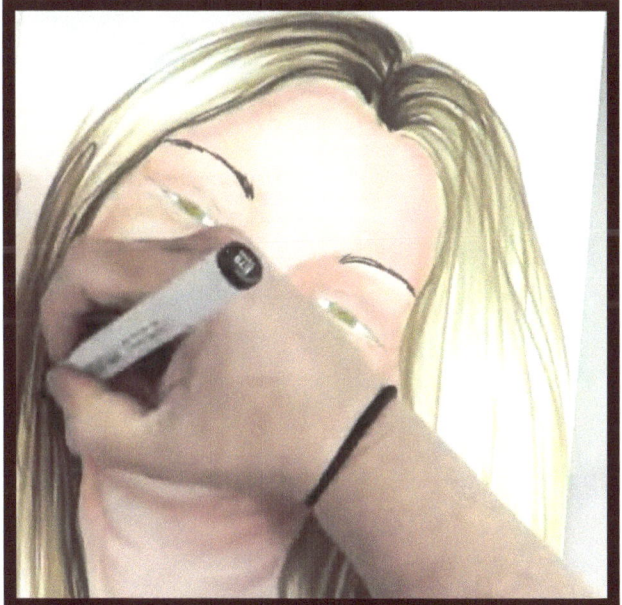

Step 8. Use a third and even darker shade of brown to once again color the roots and tips. Use this color to draw eyebrows. Color the eyes with a green and golden brown color.

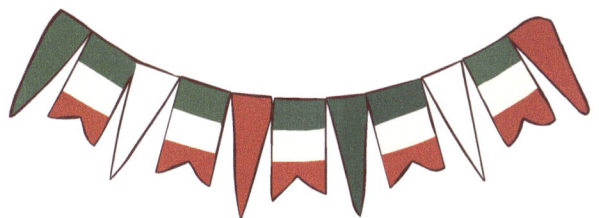

Italian

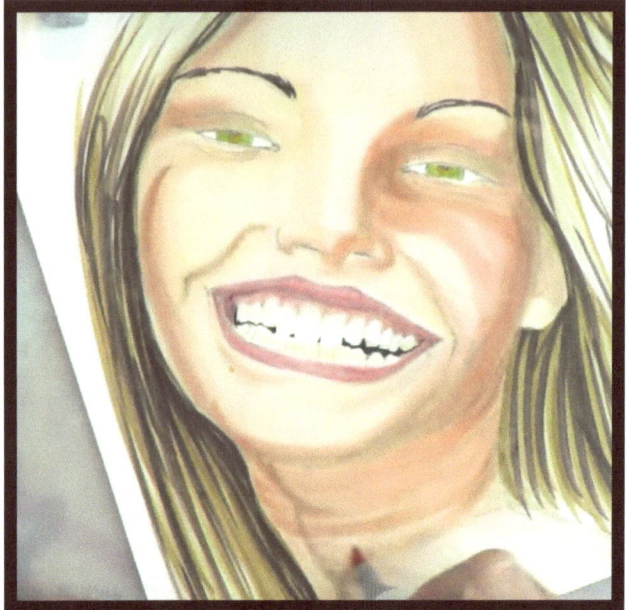

Step 9. Use another darker pink shade to further shade of the right side and neck.

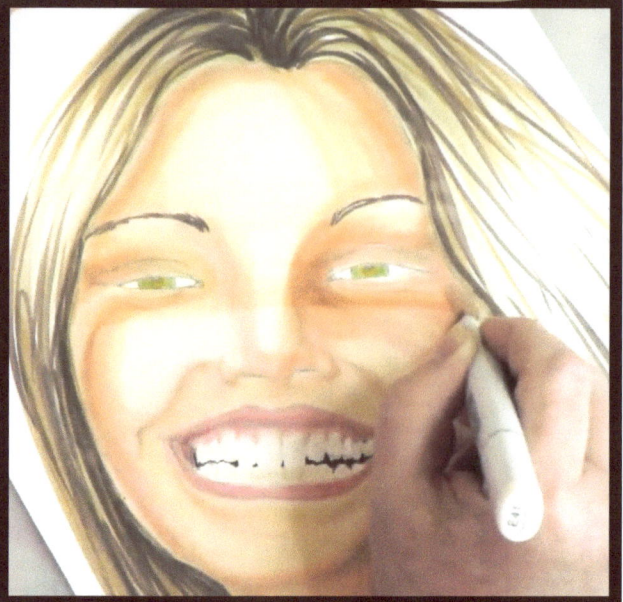

Step 10. To blend the face colors together, use a light shade and go over the entire face.

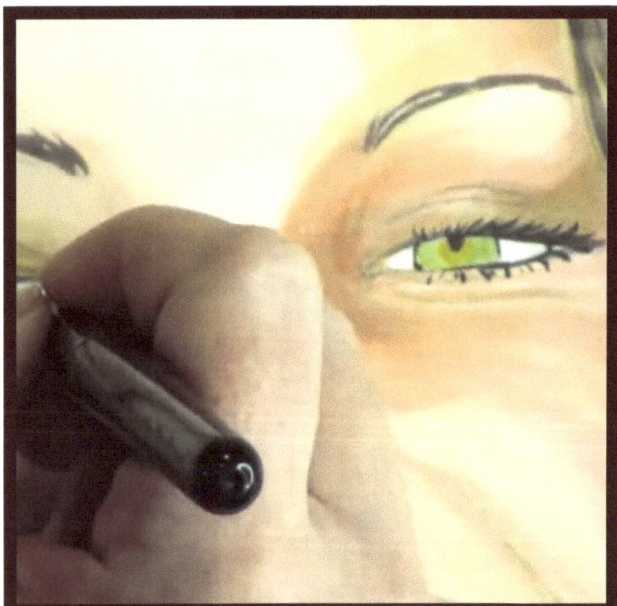

Step 11. Use a black brush pen to color in the pupil and eyelashes.

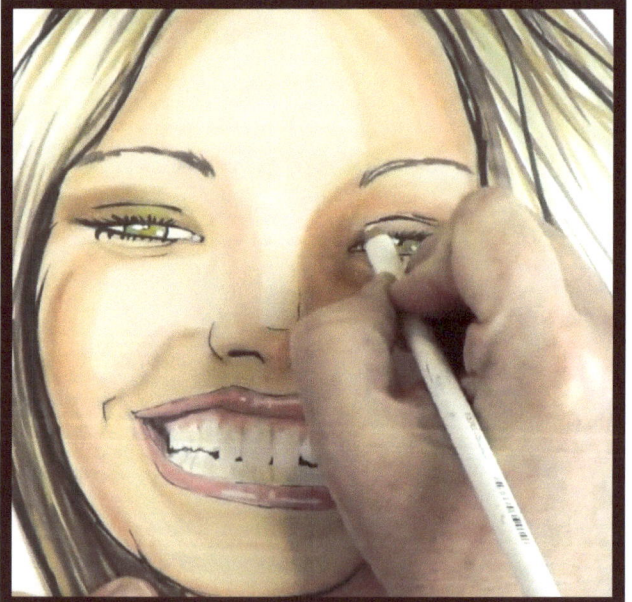

Step 12. Use colored pencils to punch up the highlighted regions like her brow bone, nose bridge and any teeth that are too dark.

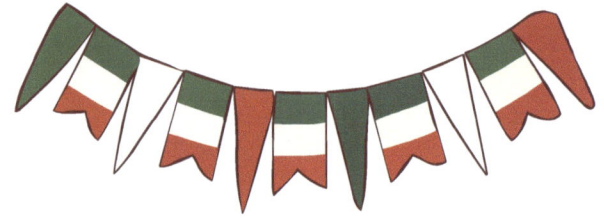

Italian

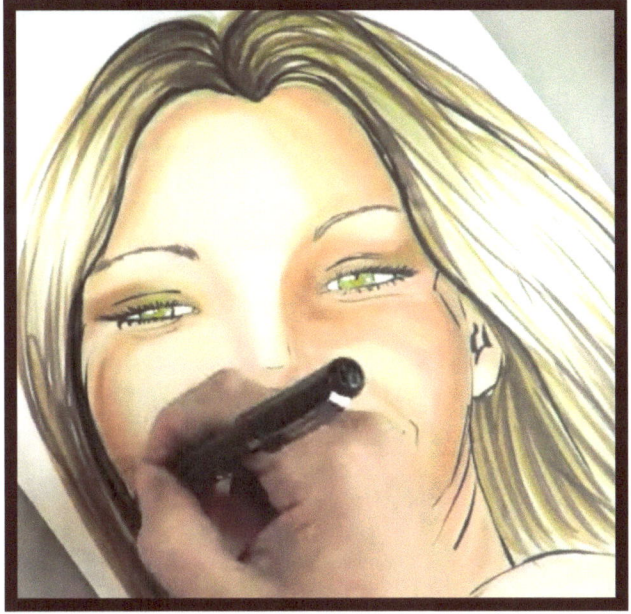

Step 13. Outlining is always optional but if you choose to do it, go everwhere with it!

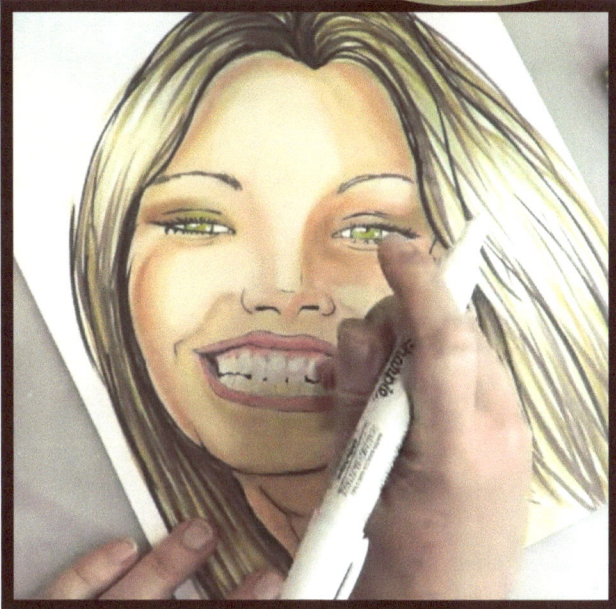

Step 14. Use a white paint marker to add more highlights to the lips and teeth.

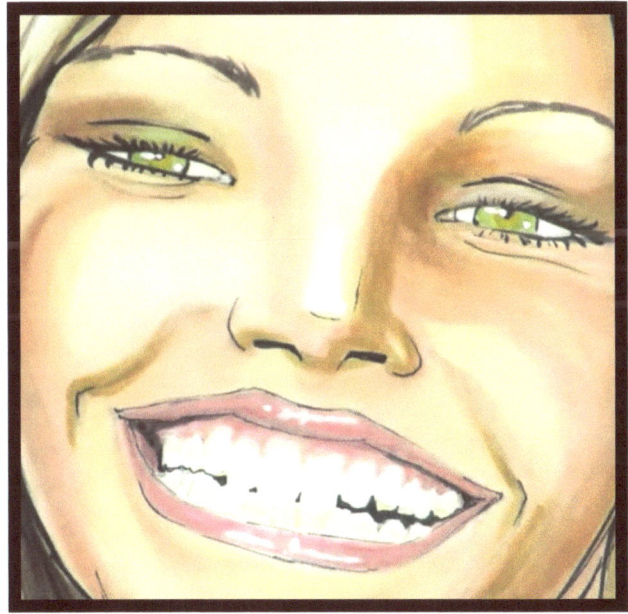

Step 15. Use a thin fine liner to accent the nose bridge, nostrils and laugh/mouth lines.

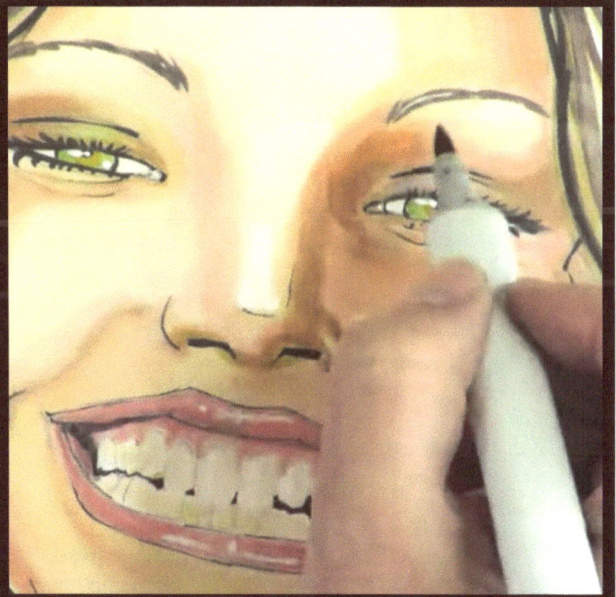

Step 16. Add any deeper shadows around the eyes, under the chin, along the right side of the nose bridge and along the apples of the cheeks! Anywhere you want more drama!

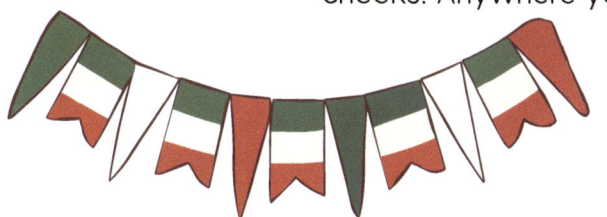

Student Spotlight

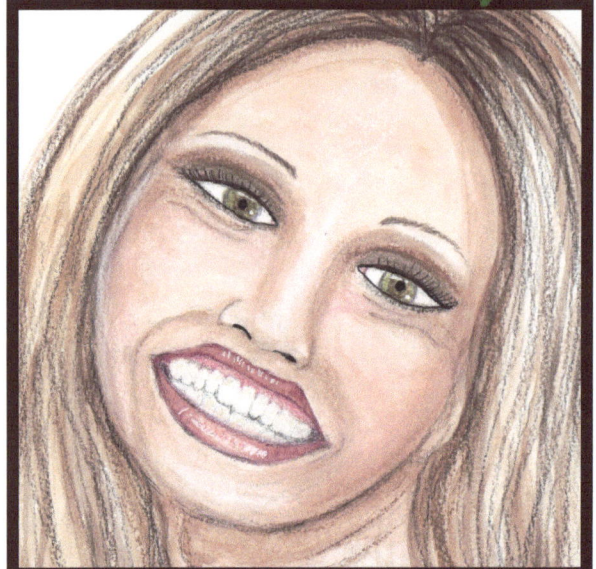

Debi Ledford. Watercolor with a little hard pastel and pencil. *"I like mixing my media to get the look I want to achieve."*

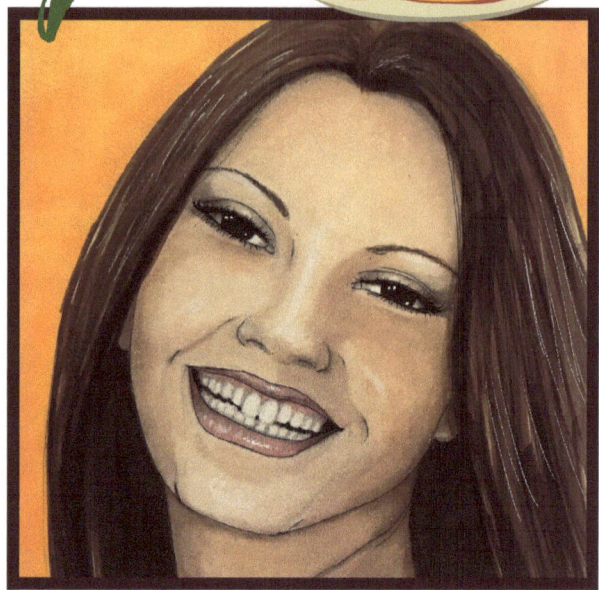

Darlene Hannah. Copic markers, watercolour Pencils, fine liner. *"I love the blend of the markers, just beautiful!"*

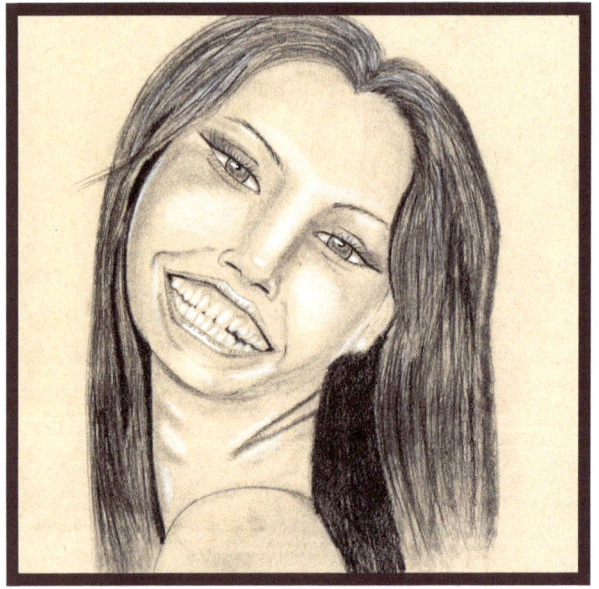

Melanie Stringer. Graphite, colored pencils and white paint marker for the shine in the eyes and on the lips. *"I really love the look I achieve with graphite."*

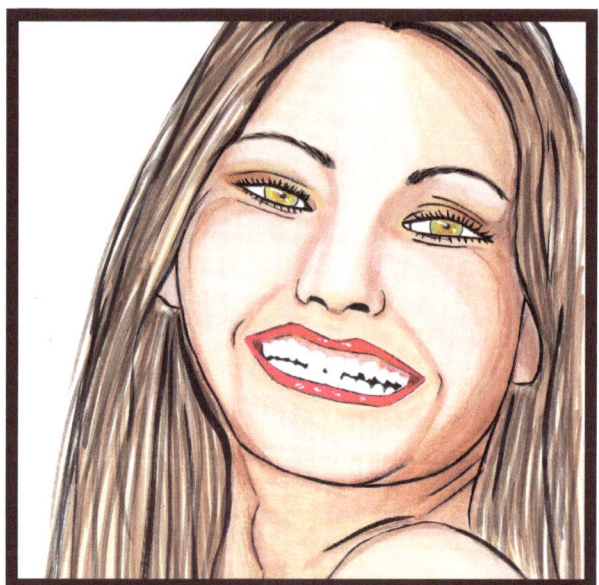

Bonnie Friesen. Ohuhu markers, pens. *"I love how the markers give a bold vibrant look."*

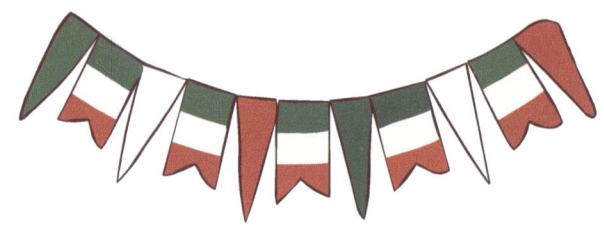

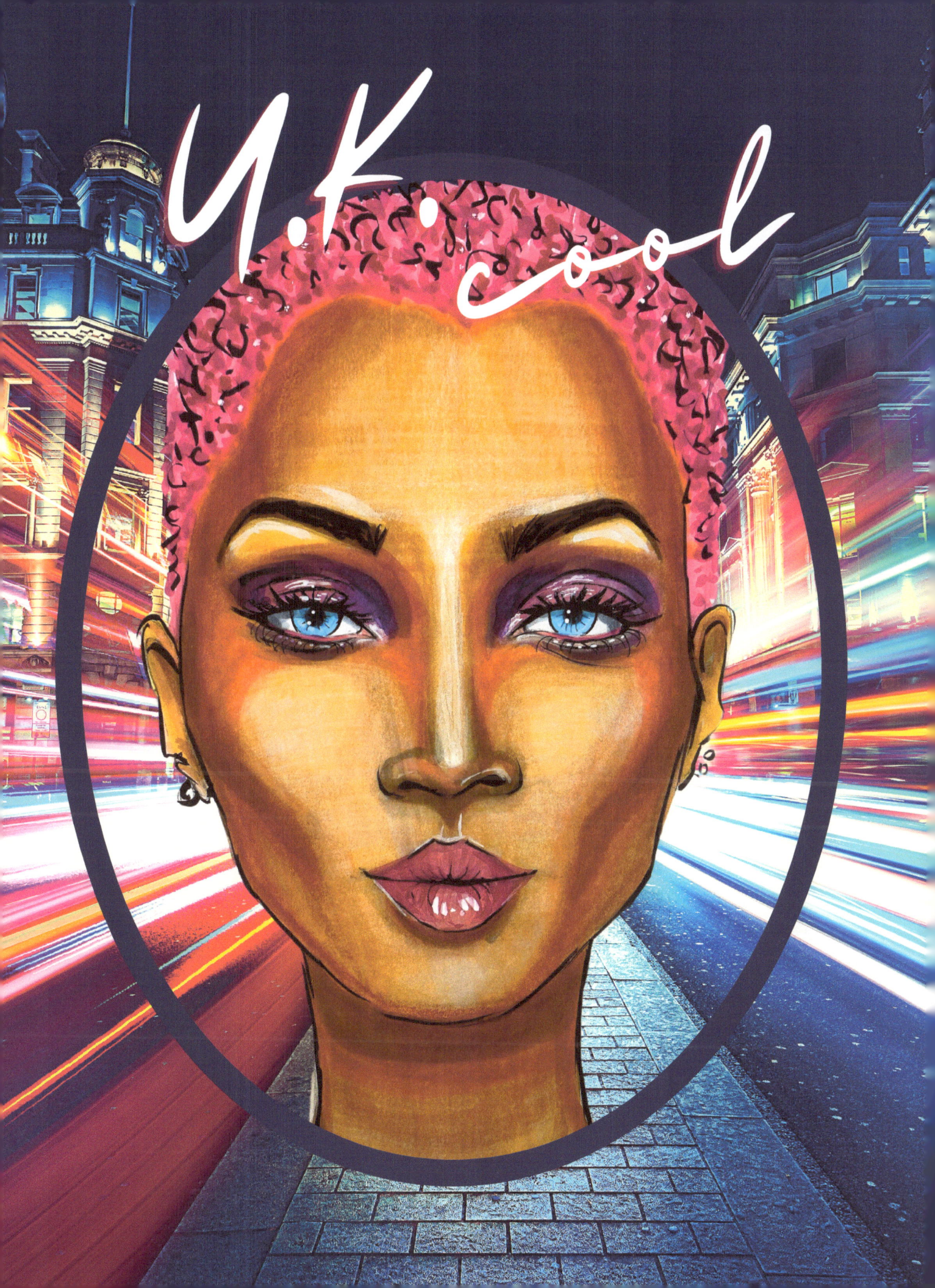

United Kingdom

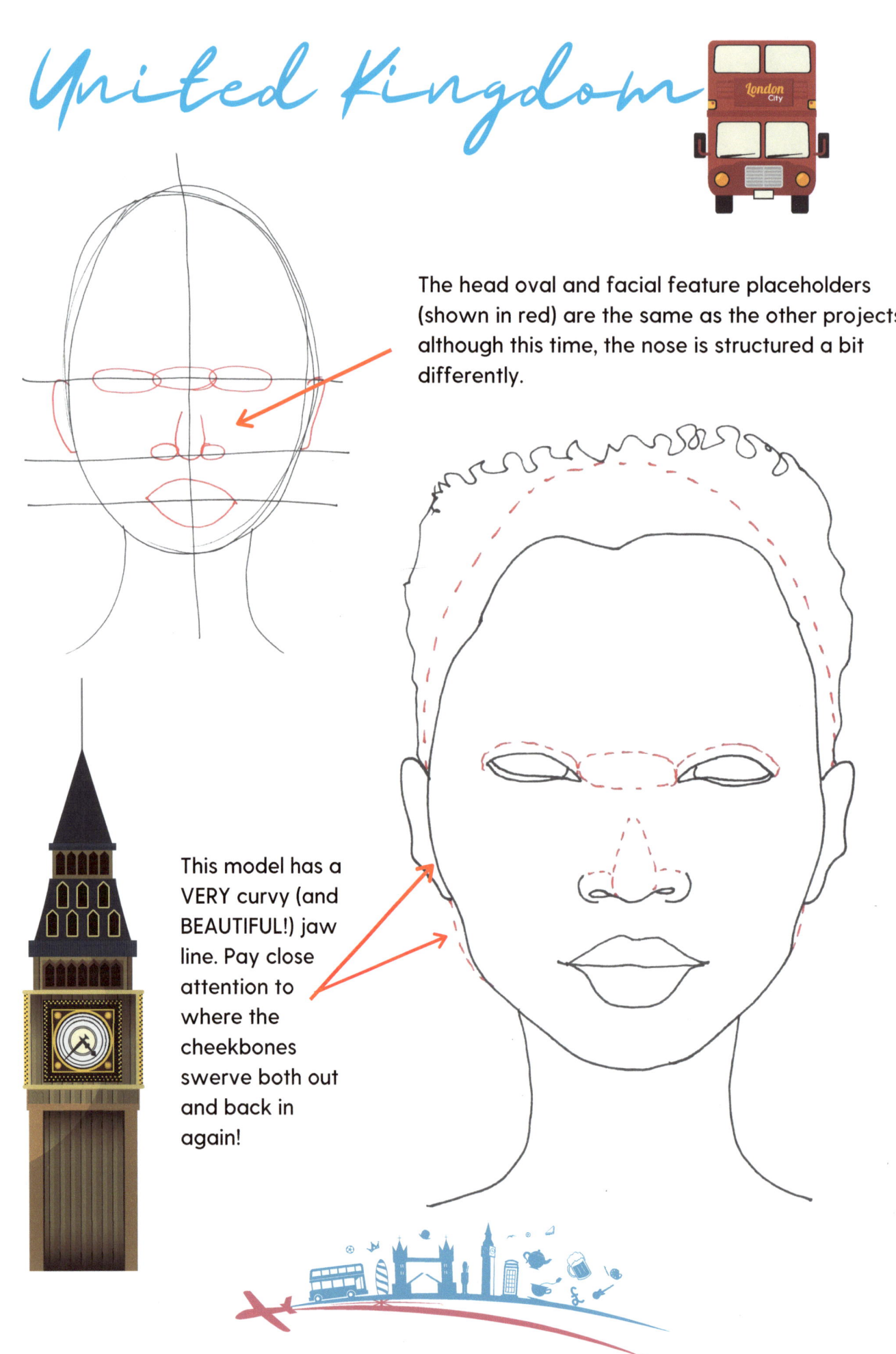

The head oval and facial feature placeholders (shown in red) are the same as the other projects although this time, the nose is structured a bit differently.

This model has a VERY curvy (and BEAUTIFUL!) jaw line. Pay close attention to where the cheekbones swerve both out and back in again!

United Kingdom

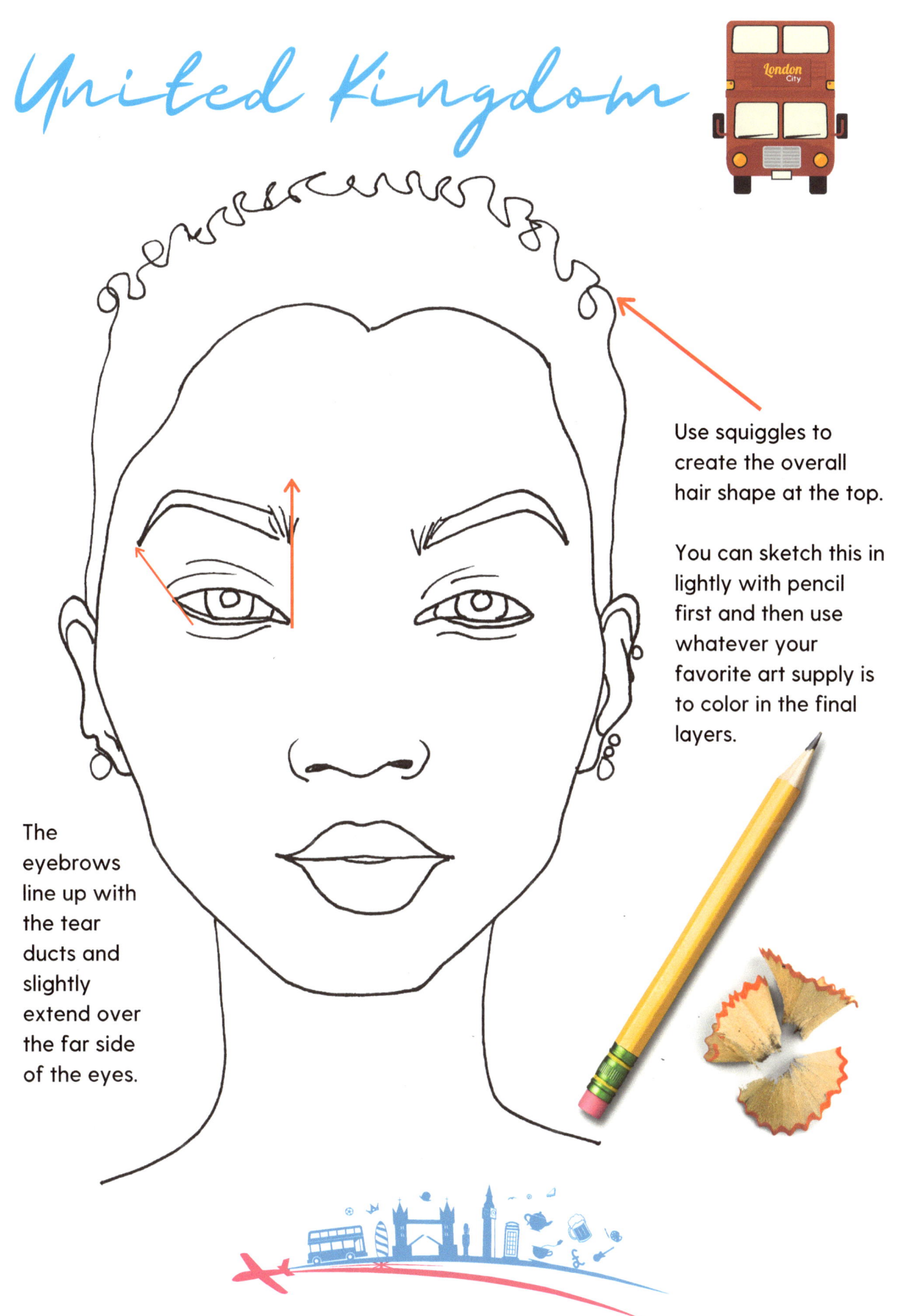

Use squiggles to create the overall hair shape at the top.

You can sketch this in lightly with pencil first and then use whatever your favorite art supply is to color in the final layers.

The eyebrows line up with the tear ducts and slightly extend over the far side of the eyes.

United Kingdom

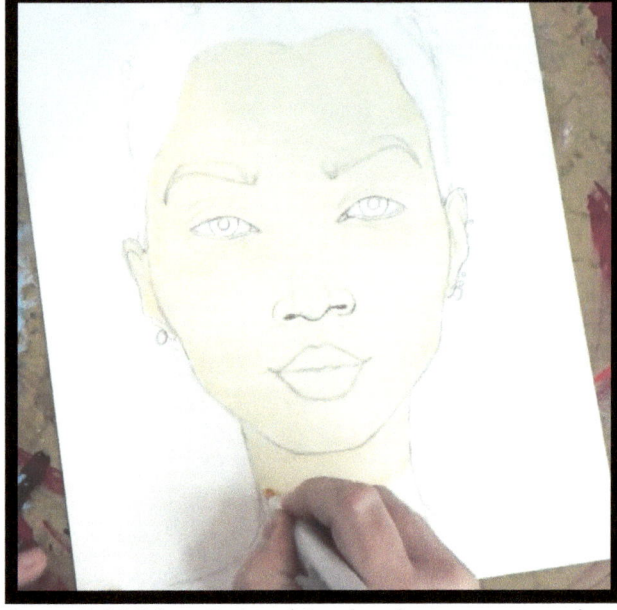

Step 1. With a light skin shade to start, color the entire face and neck area.

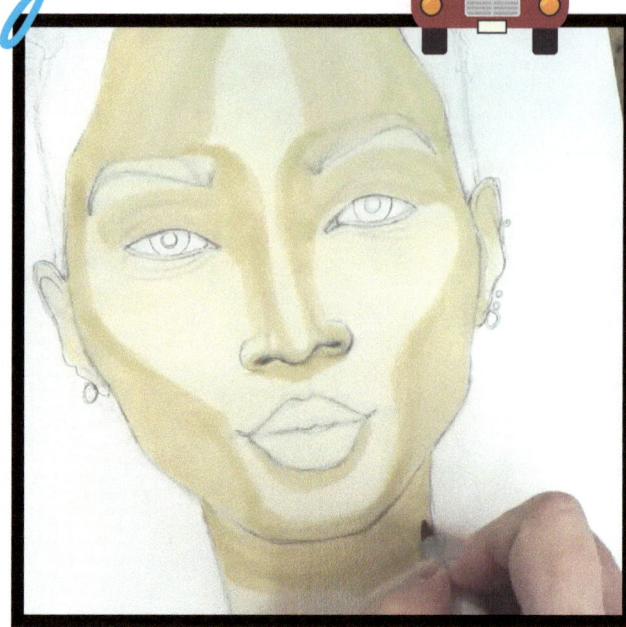

Step 2. Using a slightly darker shade, color in the areas shown.

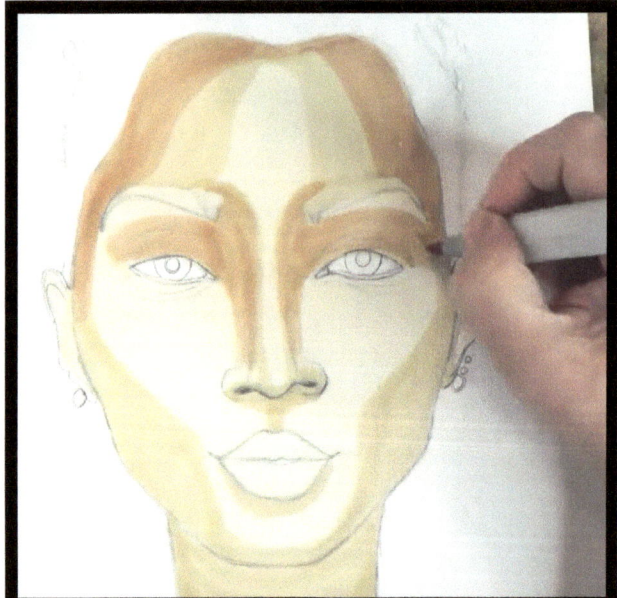

Step 3. Use a third shade to accentuate the shadows even further.

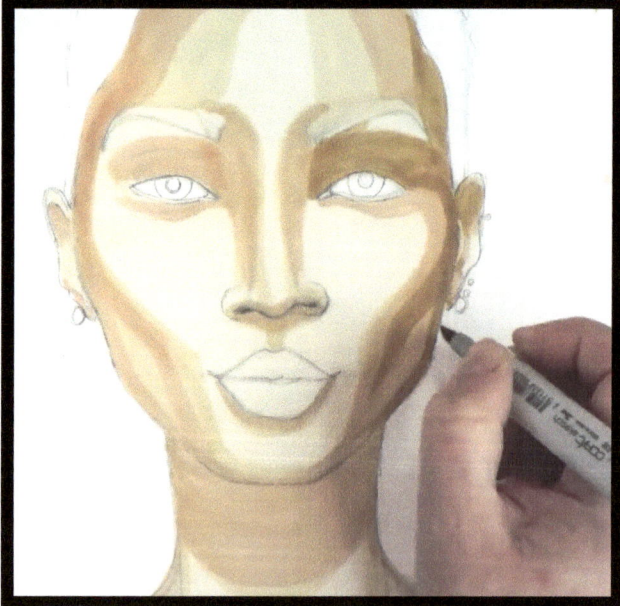

Step 4. Now go in with a fourth darker shade and add it to the eye area, cheeks, nose bridge, and under the mouth and chin.

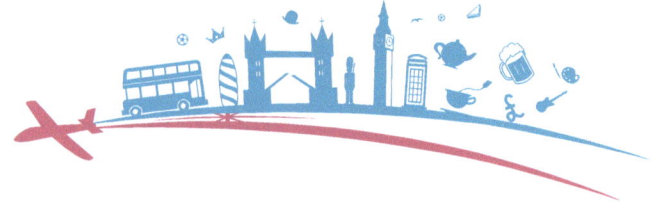

United Kingdom

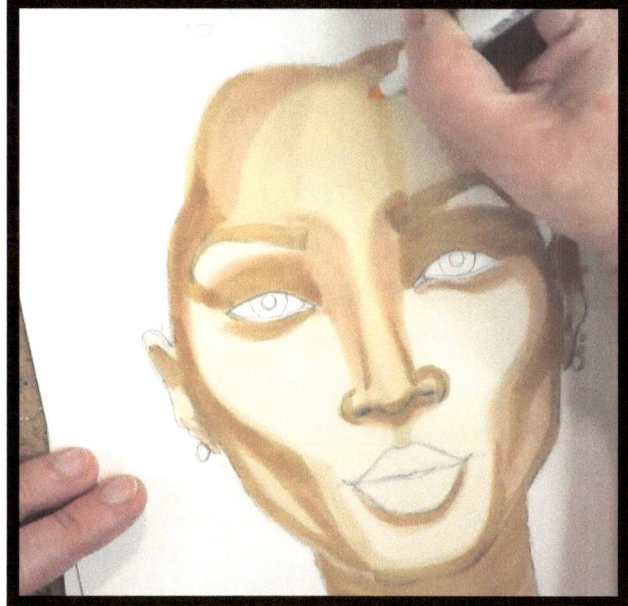

Step 5. Now with a light shade, go over the ENTIRE face to blend all the colors together.

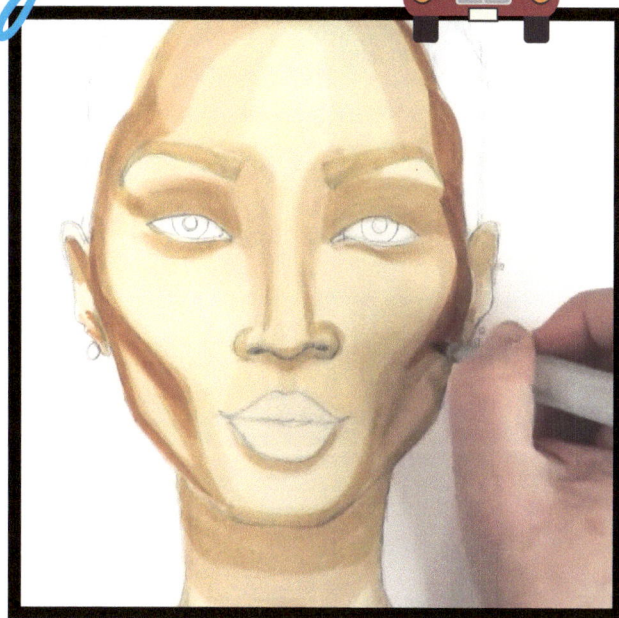

Step 6. To add even more drama, add yet another darker shade!

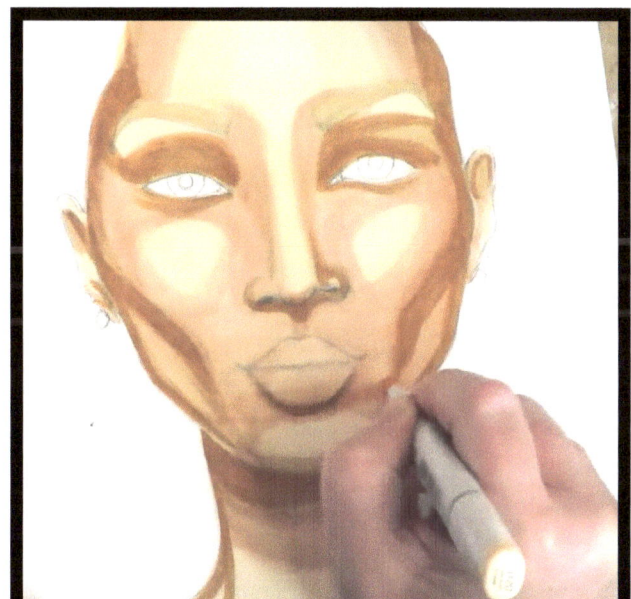

Step 7. Use a medium shade to cover ENTIRE face and blend all the layers and colors together again.

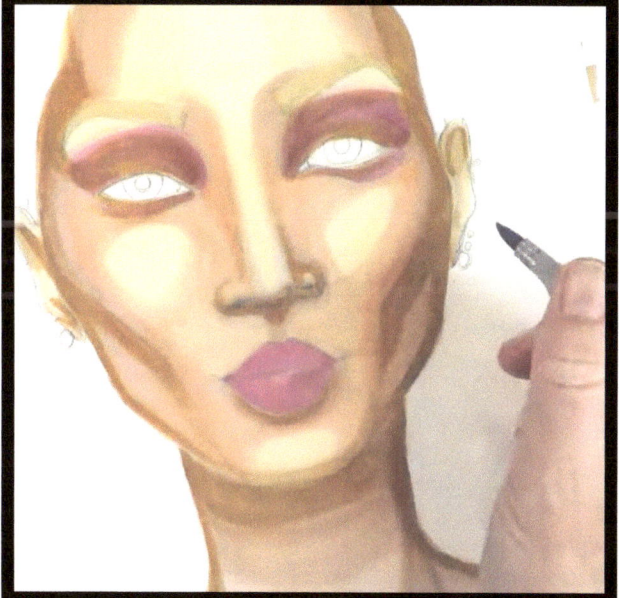

Step 8. Add a purply pink to the eyeshadow area and lips. Color in the eyes light blue.

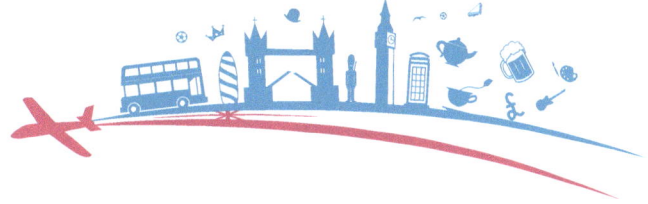

United Kingdom

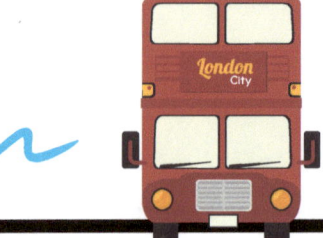

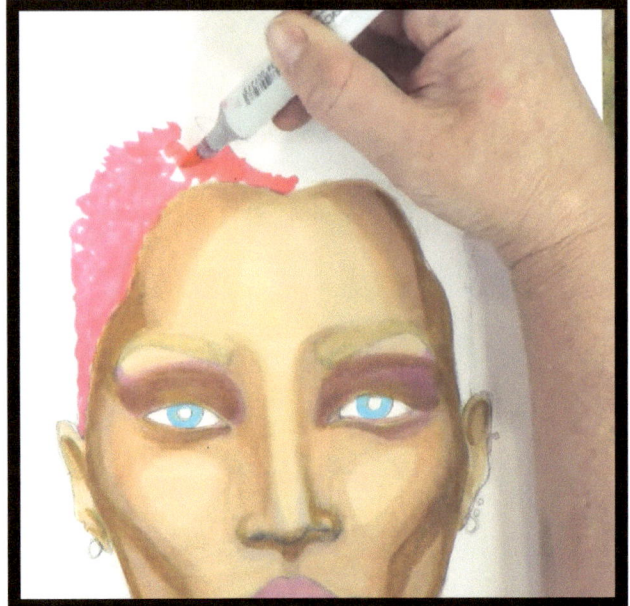

Step 9. Choose 3 shades of pink. Add the lightest shade first, using squiggle motions.

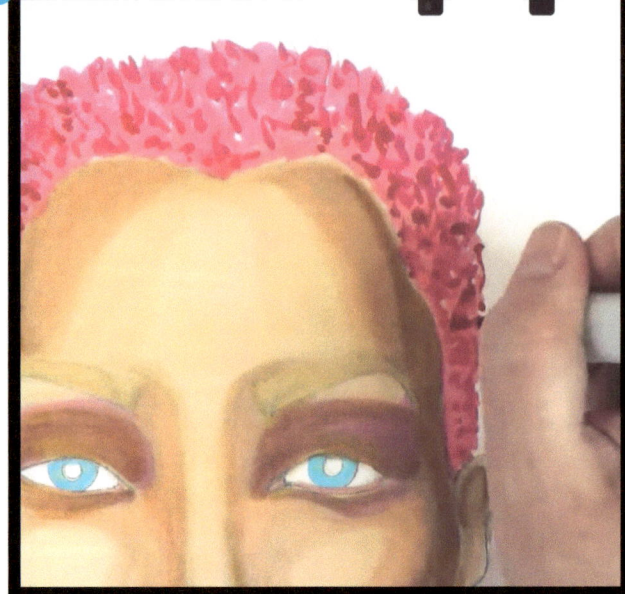

Step 10. Use the second and third shades in the exact same way.

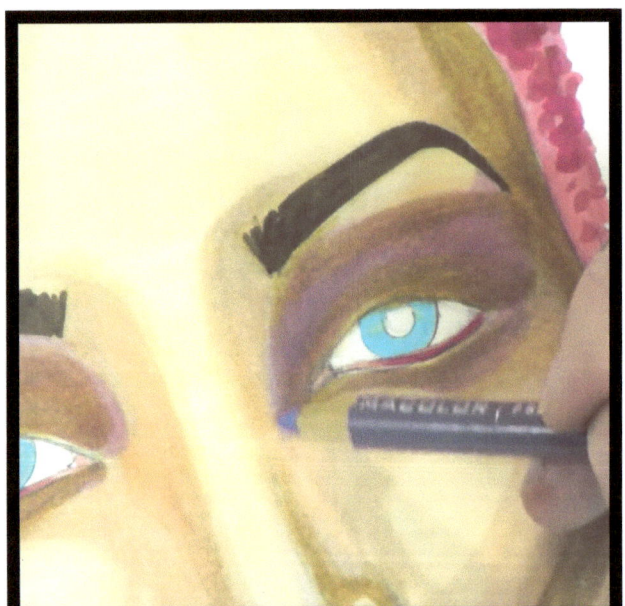

Step 11. Use colored pencils in the same colors as your markers to accentuate any areas that you like! I'm using purple for the eye shadow and then white to the eyelids to create a rounded effect.

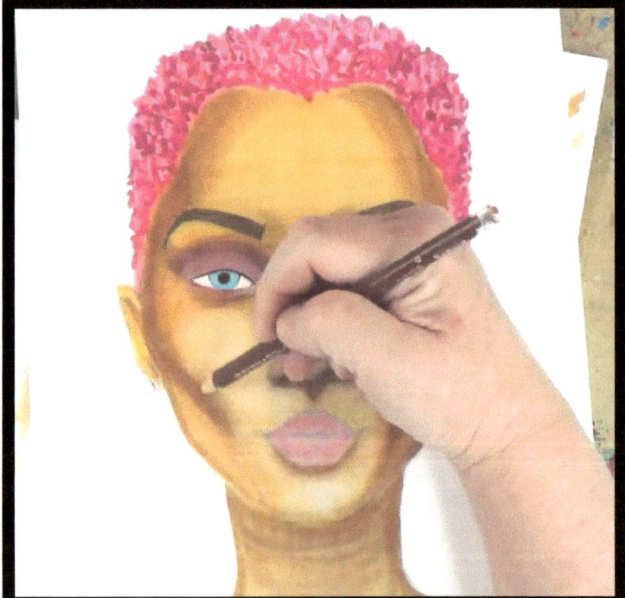

Step 12. You can see here how I use a brown colored pencil to smooth out the transition between the shades of marker.

United Kingdom

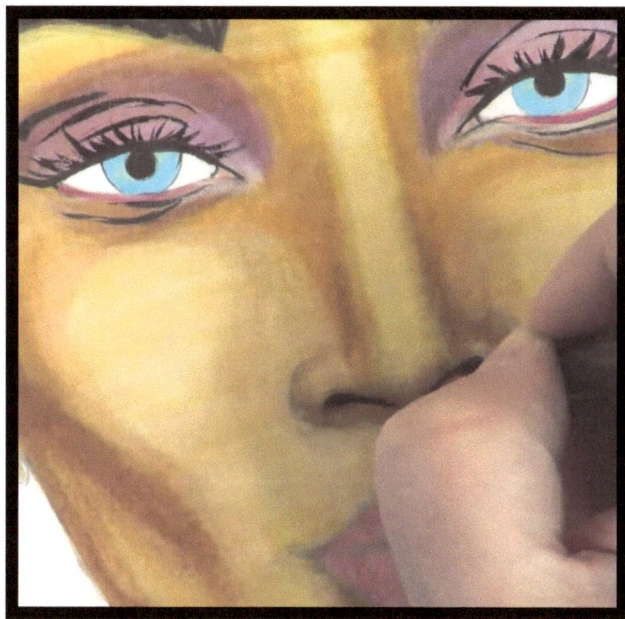

Step 13. Use a brush pen to add lashes and outlines!

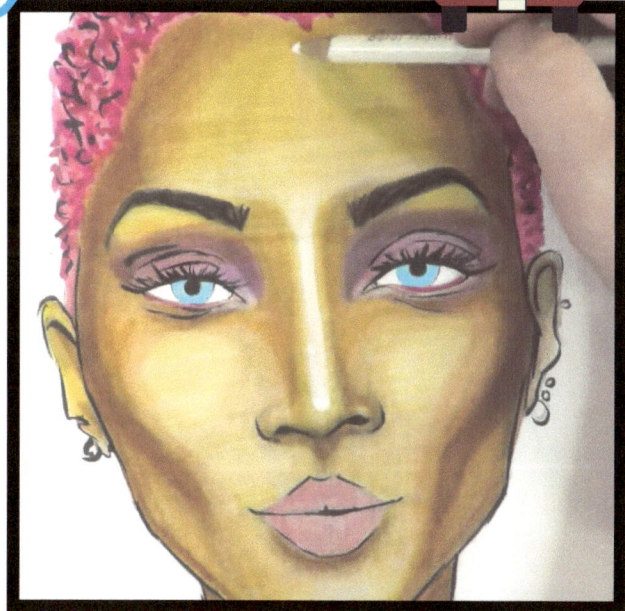

Step 14. Use a white colored pencil and white paint marker to add striking highlights!!

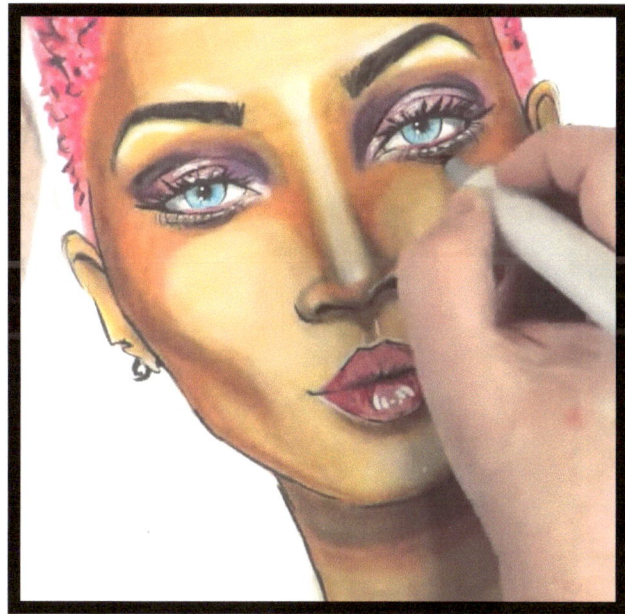

Step 15. Use markers one last time, anywhere you want to punch up the make-up or add more definition or shading drama! You can even use markers over the areas you shaded in colored pencil!

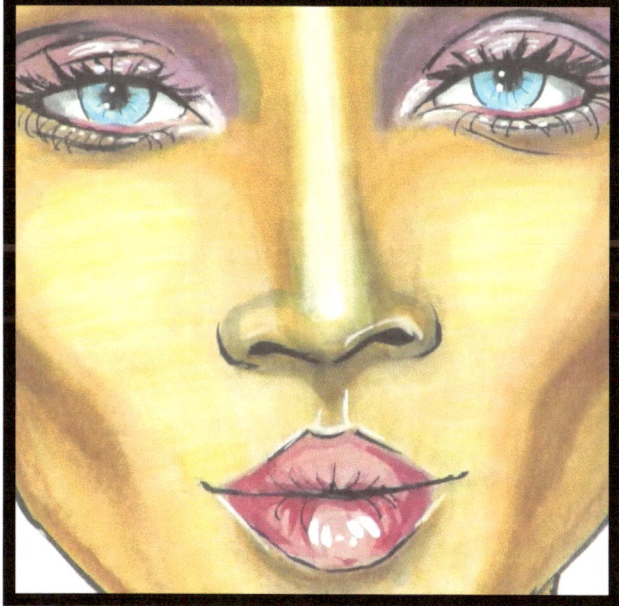

Step 16. Use this close-up to help you figure out where great places are to add highlights! Eyelids, the ball of the nose and the lips are a must in every project (at least to me!).

Student Spotlight

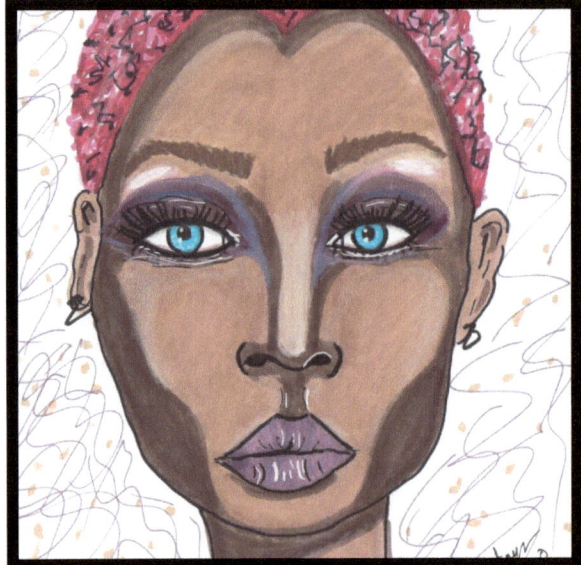

Kathryn Thomas. Mixed media. *"Having fun with markers. Working on blending. OMG her eyes - love the POP of color."*

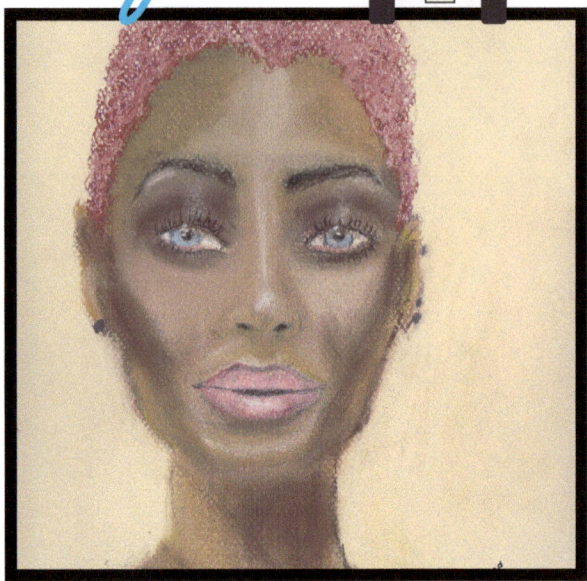

Linda Fitch. Soft pastels. *"I decided to challenge myself to use this beautiful medium. I love the feel and sound of soft pastels on paper!"*

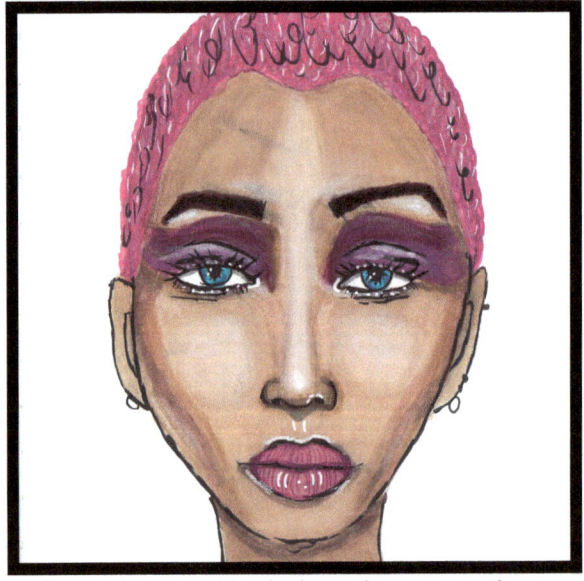

Jackie Klassen. Alcohol markers, pencil crayons, gelatos, and Posca pens for shading and highlights. *"I wanted to use the alcohol markers because I haven't used them very much and would like to get better at them."*

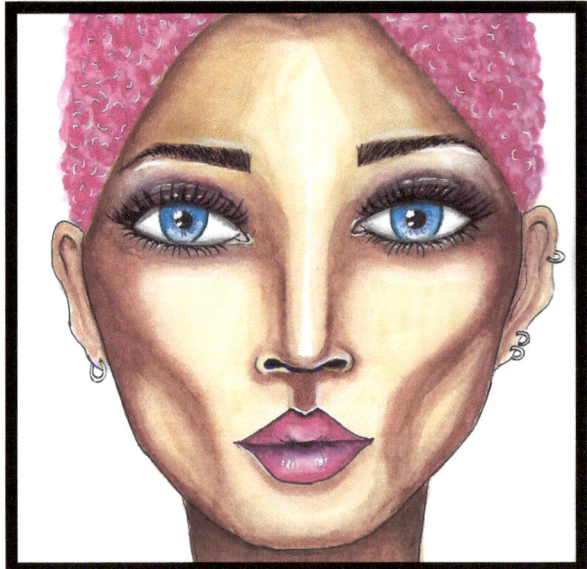

Karina Aguirre. Watercolors, Stabilo Carbothello, Ecoline Brush and Posca Pens. *"I love watercolor effects and I decided to add some carbothello pencils to soften the transitions and achieve the eye make-up."*

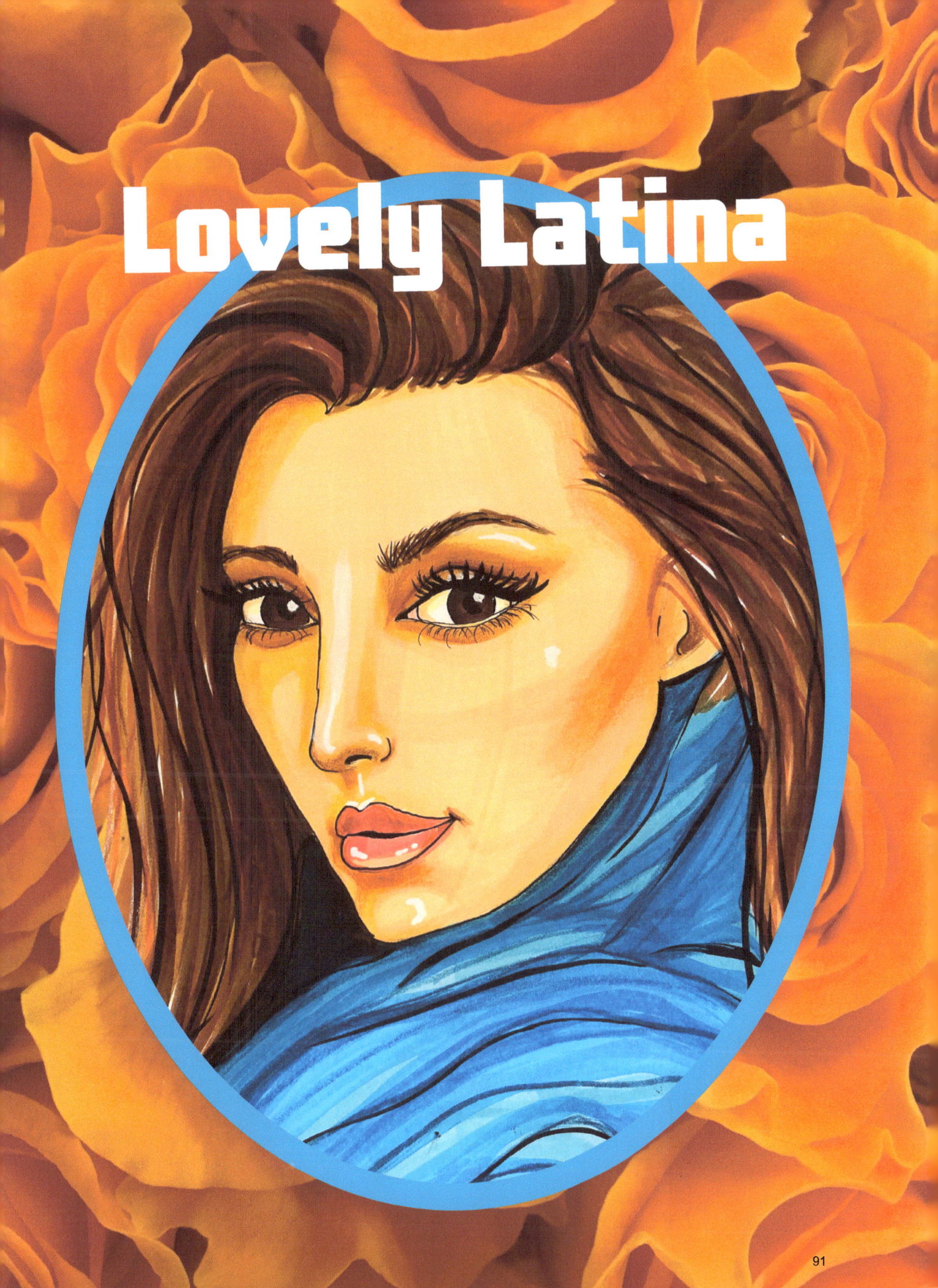

Lovely Latina

This 3/4 face starts with a circle.

The facial feature guidelines are the same as the ones for forward facing except they curve up a bit on the right to represent the curve of the face.

Then from either side of the circle, extend lines to create a soft "V" shape that ends slightly to the left side of the circle's center.

At the intersection of eye-line and circle, draw a curved indentation to represent the cheek bone.

Add the ovals and rounded shapes to map out where the facial features will go relative to the vertical curved line.

Note the vertical line is curved and placed approximately 1/4 from the far side of the face (or 3/4 from the closest).

Lovely Latina

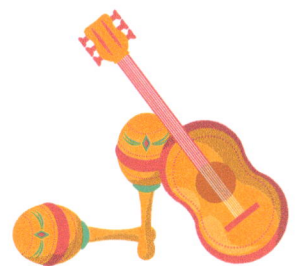

Draw the outline of the hair.

She is wearing a puffy jacket so draw curved sweeping lines to indicated the fabric folds.

Break up the hair into more sections to make coloring a bit easier!

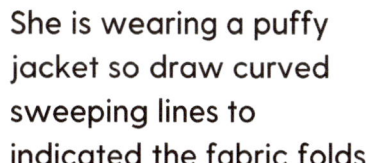

Add eyebrows, eye lids and pupils.

On this drawing we will draw the nose bridge as a line.

However, you can also opt to show the nose bridge using the same shading practices we've been using for the other drawings. The choice is yours!

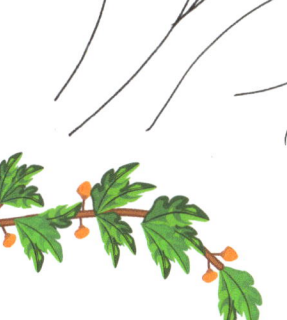

Latina

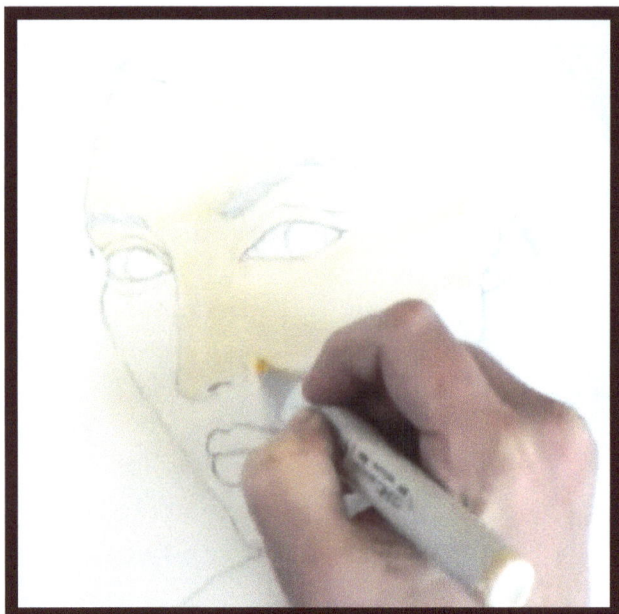

Step 1. Sweep a light color over the entire face in smooth, even motions.

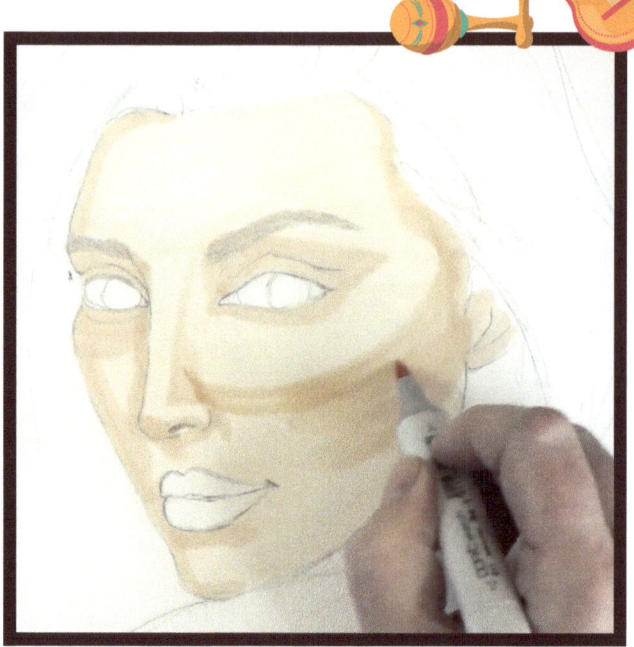

Step 2. With one shade darker, fill in the areas as shown.

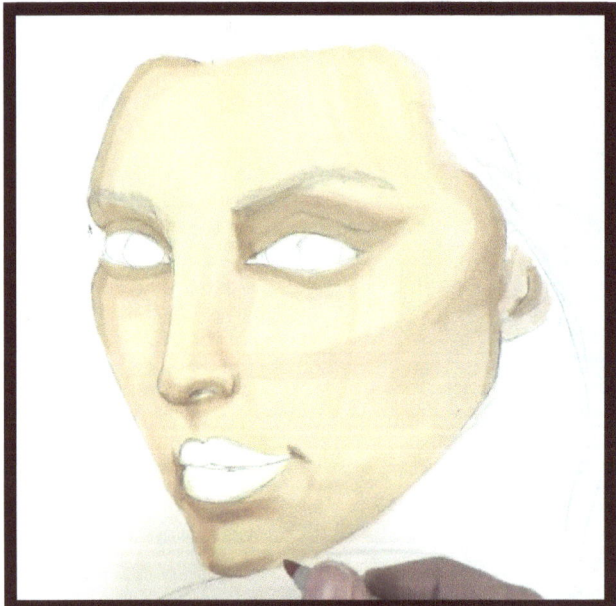

Step 3. Using one shade darker still, apply to the areas along the far hairline, around the eyes, under the nose and mouth and by the ear and cheek closest to you.

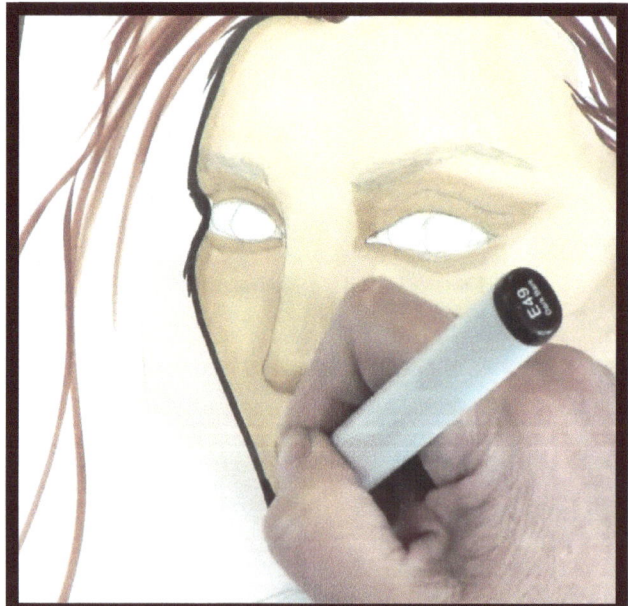

Step 4. Pick 3-4 shades of hair color. Start with the medium shade and create strands that start at the part. Apply the darkest shades against the face so the face pops!

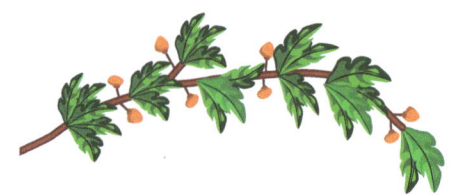

Latina

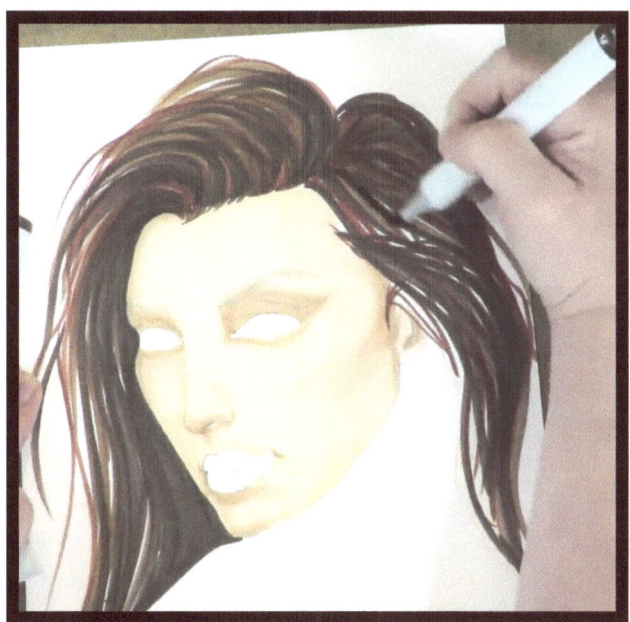

Step 5. Sweep all 4 shades of hair from part to ends, alternating colors as you go.

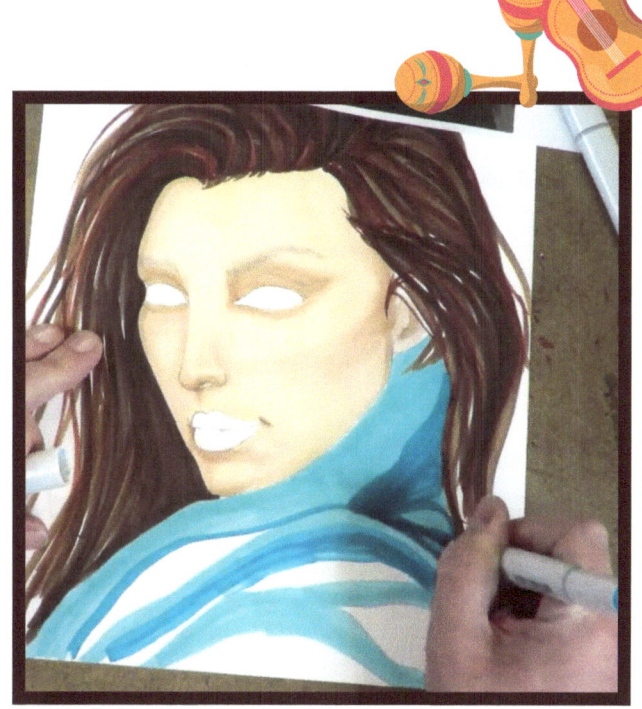

Step 6. Use 2 shades of turquoise to create the look of fabric for the coat.

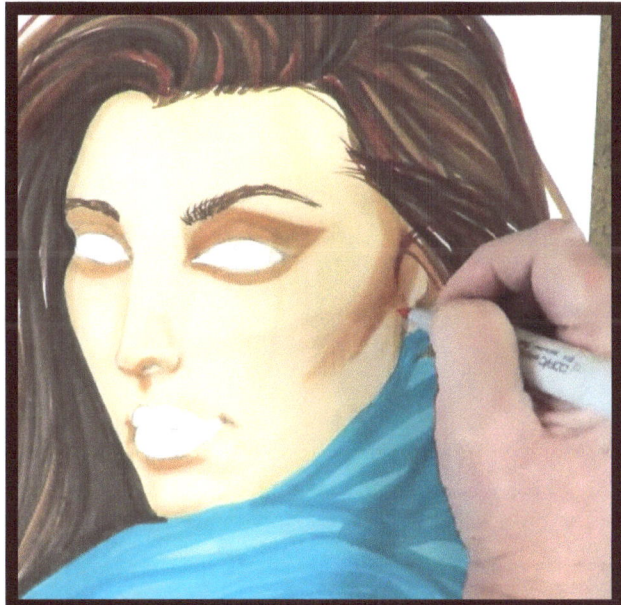

Step 7. With the darkest skin tone yet, add color around the eyes, under the nose and mouth and along the closest cheek bone.

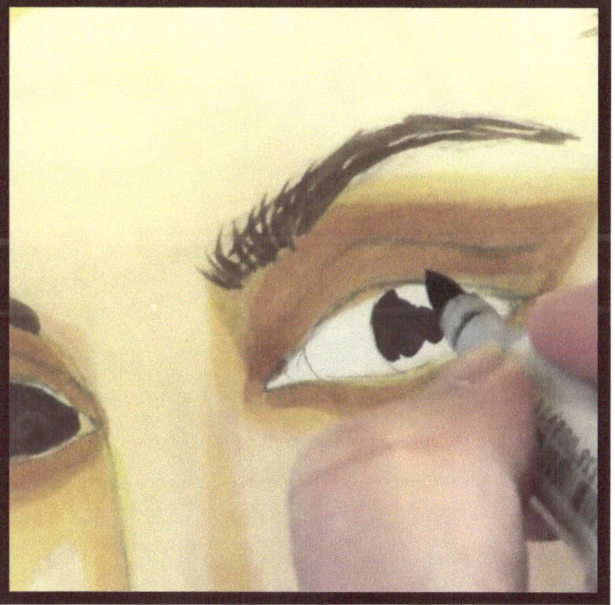

Step 8. Color in the irises. Use more than one color if you can! Then shade the whites of the eyes with a pale yellow or a super light grey. Color the tear duct with a pale pink.

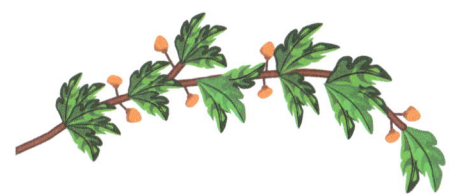

Latina

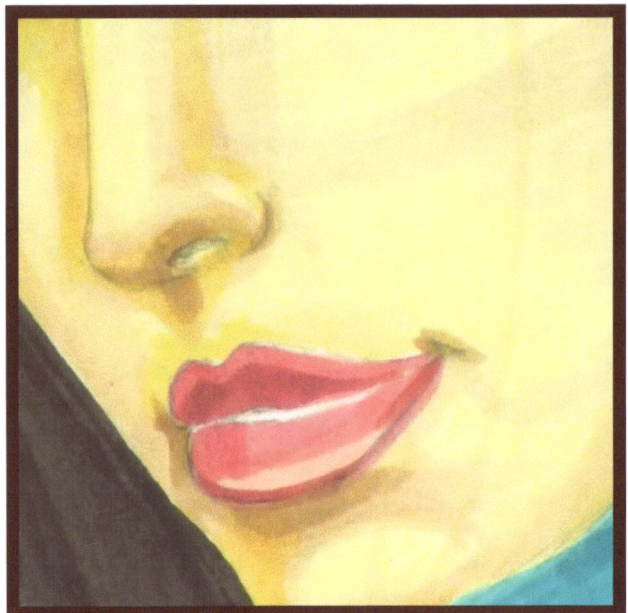

Step 9. As with every feature, the more shades you apply, the more depth you will create. Use 3 shades for the mouth as shown.

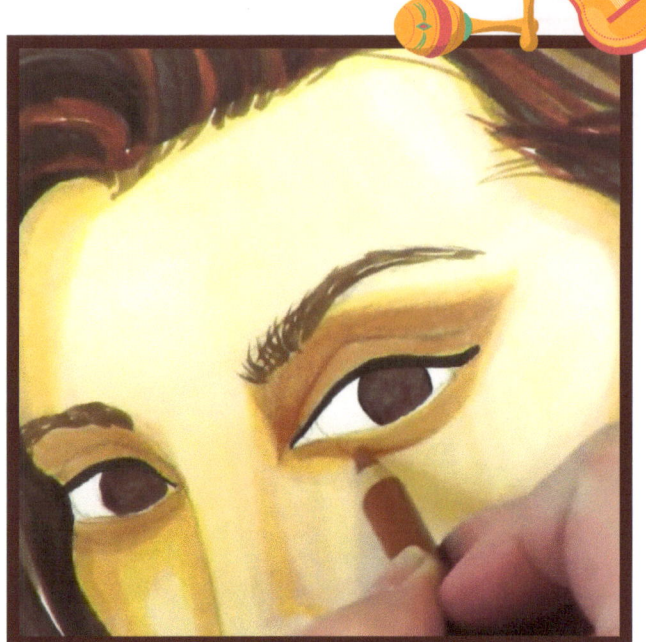

Step 10. Colored pencil can be used to create more dimension and details around eyes.

Fineliners like these from Molotow are great because they are pigment based so are permanent and won't bleed with your alcohol markers!

They're also great because they come in a ton of different nib sizes so you can pick the perfect one for the job!

Brush pens like this one from Pentel are great for creating realistic looking lashes.

It takes a bit of practice so don't be discouraged!

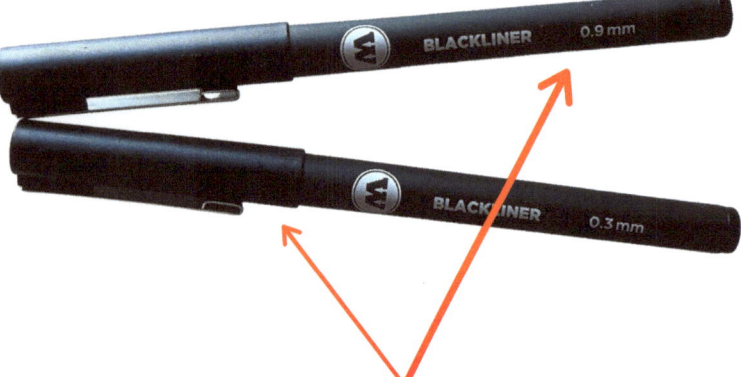

Latina

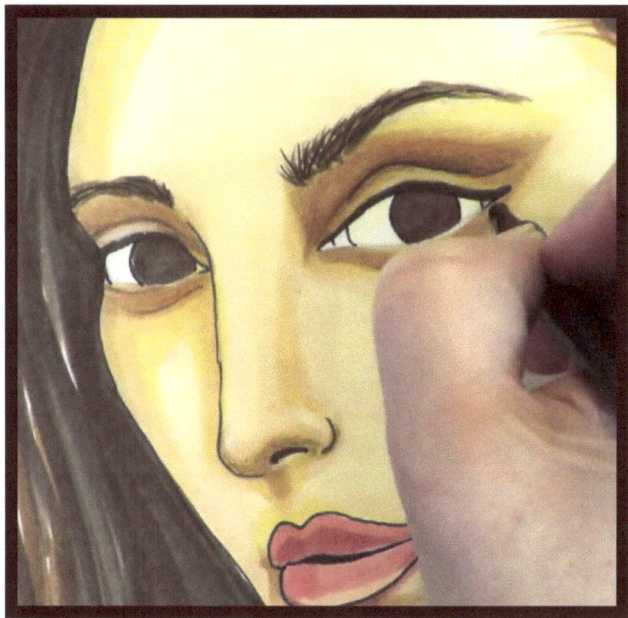

Step 11. Use a fine liner to outline eyes, nose, mouth and face shape.

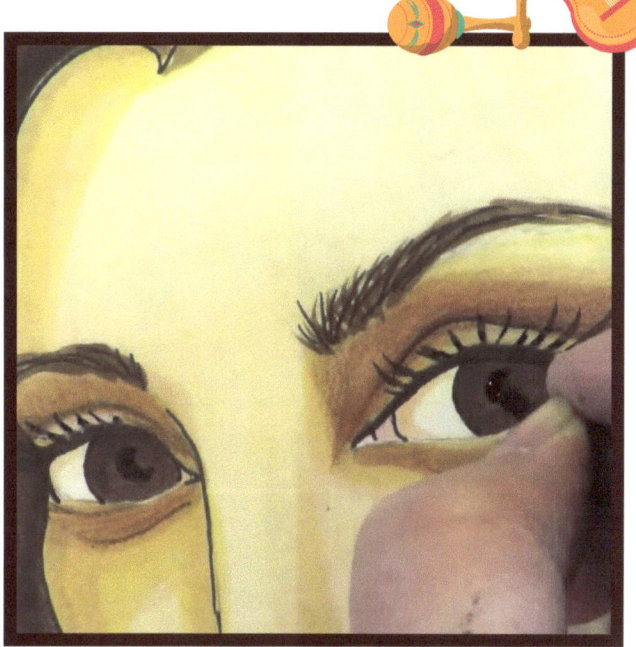

Step 12. Use a brush pen to create the lashes, brows, and dark strands of hair on her head.

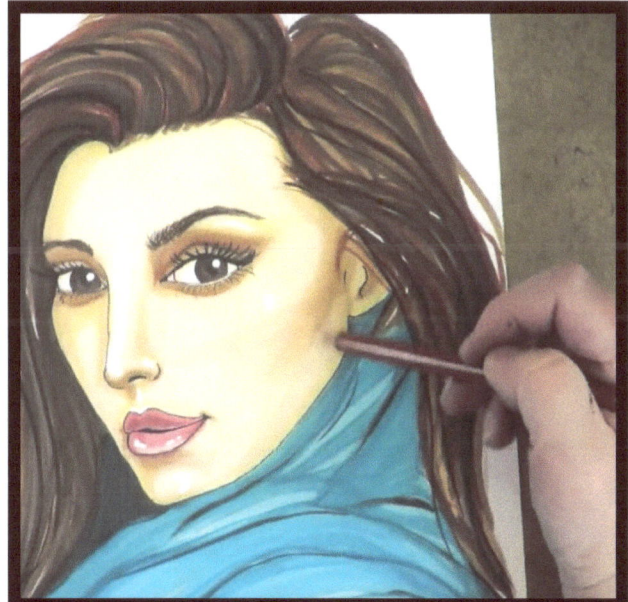

Step 13. Use colored pencils to soften transitions between marker colors, add texture to the hair and definition to the fabric of her coat.

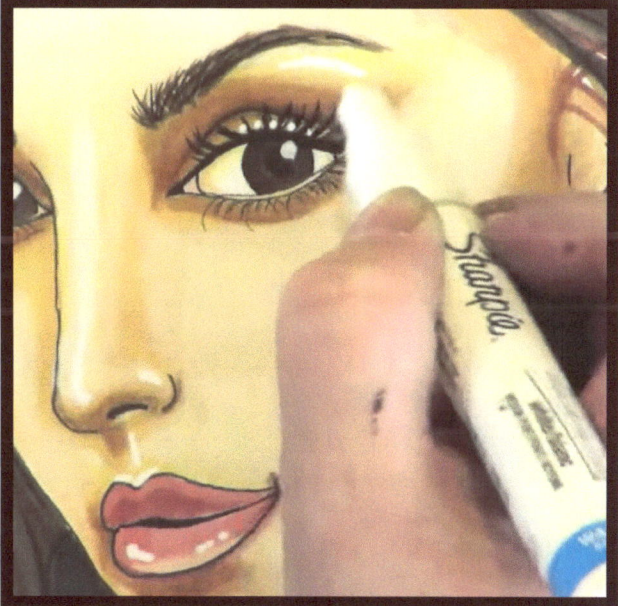

Step 14. Use a white paint marker to add pops of white on the brow bone, pupil, along the nose bridge and on lips! So fun!

Student Spotlight

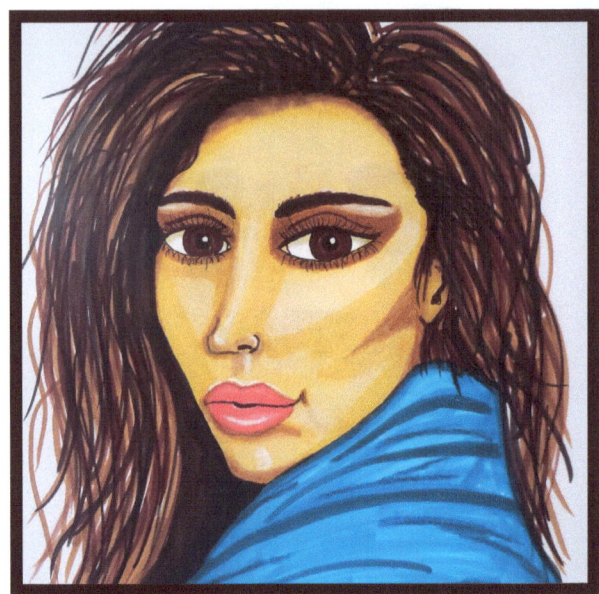

Judy Middleton. Alcohol markers, colored pencils. *"Everyone of these women has been a challenge, which makes learning a fun process."*

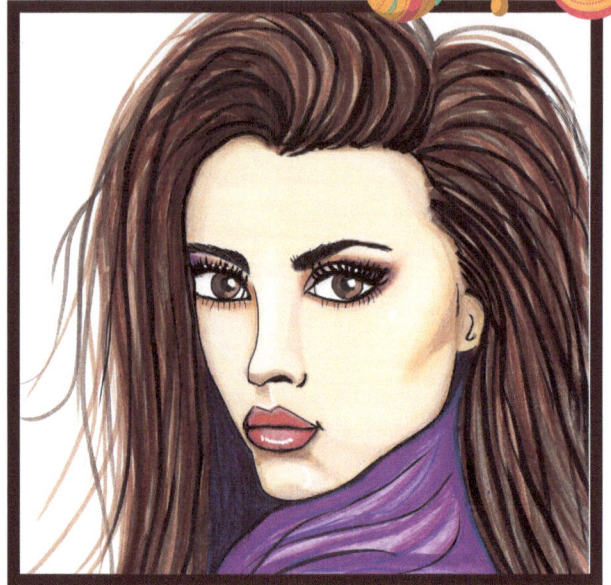

Bonnie Friesen. Alcohol markers, colored pencils, brush pen and white paint pen. *"I love how the markers give a bold vibrant look."*

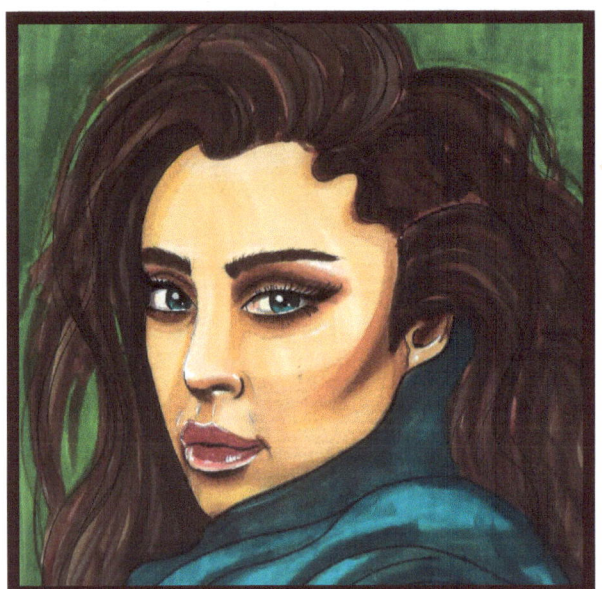

Bryn Nguyen. Copics, colored pencils, brush and Posca pens. *"I love working with mixed media, and I wanted more practice with alcohol markers to develop my skills."*

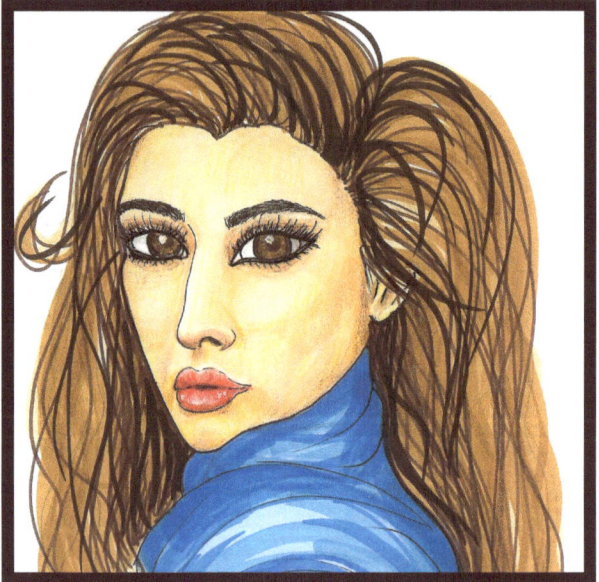

Isabel Yuvienco. Alcohol markers, watercolor pencils and colored pencils. *"I am still learning to use alcohol markers; hence, I feel the need to always blend with my colored pencils."*

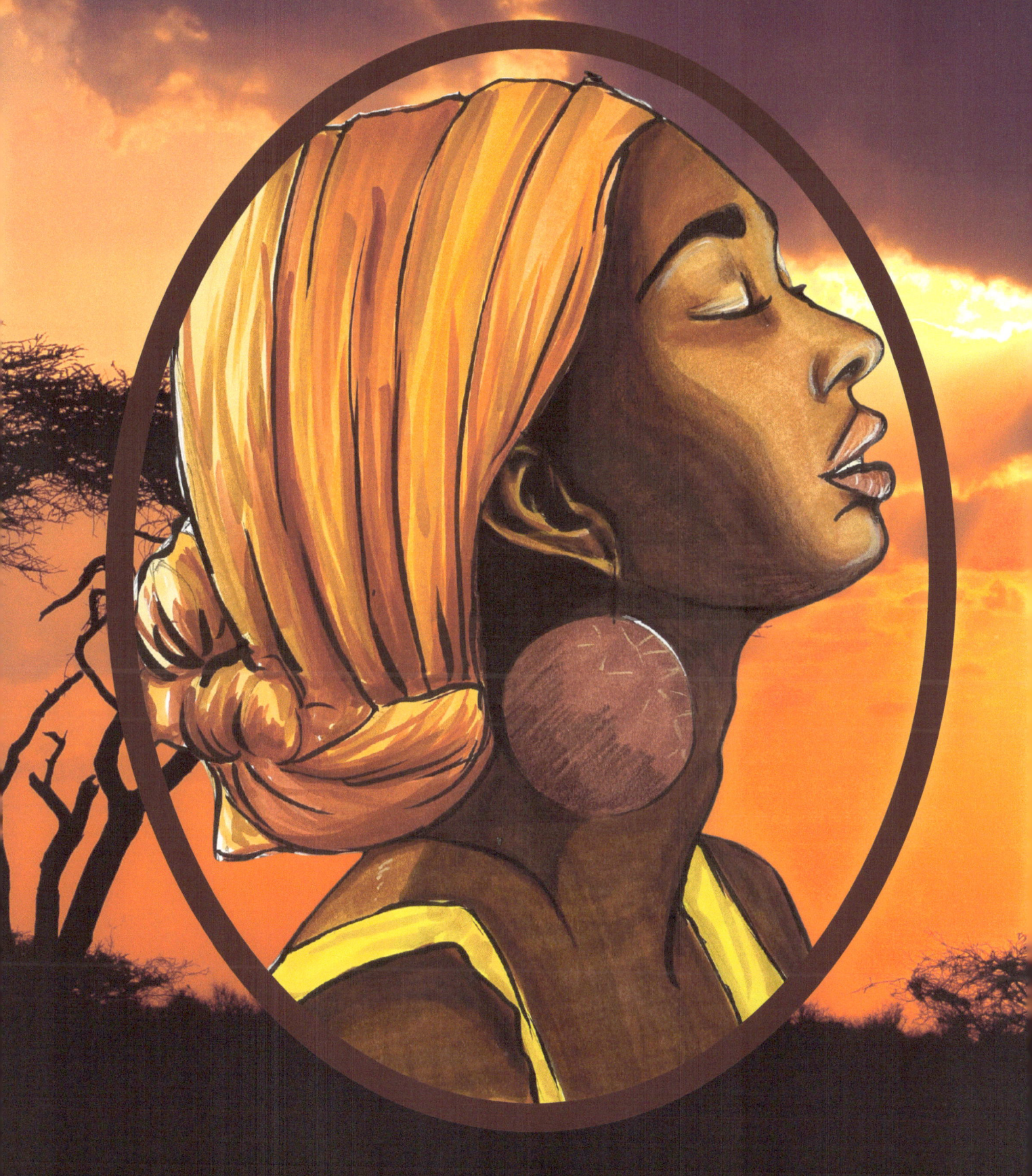

AFRICAN

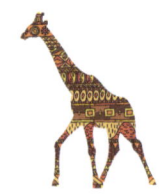

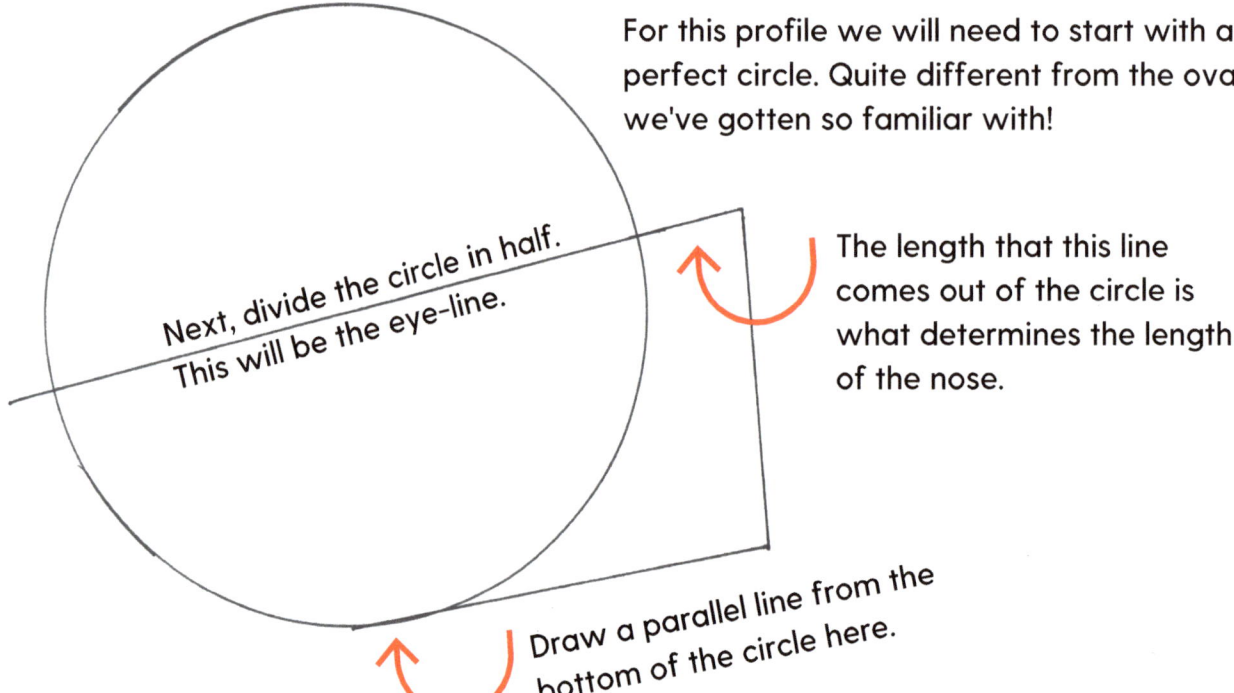

For this profile we will need to start with a perfect circle. Quite different from the oval we've gotten so familiar with!

Next, divide the circle in half. This will be the eye-line.

The length that this line comes out of the circle is what determines the length of the nose.

Draw a parallel line from the bottom of the circle here.

Place holding ovals line up right along this line.

Add the facial feature placeholders in this step, just as we did with the front facing drawings.

Ovals are a great shape that help us form the proper features in the next step.

Make a circle for the chin. Every human's profile is different! All of these proportions can vary so just do your best and approximate their placement. It's all good!

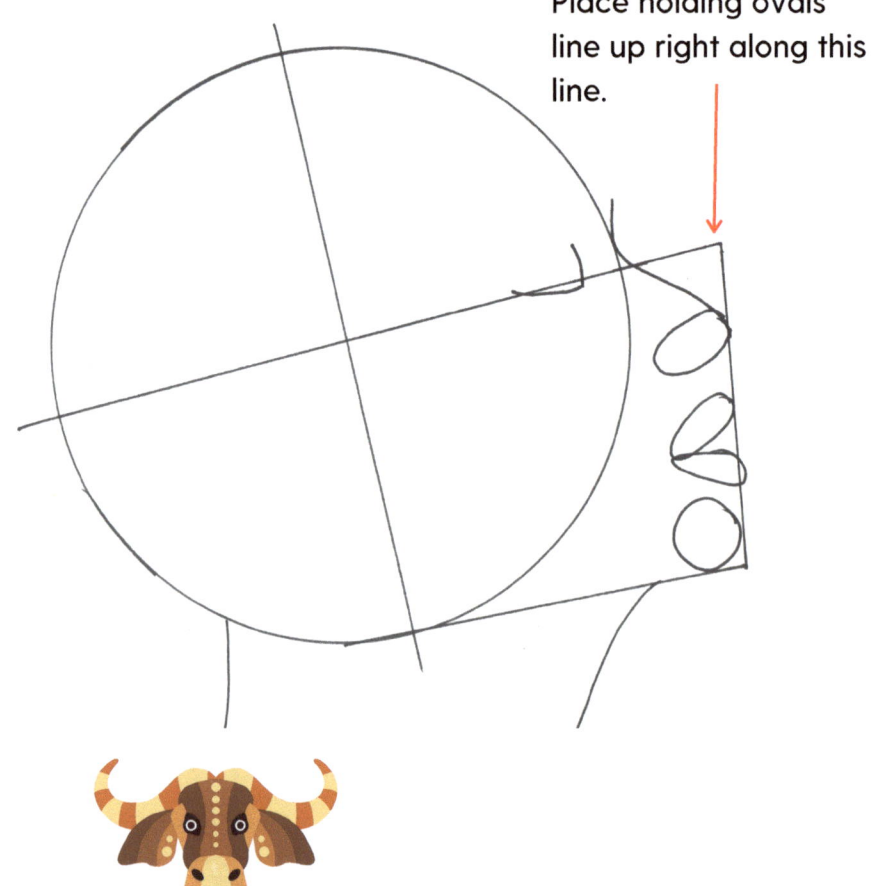

AFRICAN

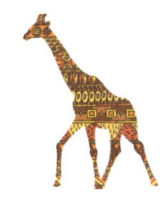

Connect the ovals with small, curved lines to complete the profile.

Add the headscarf and ear.

Note the placement of the ear in relation to the vertical line of the circle and how much volume the headscarf has at the back!

Erase the guidelines.

Add the eyebrows and nostril.

Add the shirt sleeves and a long, circular earring.

I suggest tracing a circle or using a template so it doesn't look wonky like mine!

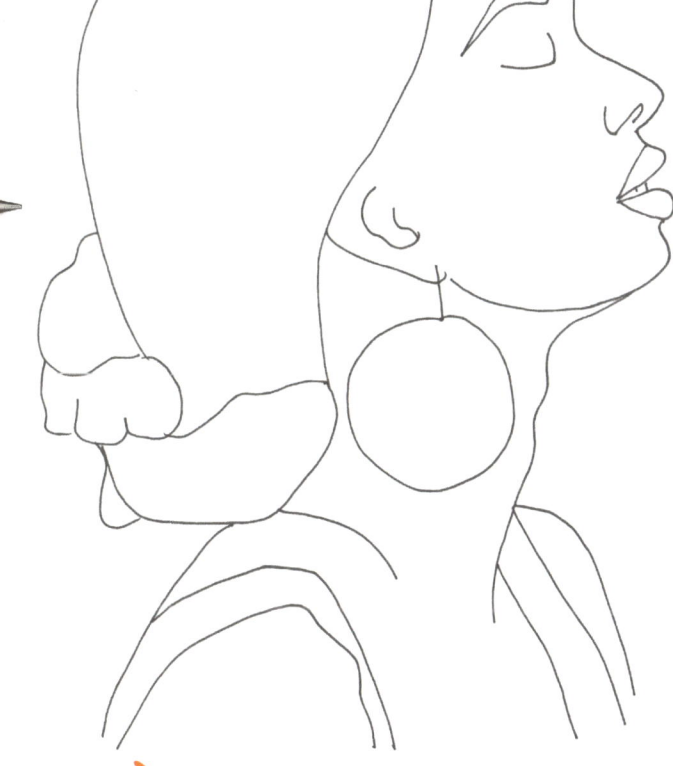

AFRICAN

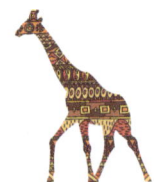

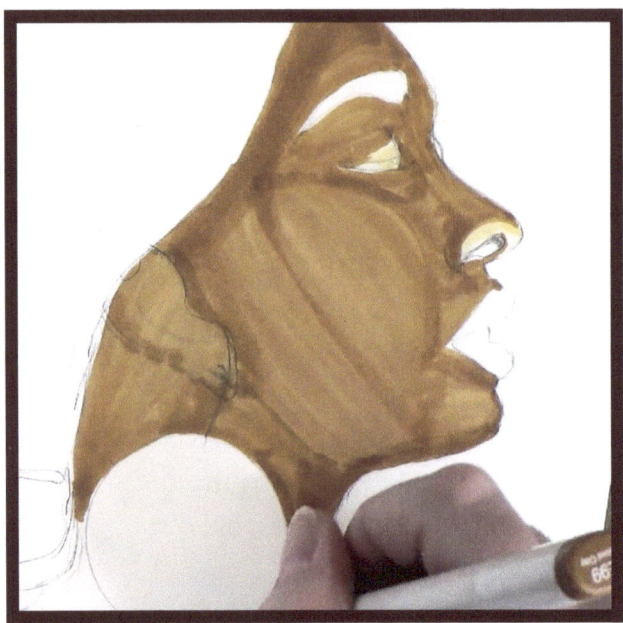

Step 1. Sweep a medium brown over the entire face, neck and shoulders.

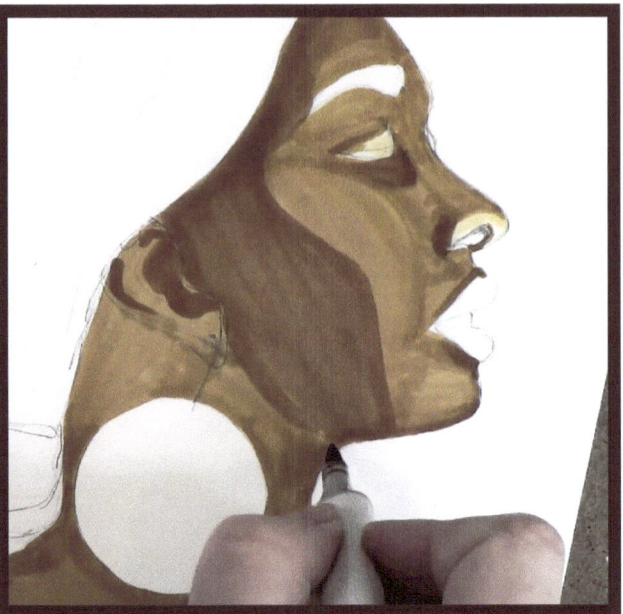

Step 2. Add a darker shade to the areas show. Continue down to neck and shoulders.

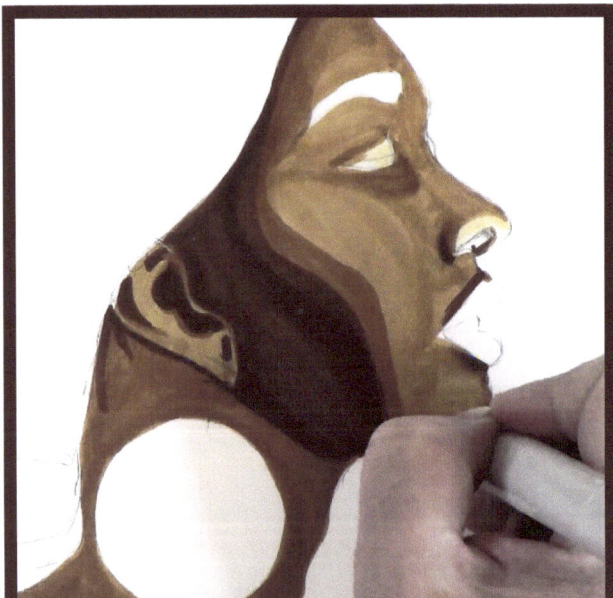

Step 3. Do the same process but use an even darker shade still. Every time you add a darker shade, leave some of the color before it exposed a little more.

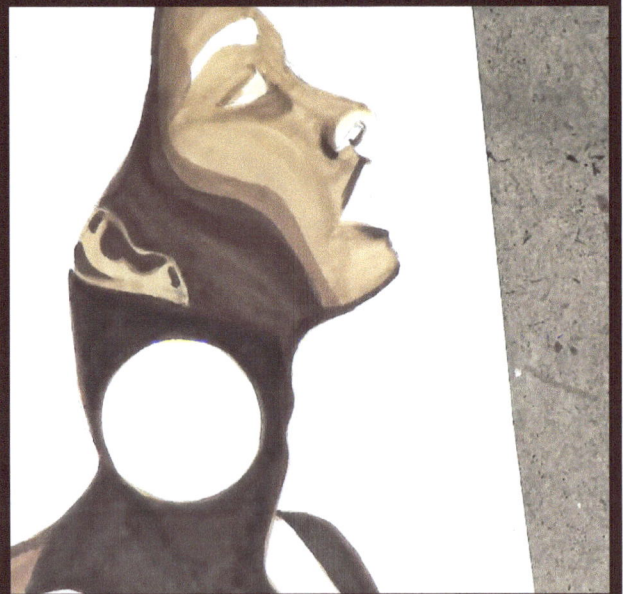

Step 4. Add the 4th shade to the neck down. You can see how each shade is layered one after another. Next, take a light shade and apply it over the entire face to blend.

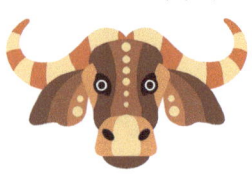

AFRICAN

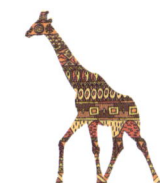

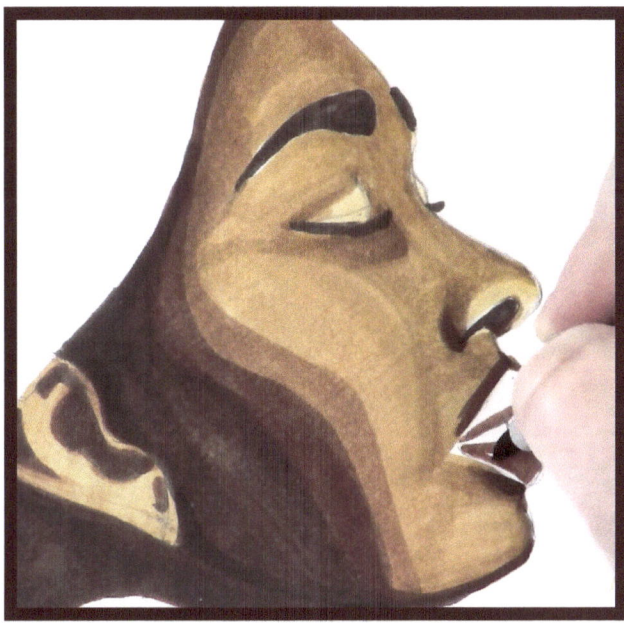

Step 5. Color in the eyebrow and eyelashes in brown and lips in a deep pink.

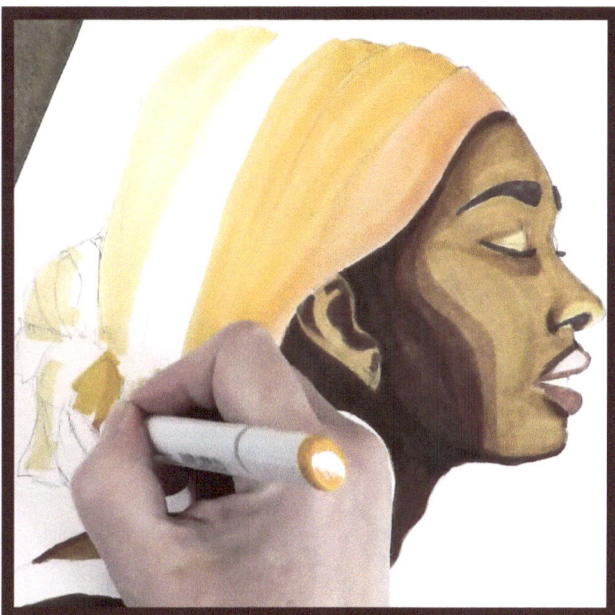

Step 6. Use 3-4 Shades of yellow/orange to color in the headscarf. Alternate colors.

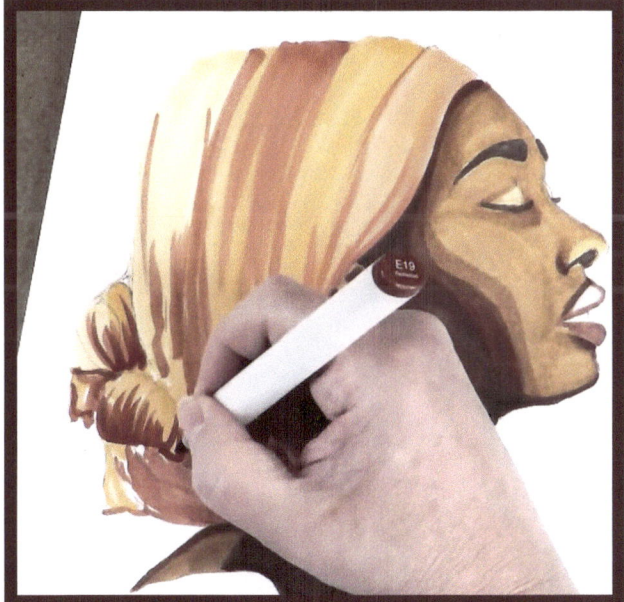

Step 7. Use a deep orange/red to color the folds of the fabric.

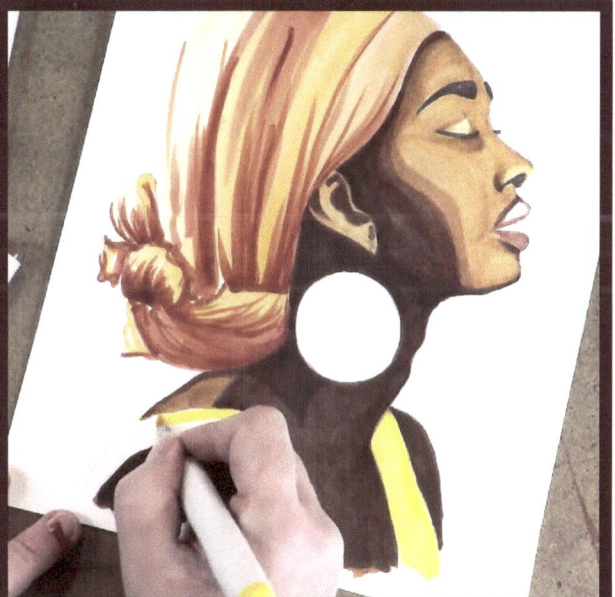

Step 8. Color the shirt with a bright yellow.

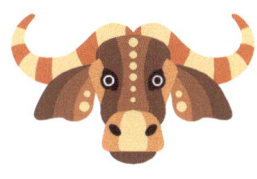

AFRICAN

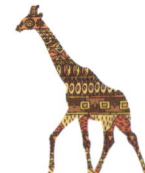

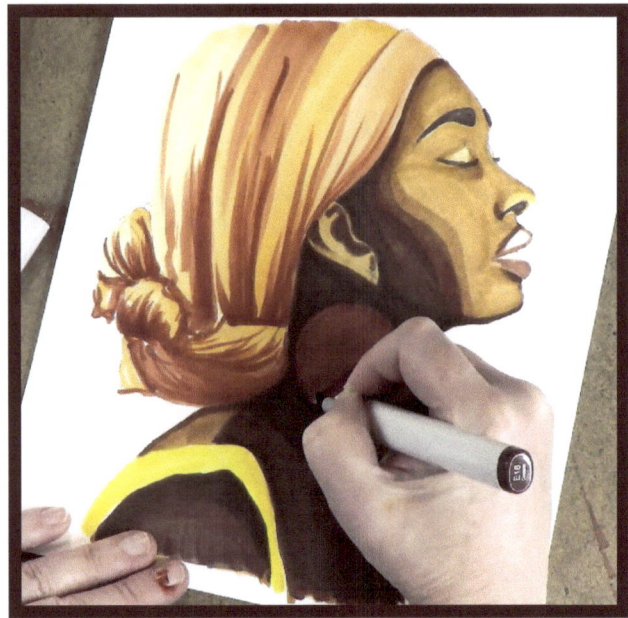

Step 9. Color the earring in with a coppery brown that is lighter than the skin around it.

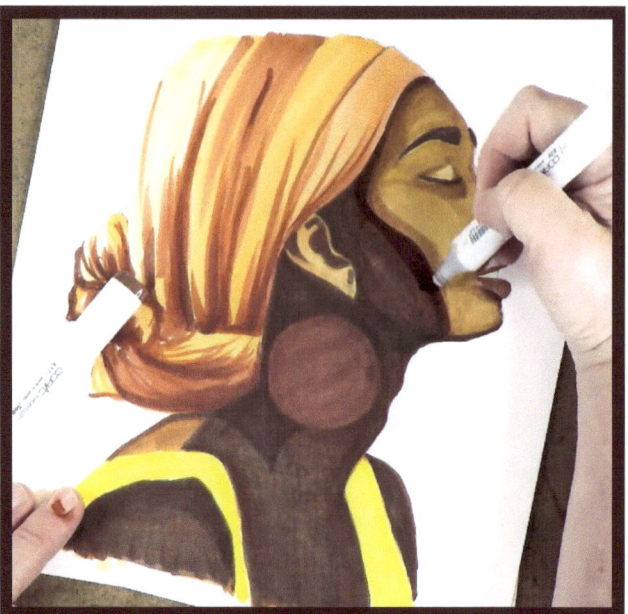

Step 10. Use the 4th darkest shade to layer over the existing dark layers.

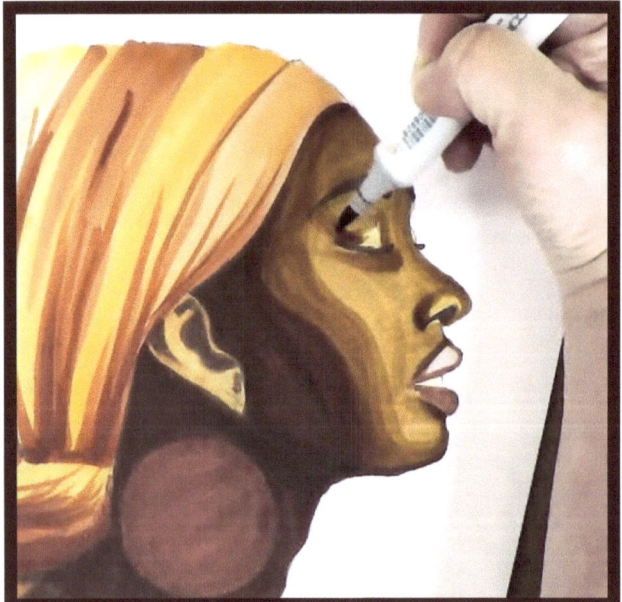

Step 11. Sweep the 3rd darkest skin shade to more areas on the face including around the eyes, more on the cheek, on the nostril and under the lips.

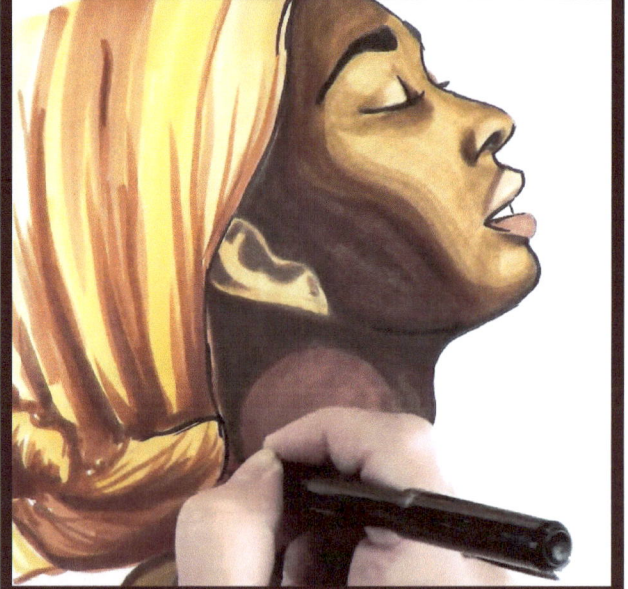

Step 12. With a brush pen or fine liner, outline her face, features and headscarf. Use a gentle touch to create a sketchy line.

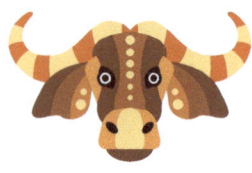

AFRICAN

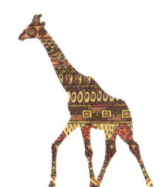

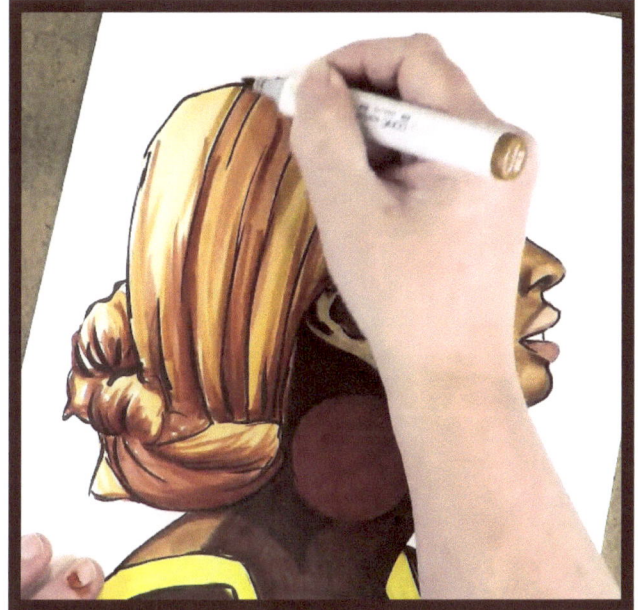

Step 13. Using the a medium brown skin shade, add some streaks onto the headscarf.

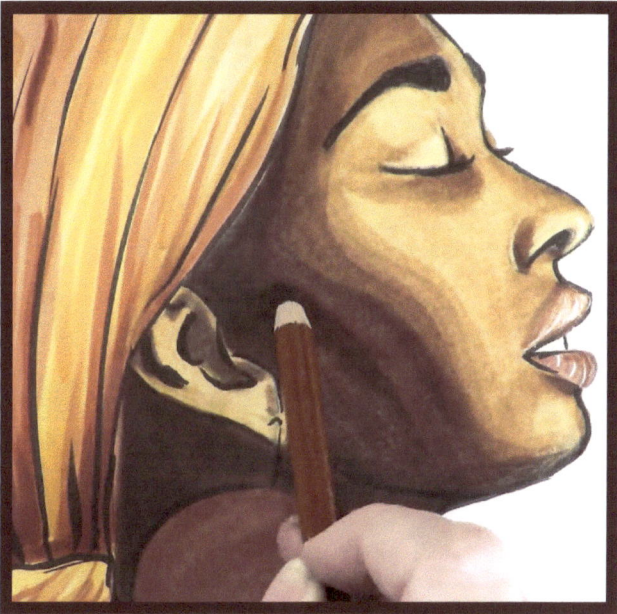

Step 14. Use colored pencils to help blend transitions and for the earring details.

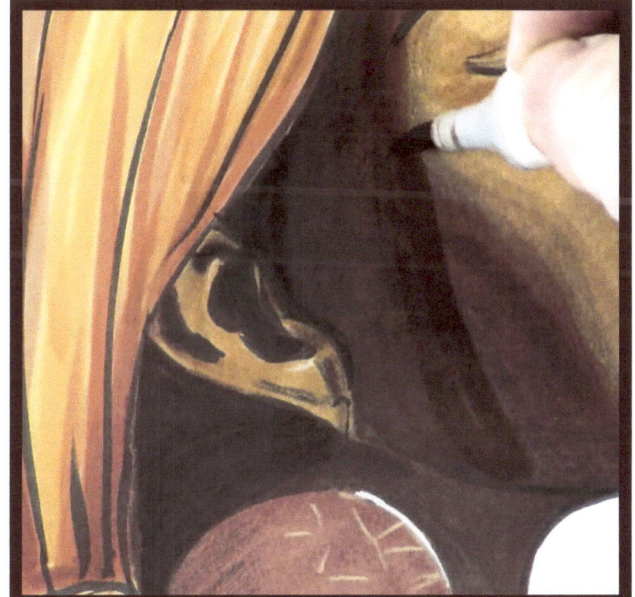

Step 15. Sweep a medium brown in vertical strokes one final time to blend all previous layers and colors together beautifully.

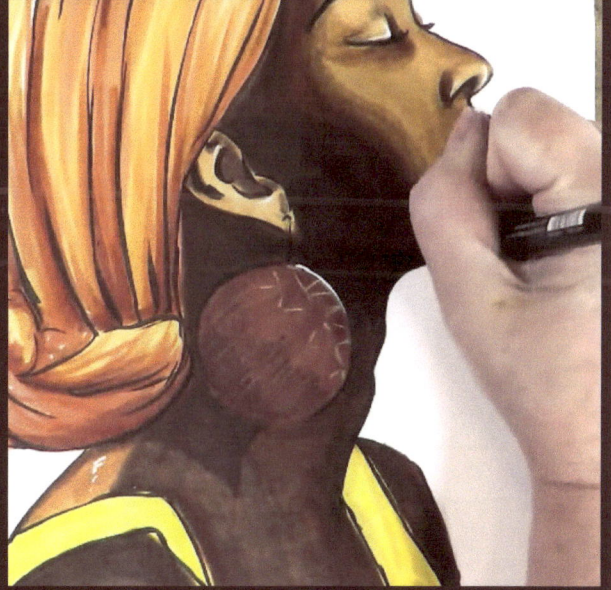

Step 16. Use a white gel or paint pen to add highlights to the earring, nose and mouth and wherever you want to create some drama!

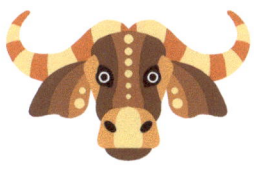

STUDENT SPOTLIGHT

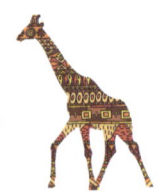

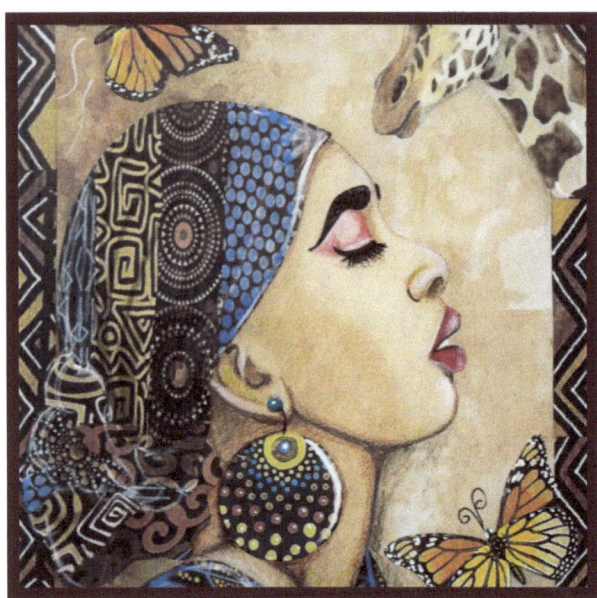

Cornelia Van Der Merwe. Mixed media. *"I love how each supply brings their own kind of magic to the piece."*

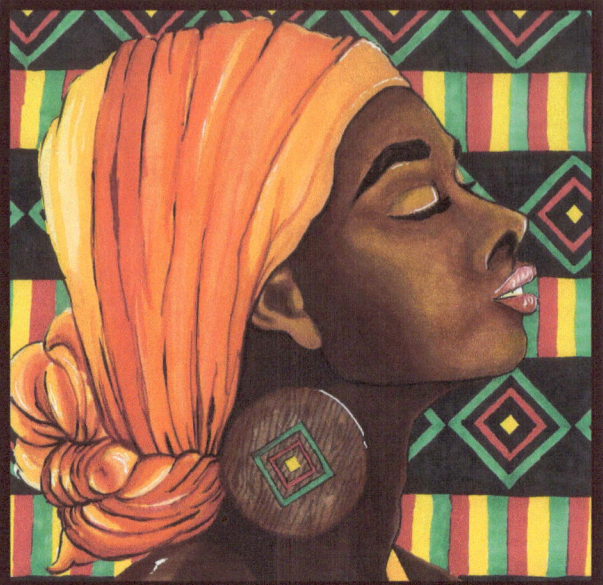

Lynn Buchi. Alcohol markers, pens. *"I love the sheer feel, the contrast, and the glowing color that alcohol markers bring to a piece."*

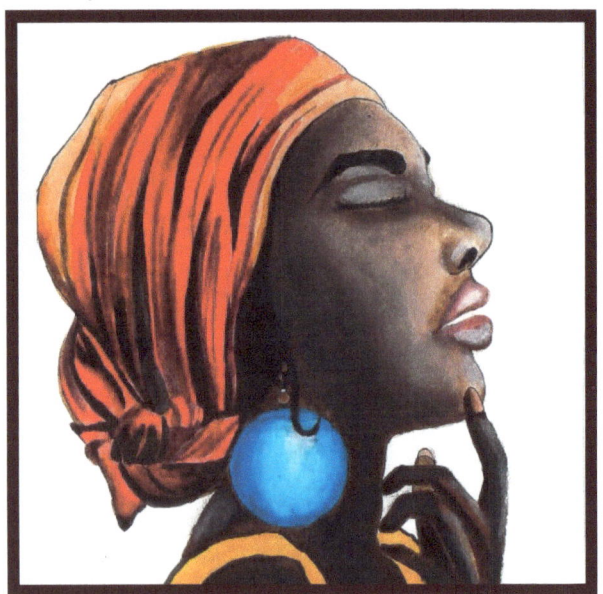

Nancy Moncada. Tombow markers and Marabu crayons. *"I used Tombows and Marabu crayons because I just love them and am better at blending with these."*

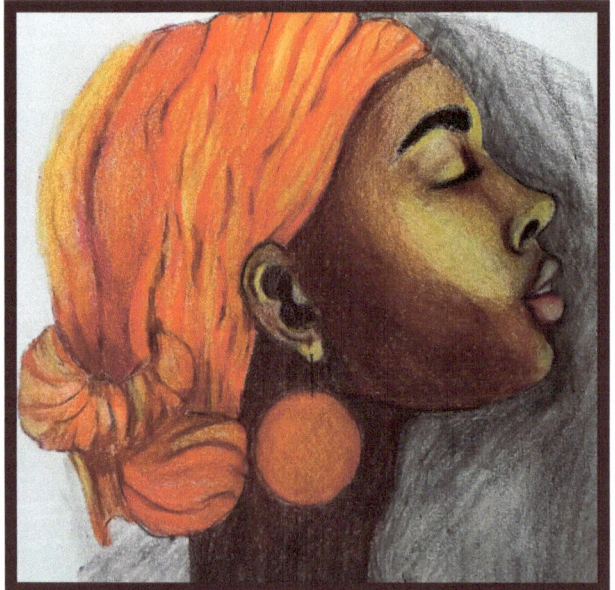

Kirsten Weidinger. Polychromos colored pencils. *"I just got them for a Christmas present so this was a great opportunity to try them out. I had a lot of fun with her!"*

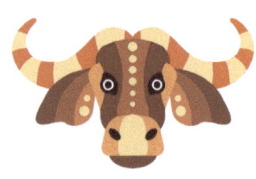

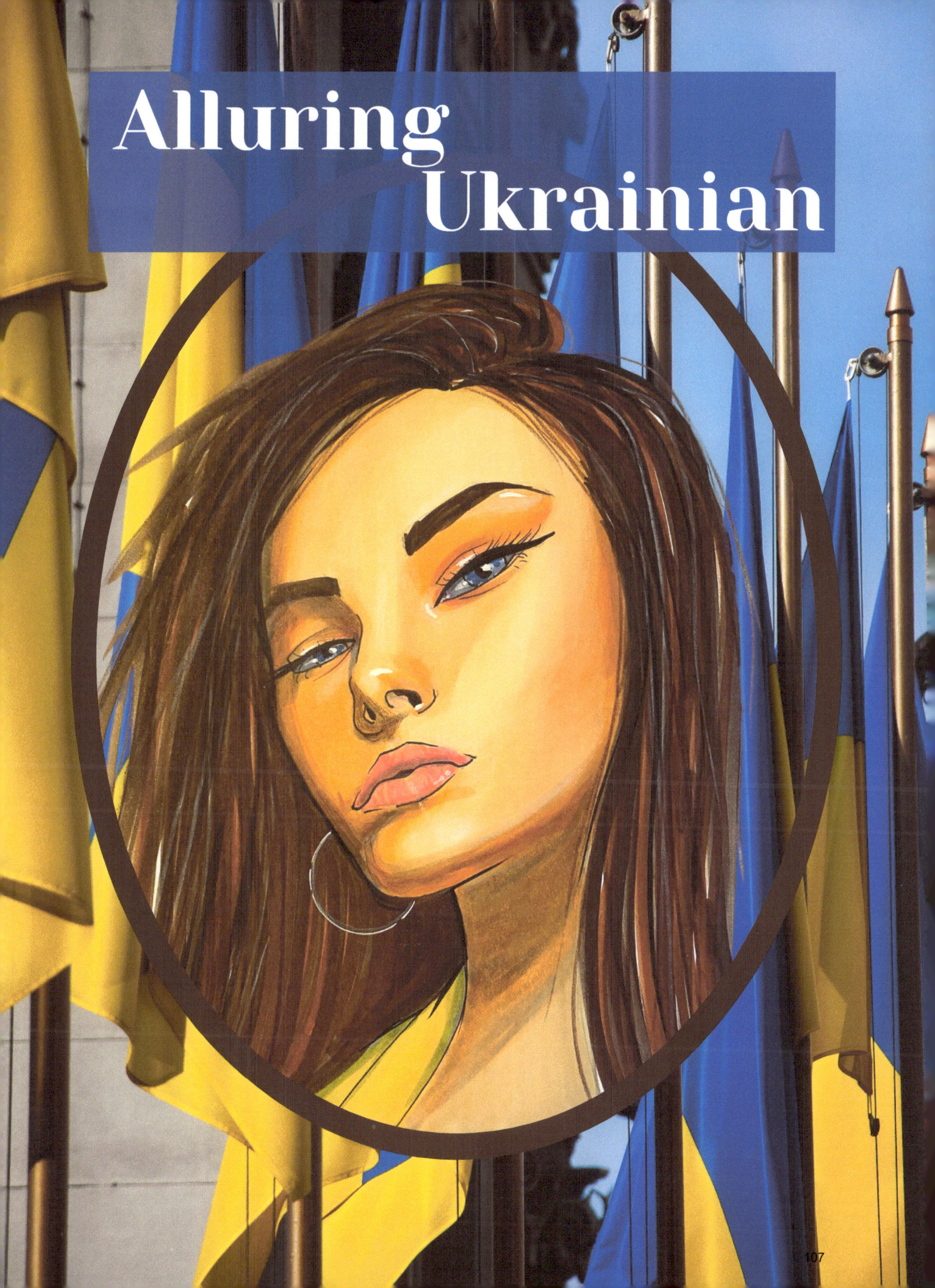

Ukrainian

We start off with a perfect circle...

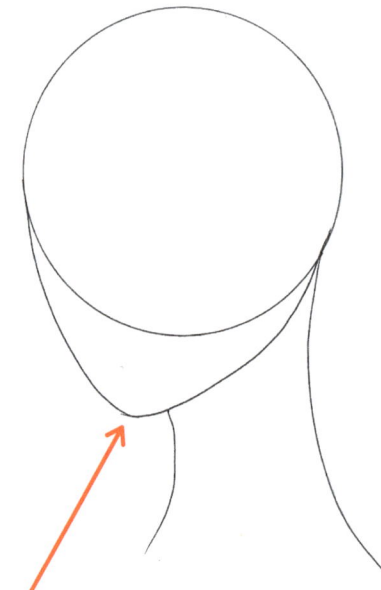

Then add the soft "V" shape to form the chin, just like we did for the Lovely Latina!

The guidelines are super weird for this girl. The curved vertical is the same as we would draw for any 3/4 portrait (like the Latina) but the angles of the eyes, nose and mouth line are what we need to make sure we get them right.

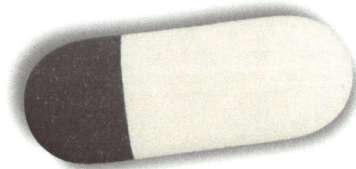

The facial feature "placeholder" shapes are also a bit funny!

The nose is almost the shape of a triangle and the eyes are tiny slits from this strange angle!

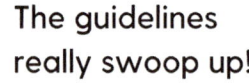

The guidelines really swoop up!

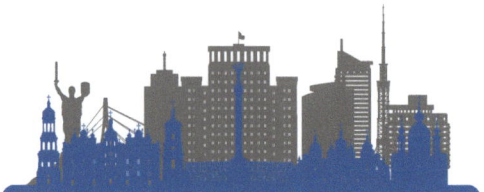

Ukrainian

Now we add the outline of her hair shape.

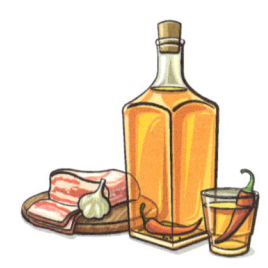

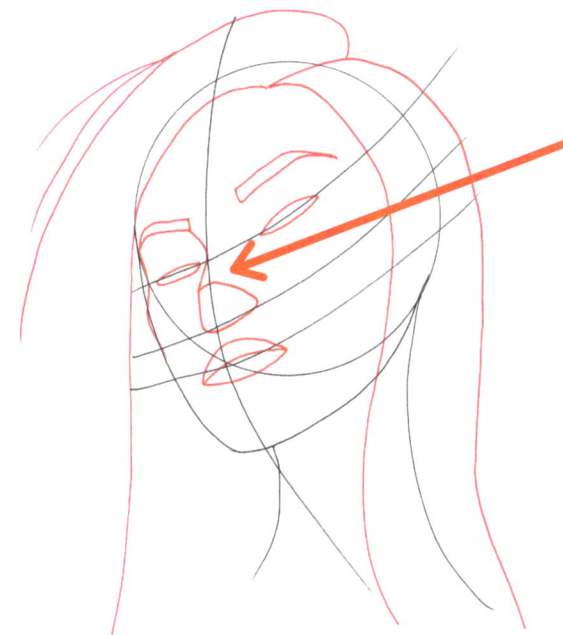

Once again you can connect the eyebrow to the nose bridge if you like! I find I do like to do this when I'm drawing 3/4 portraits. It helps me make sense of how the features relate to one another.

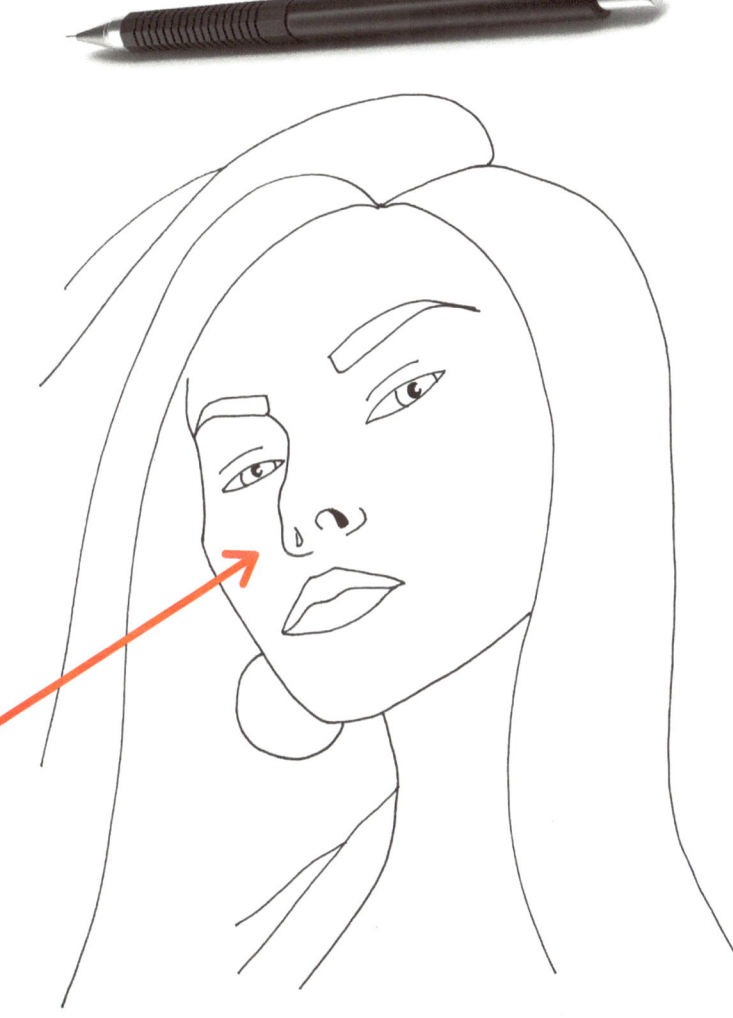

Once again, the hair has so much volume and goes way above the head circles as well as down into the face!

When you erase the guidelines for the nose you can actually keep most of the triangle shape in place!

Only the far side has been erased and the rest of the "soft" triangle is still there and becomes her nose!

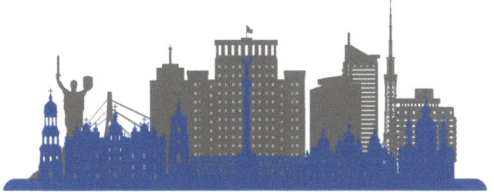

Ukrainian

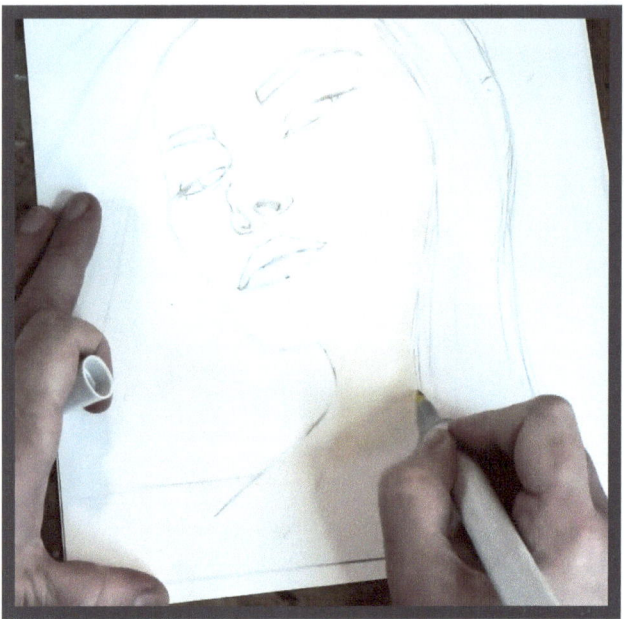

Step 1. Using a very light skin shade, color her entire face and neck with even strokes.

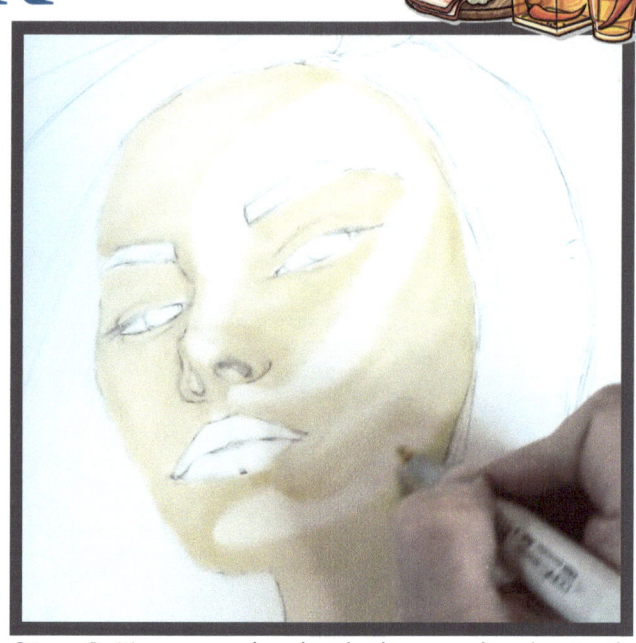

Step 2. Use one shade darker and color in the areas shown, leaving some areas lighter.

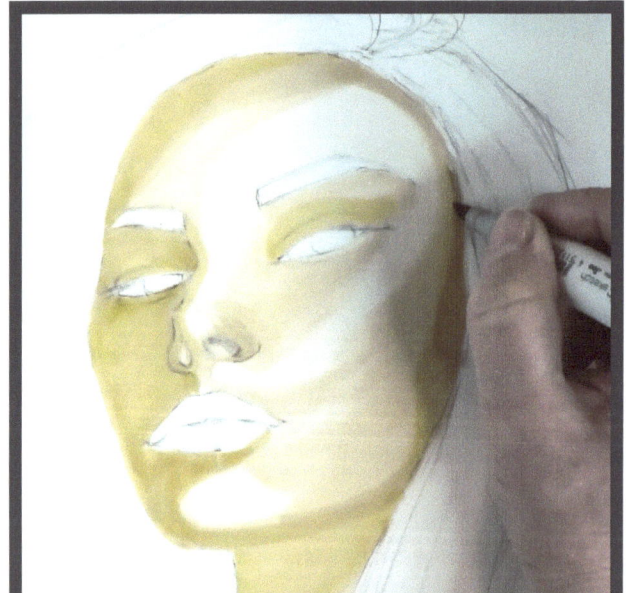

Step 3. Use a third (darker) shade and sweep it over the same areas as shown.

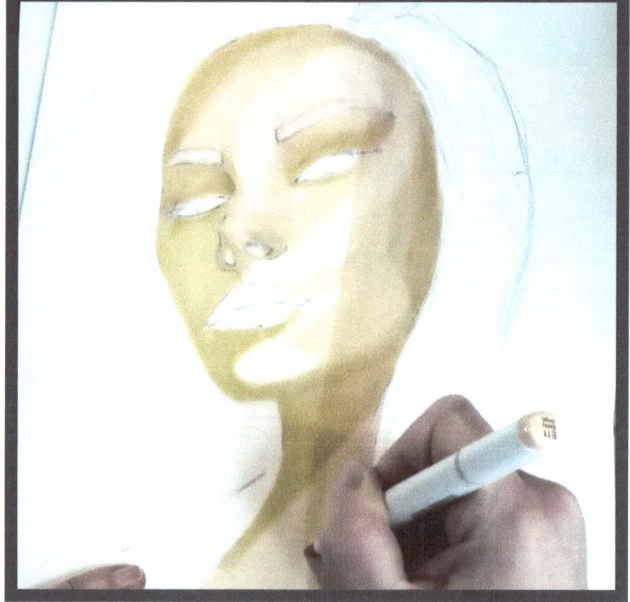

Step 4. To blend all 3 layers together beautifully, take a light neutral and color over the entire face (even highlighted regions!).

Ukrainian

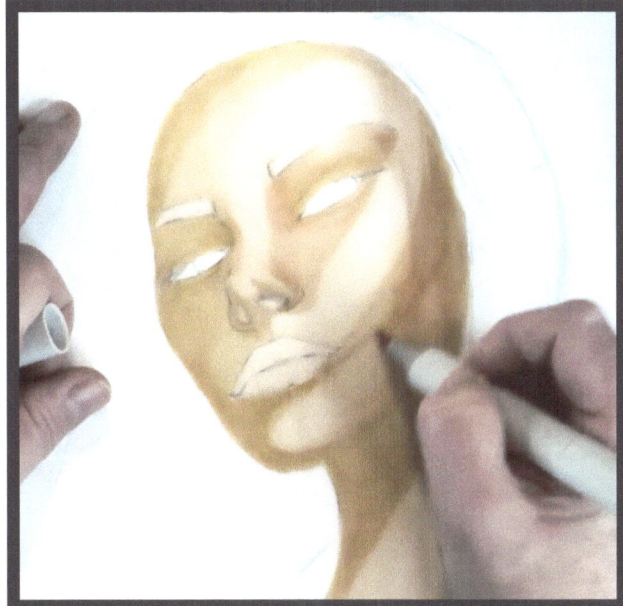

Step 5. Using a darker shade, sweep over shaded regions. Look to reference to help!

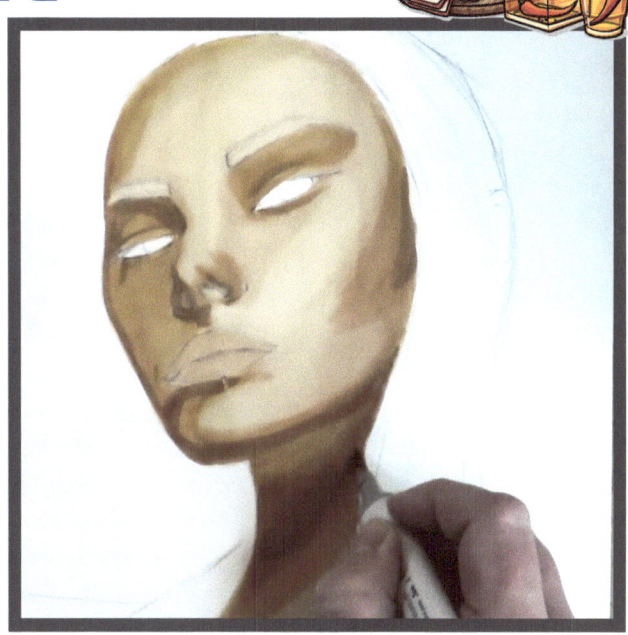

Step 6. Use one last shade (the 5th!) to add just a hint of shade to the areas shown.

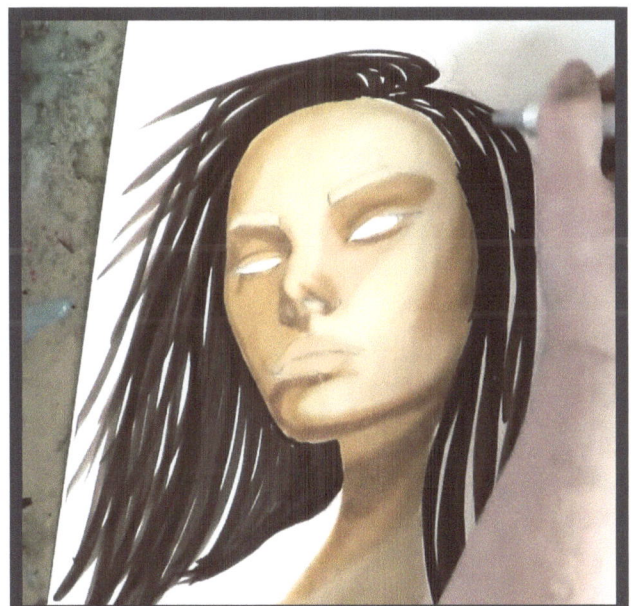

Step 7. Using the broad side of the nib, draw strands of hair from root to tip! Use long, even strokes.

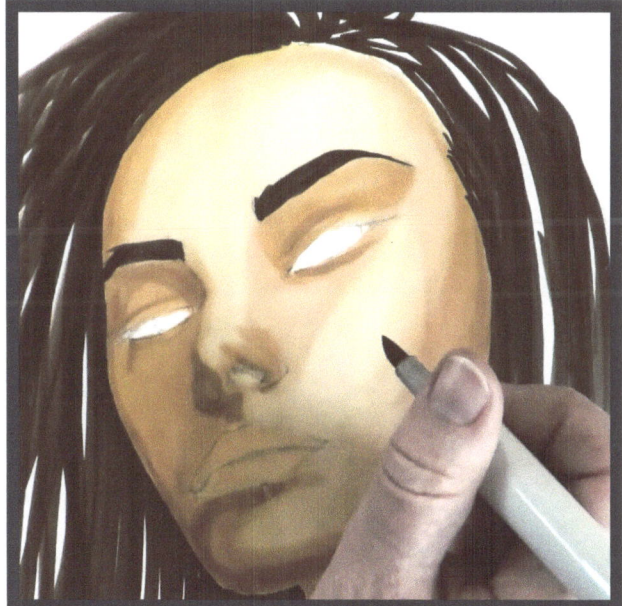

Step 8. Use same shade of brown to color in her eyebrows.

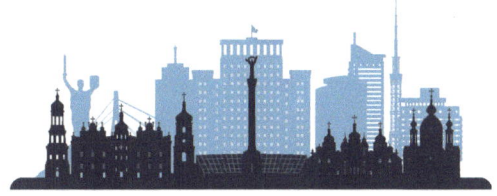

Ukrainian

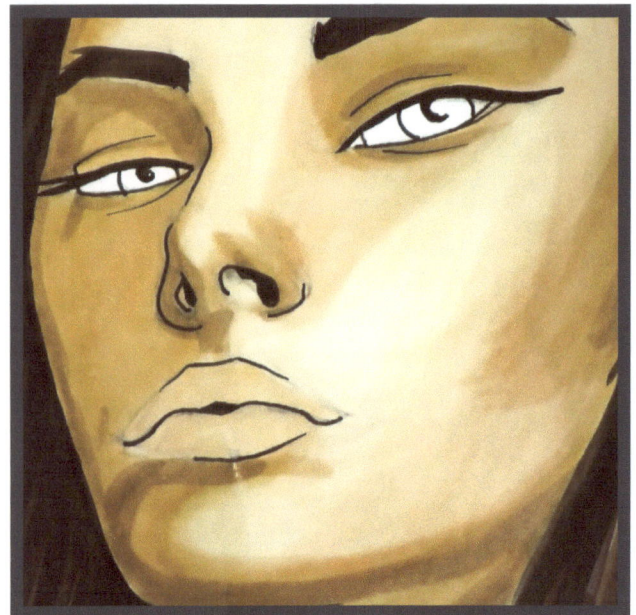

Step 9. Use a fine liner to outline her features. Color the eyes a light blue.

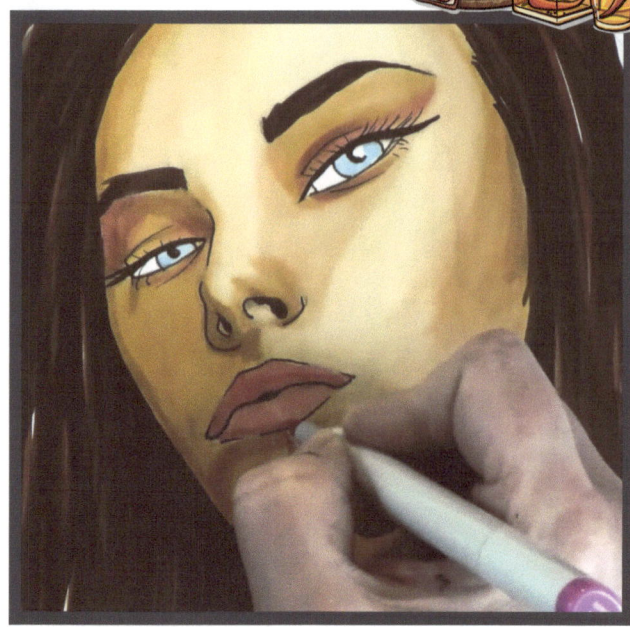

Step 10. Use the same pink to color her lips and around the eyes for drama!

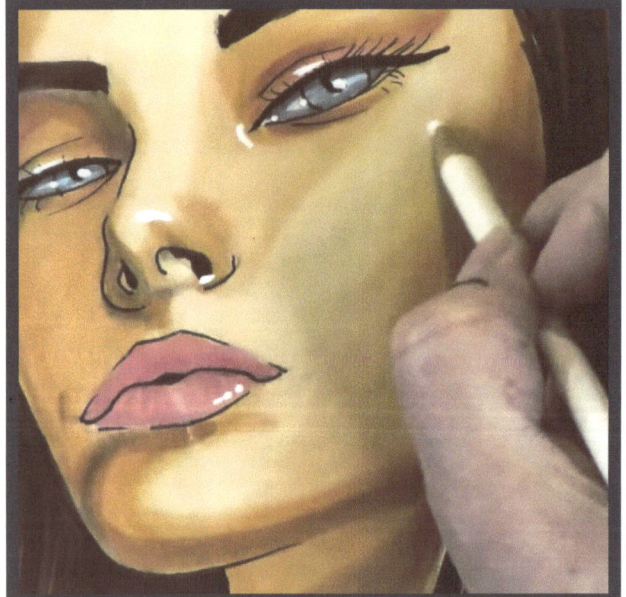

Step 11. Add dark grey to the whites of the eyes. Then use a white paint marker to create bold highlights! A white pencil creates softer ones to cheeks.

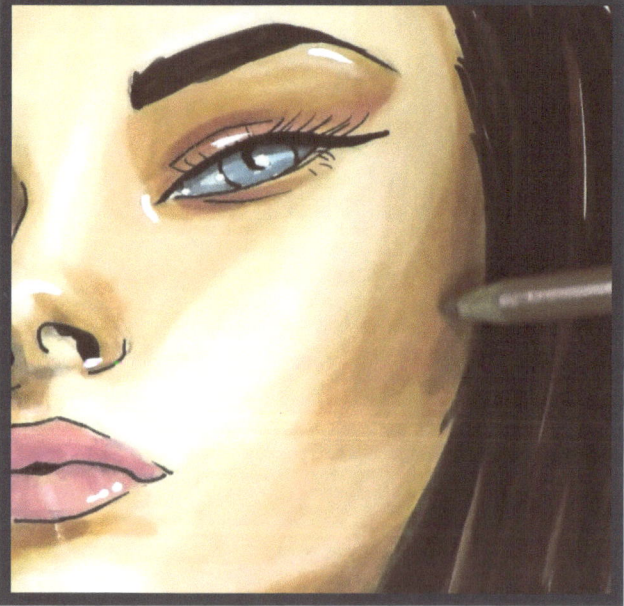

Step 12. Use darker colored pencils to accentuate shaded regions for added drama!

Ukrainian

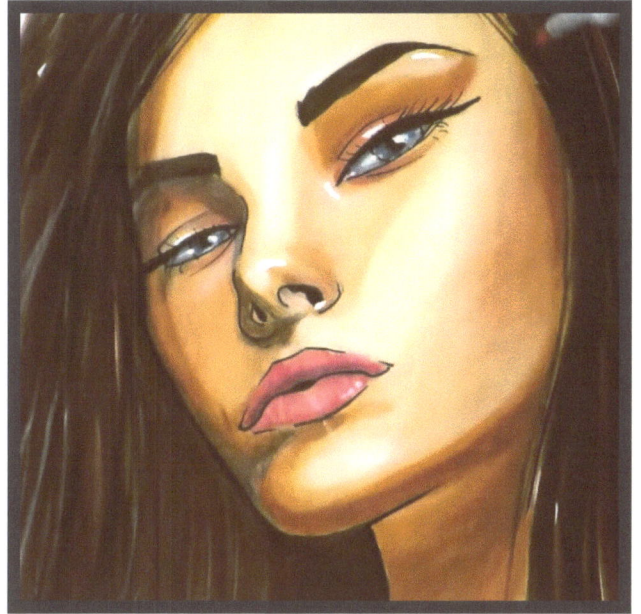

Step 13. Sweep yet one more shade of dark brown to darker areas for the MOST drama!

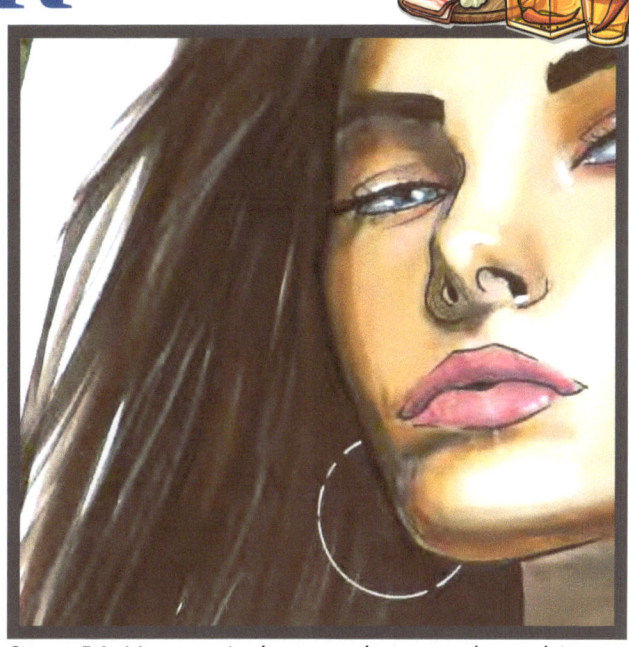

Step 14. Use a circle template and a white gel pen to create her earring!

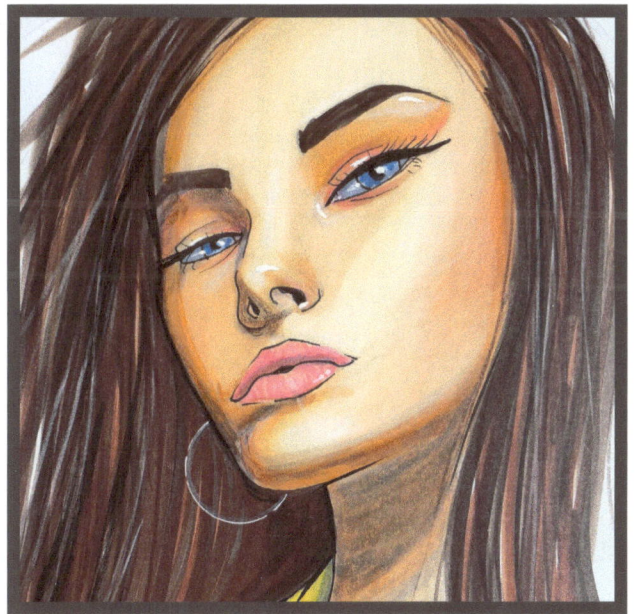

HOT TIP!!! In my final version of this drawing I used GREY for the final shades of her skin tones. DON'T make the same mistake that I did!!!

SAY NO to Grey Tones when shading skin! Grey tones make your faces and shadows appear flat and ugly.

ONLY USE SKIN TONES!
Or even blues or violets! Those make the skin appear alive, healthy and glowing!

Student Spotlight

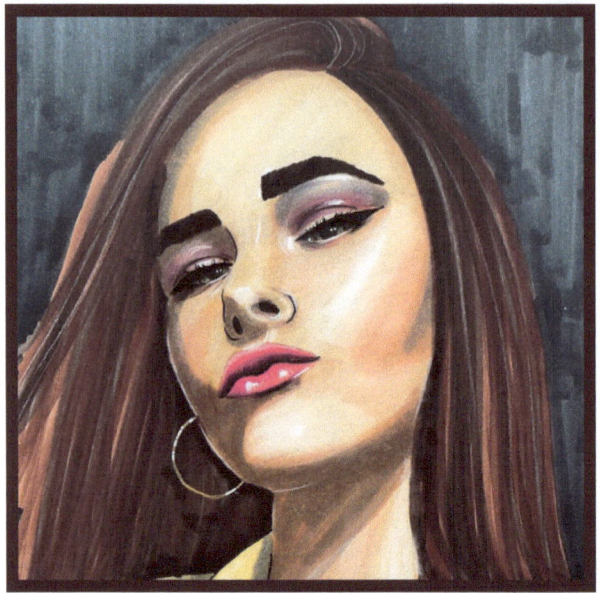

Bryn Nguyen. Copics and colored pencils, brush pen, Posca pen. *"I wanted more practice with alcohol markers to develop my skills."*

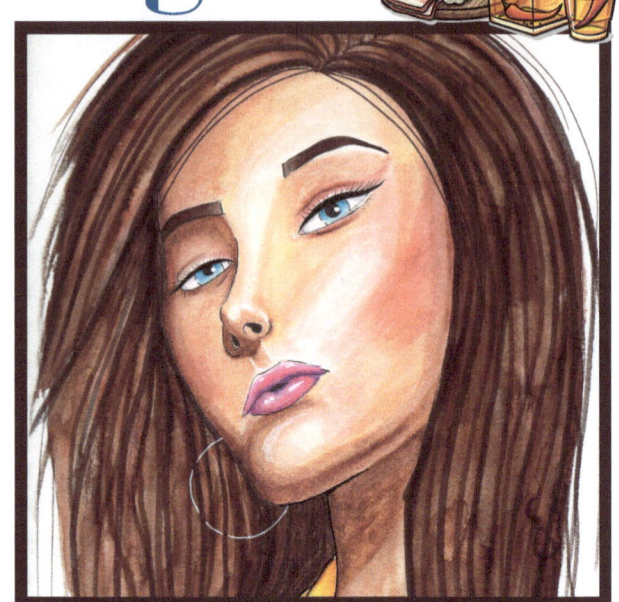

Patricia Veneman. Tombow markers and colored pencils. *"I just love how these two mediums work together."*

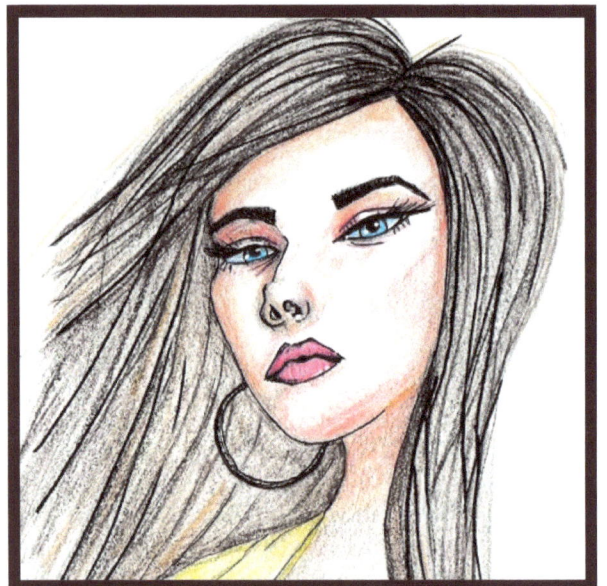

Beverly Barclay. Coloured pencils and black and white paint pens. *"I love how the pencils are soft and easy to blend for shading."*

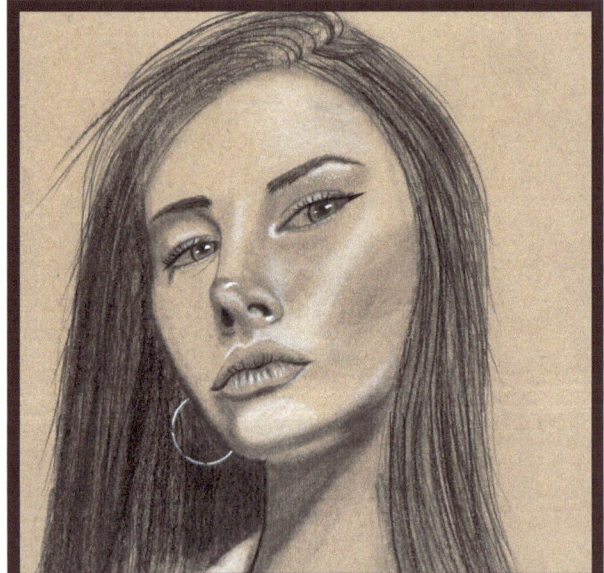

Melanie Stringer. Graphite, colored pencil and white gel pen for the brightest shine on toned paper. *"I love the look of graphite on toned paper."*

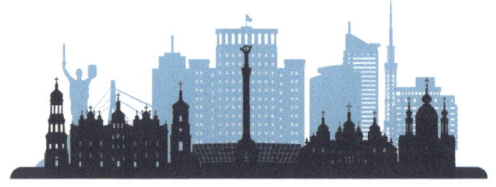

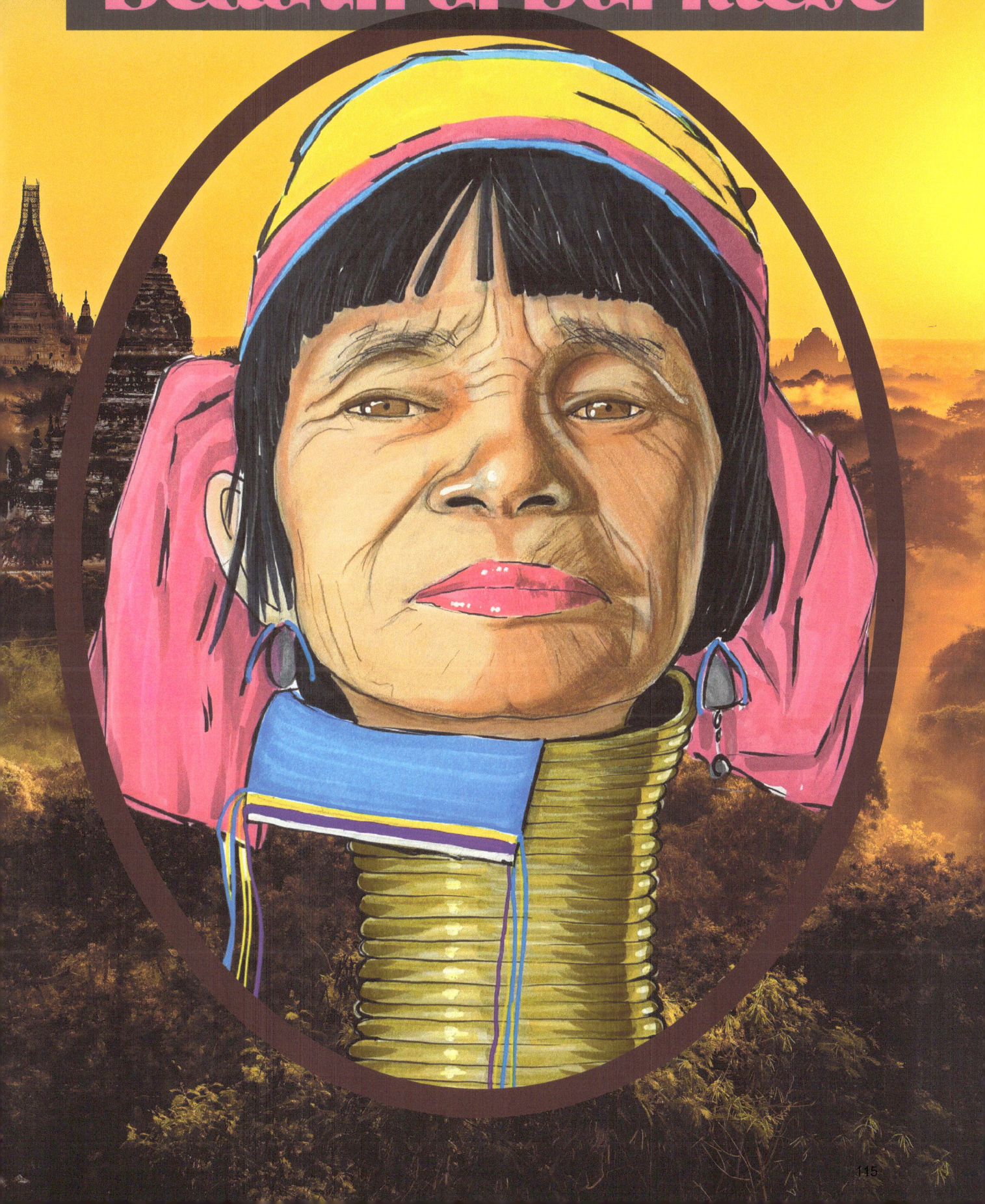

Myanmar (Burma)

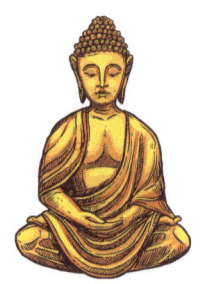

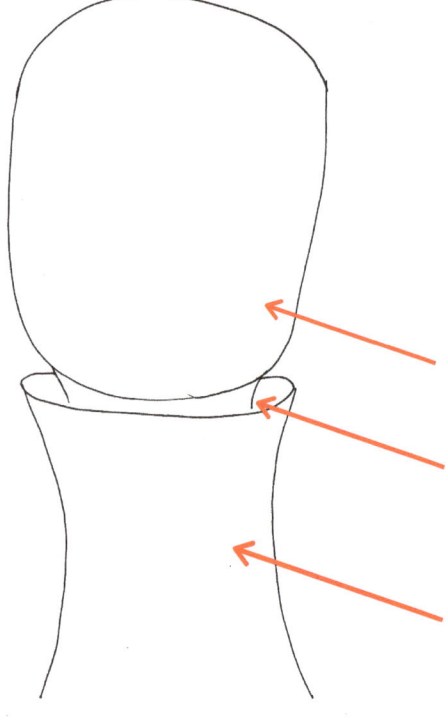

As you've probably already surmised, this drawing project is quite different (and more advanced) than the others.

No problem! As always, I'll take you step-by-step the whole way through. So instead of starting with an oval, we'll be making this soft regtanglur shape instead.

You can just barely see the neck. Put those two little lines in there too!

Then draw a large cone shape. Think of it as a giant turtleneck for now!

Due to the head-tilt and her extraordinary features, for the first time our guidelines are going to placed a little bit differently.

The first horizontal (eye) and vertical lines still slice across and down the centers, but the nose and lips lines are EQUIDISTANT from each other.

The guidelines will look like this.

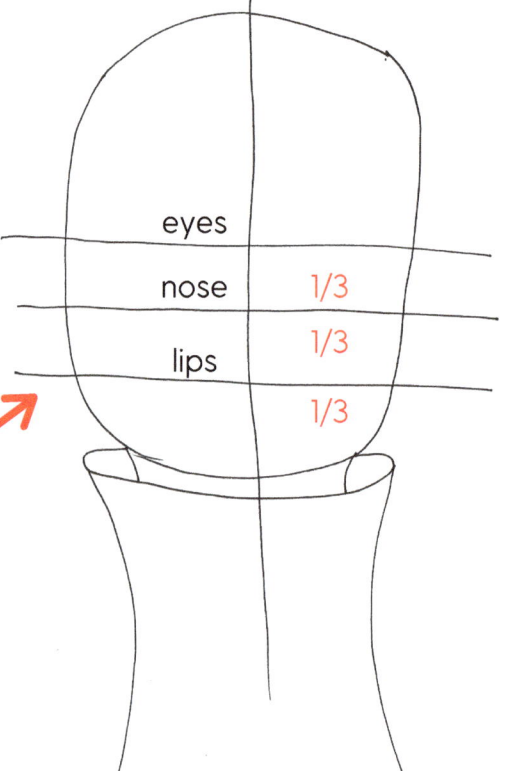

116

Myanmar (Burma)

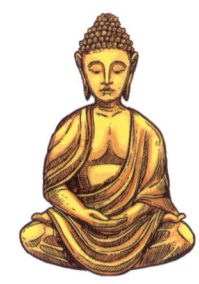

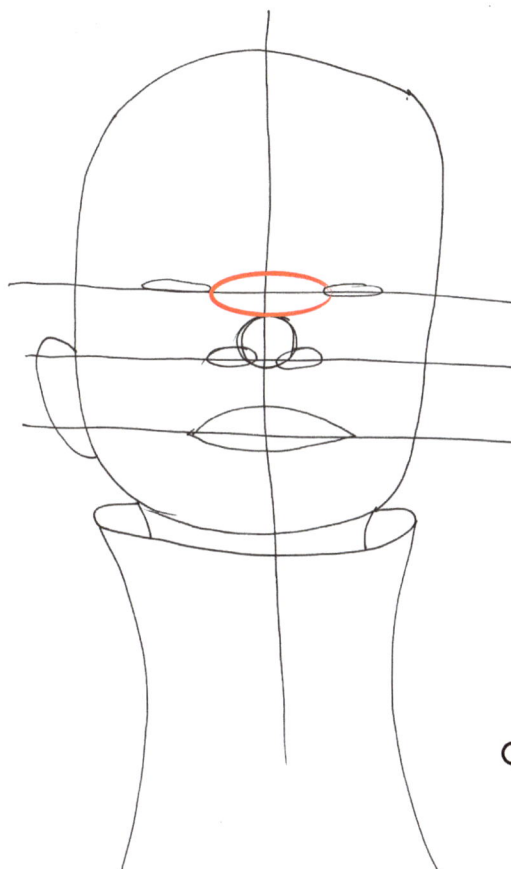

Now it's time to place the facial features.

The eyes are very narrow ovals and sit MORE than an eye-width apart (as is typical).

The nose will be made up of a large circle (for the ball of the nose) and two ovals on either side

The mouth is quite wide and reaches to the middle of each eye!.

Cap sits OFF the top of the head.

Now that the features are roughly positioned, we can draw the outline of the headpiece and hair.

As we've learned, the hair (and this case head piece) have volume so must be drawn up and away from the head shape as well as down into the face area.

The head piece flops over to each side. Approximate these shapes as best you can! Loose rectangles is what I see!

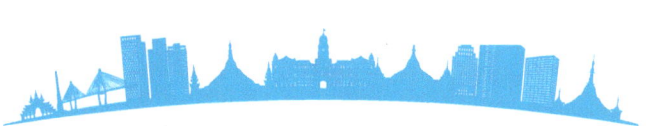

Myanmar (Burma)

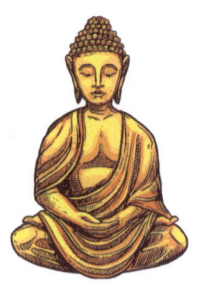

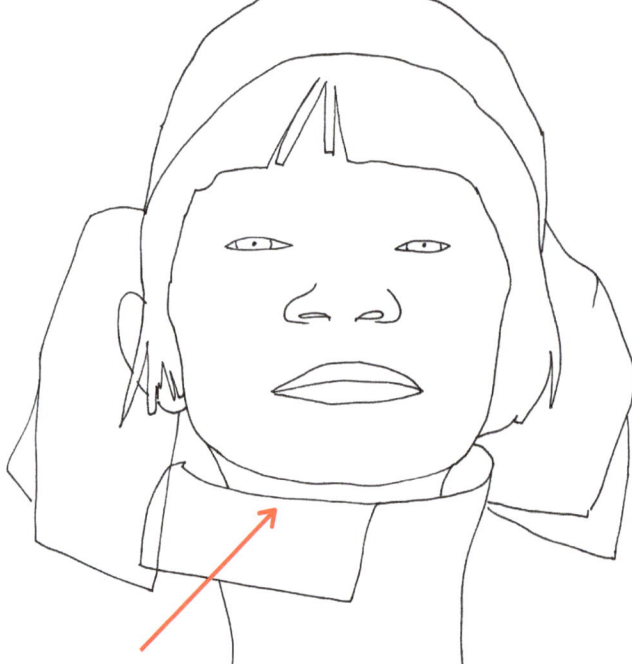

Add fabric flap!

Now it's time to refine the facial features.

No problem!! Just add irises to the eyes and tiny pupils. Then replace the nose ovals with simple nostrils as shown.

Add the center of the mouth as a straight line.

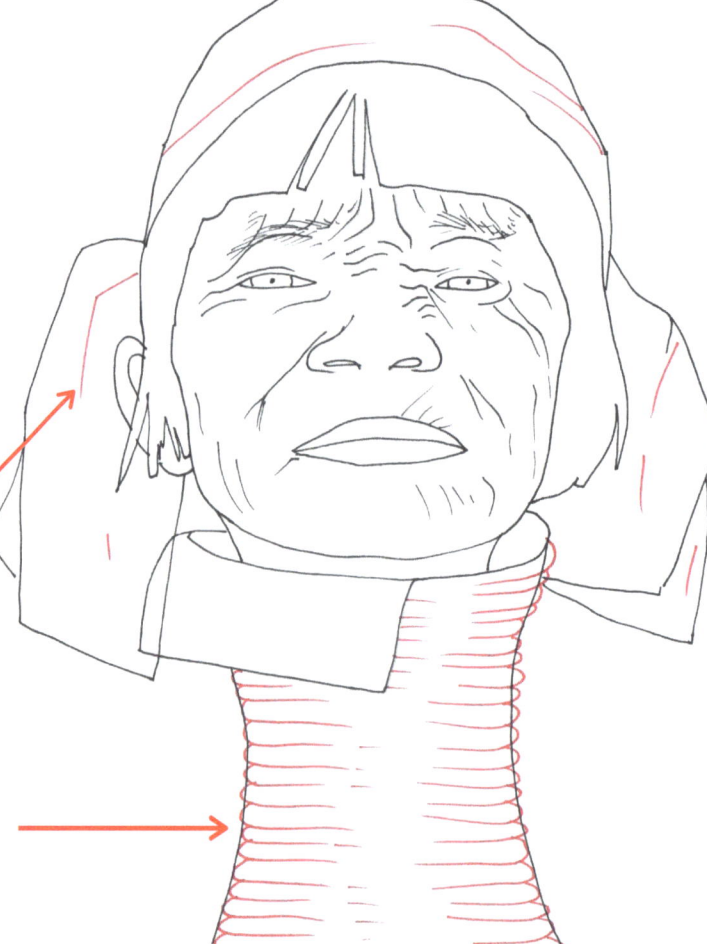

It's now detail time!

Every fold of fabric can be sketched in.

Every wrinkle needs to be drawn.

Every brass ring needs to be outlined as well! Notice I just drew the edges of the rings. Those middle areas will get colored in by the markers so I'm leaving them a little unfinished!

Remember to always check back to the reference to see just what goes where!

Myanmar (Burma)

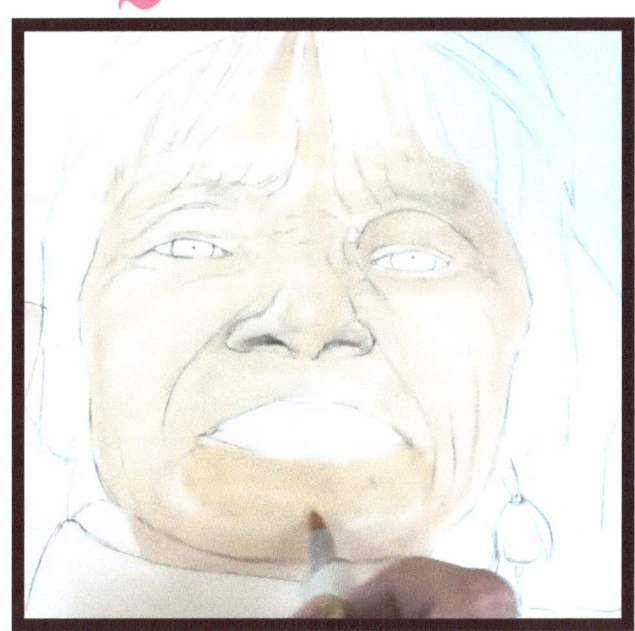

Step 1. With even strokes, color the entire face with a netural skin tone.

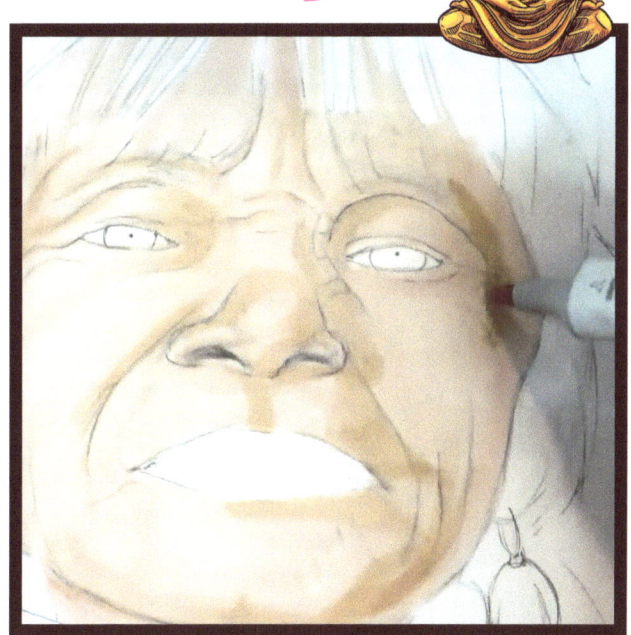

Step 2. Now with a slightly darker shade, add a second layer to the areas shown.

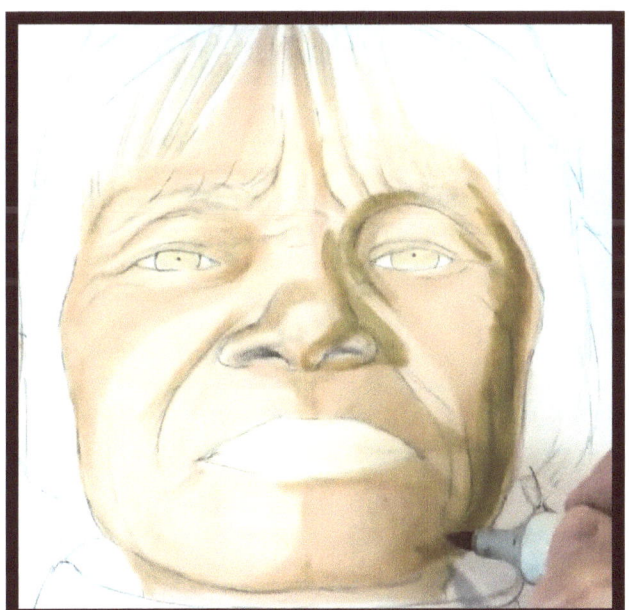

Step 3. Sweep a third shade everywhere (even irises) but leave pockets of lighter tones as shown. Next, add a 4th shade to only these areas shown (right side of the face).

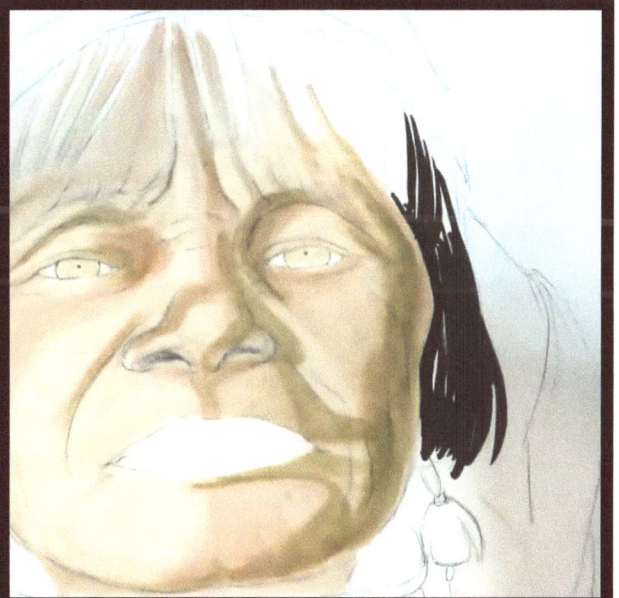

Step 4. Use black and, starting with tips of the hair, flick your marker up towards the roots.

Myanmar (Burma)

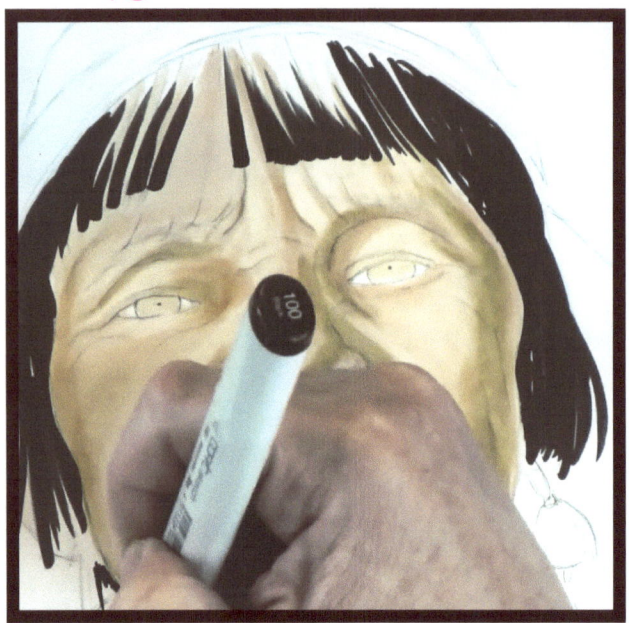

Step 5. Work the color all the way around the entire head of hair.

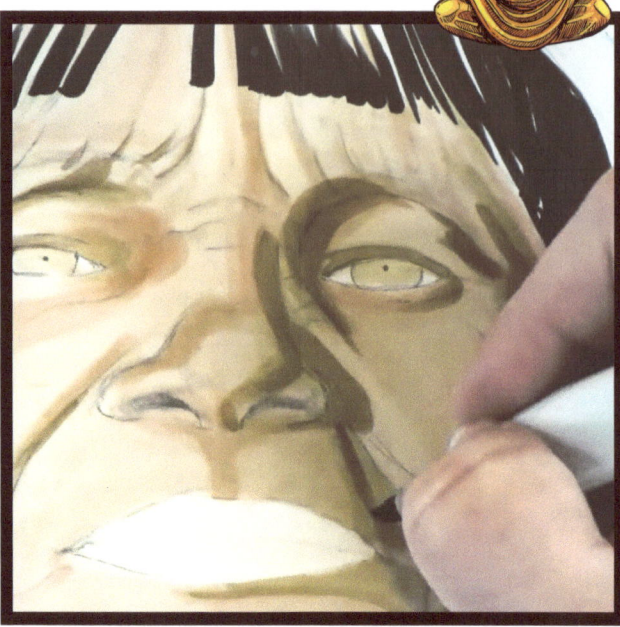

Step 6. Next, go over the darkest regions of the face one more time with a dark skin tone.

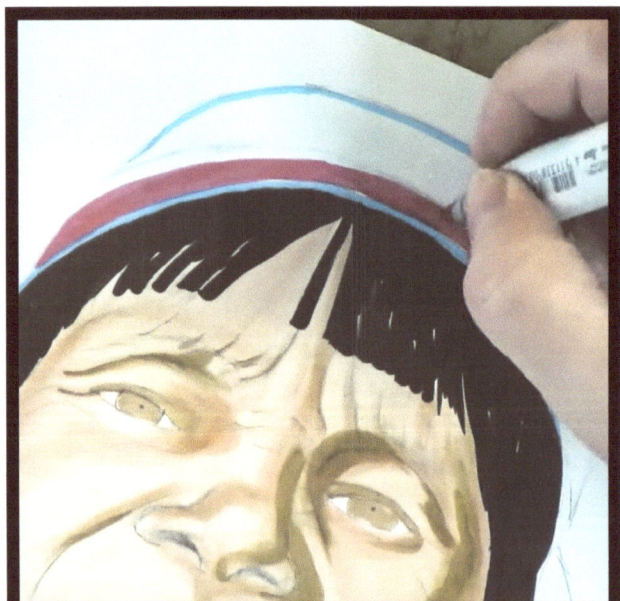

Step 7. Take a break from the skin and hair to color her head piece in with bands of pink, blue and yellow.

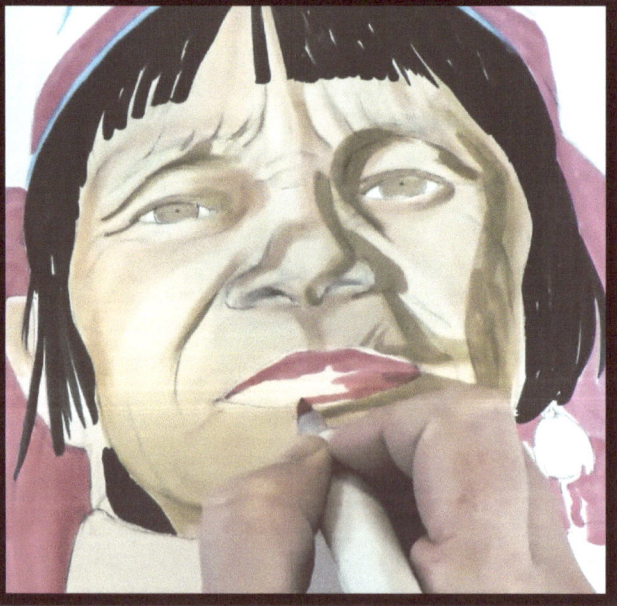

Step 8. Use the same shade of pink you used for the headpiece for the lips!

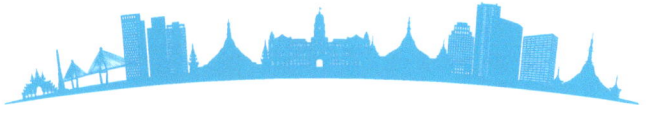

Myanmar (Burma)

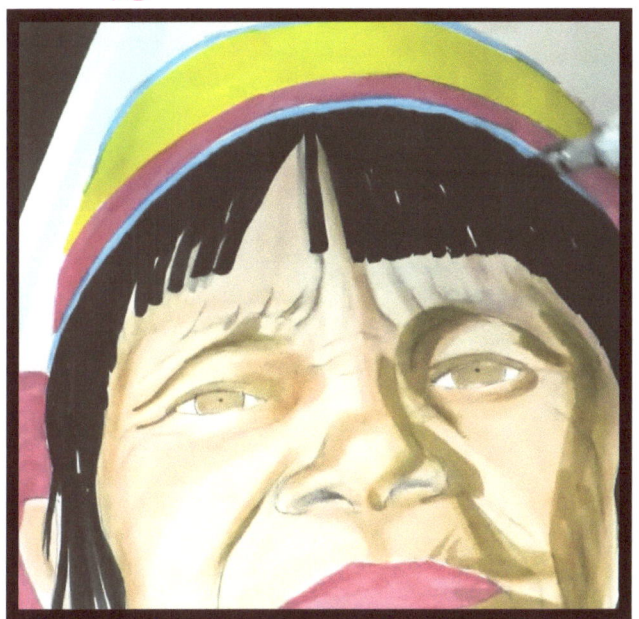

Step 9. Make sure the hair has been filled in and the head piece is fully colored.

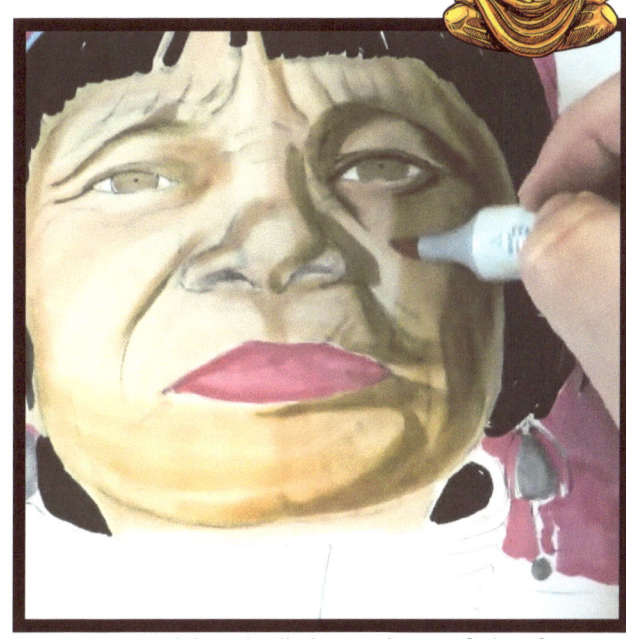

Step 10. To blend all the colors of the face together, sweep a light tone over everything.

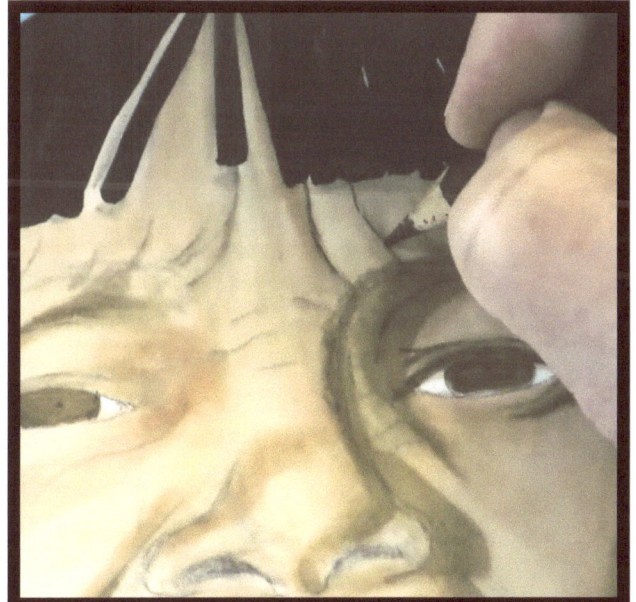

Step 11. Take a very sharp brown colored pencil and outline all of the wrinkles.

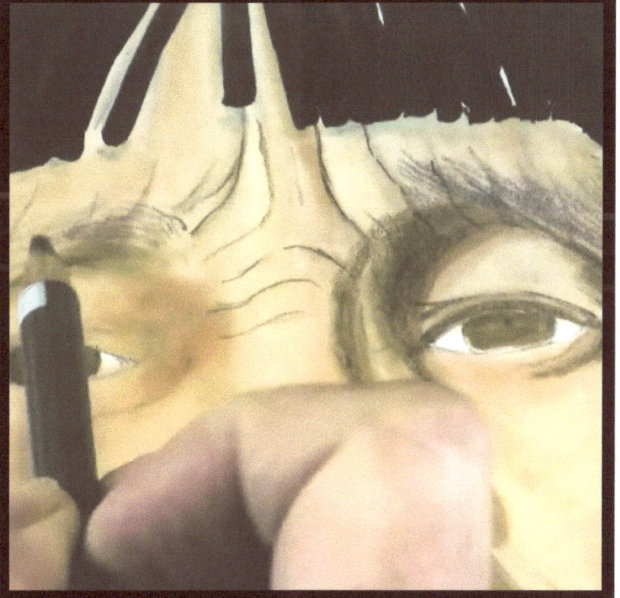

Step 12. Use the same brown pencil to sketch her eyebrows on.

Myanmar (Burma)

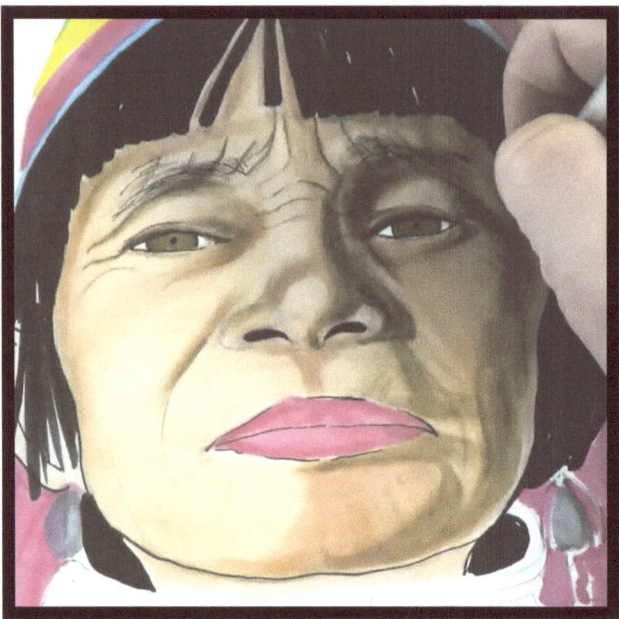

Step 13. Sweep peach under her bangs and along the right side of her face only.

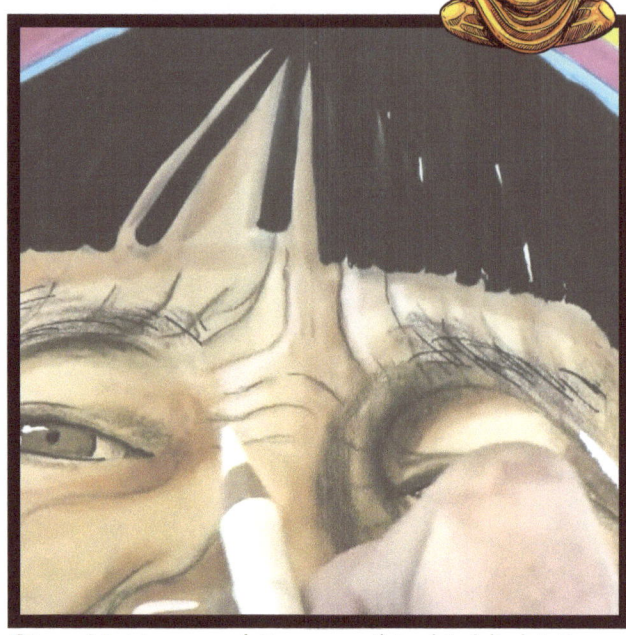

Step 14. Use a white pencil to highlight the areas *between* the wrinkles.

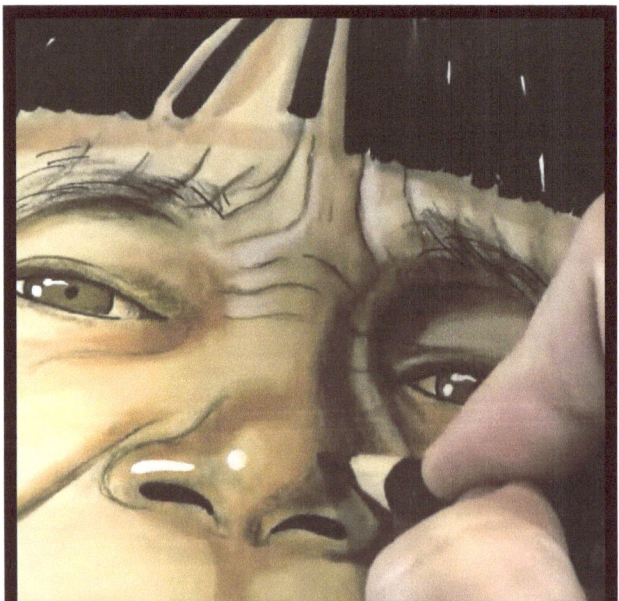

Step 15. Add highlights to her nose and eyes with a white paint marker. Accentuate her shaded regions with a dark brown pencil.

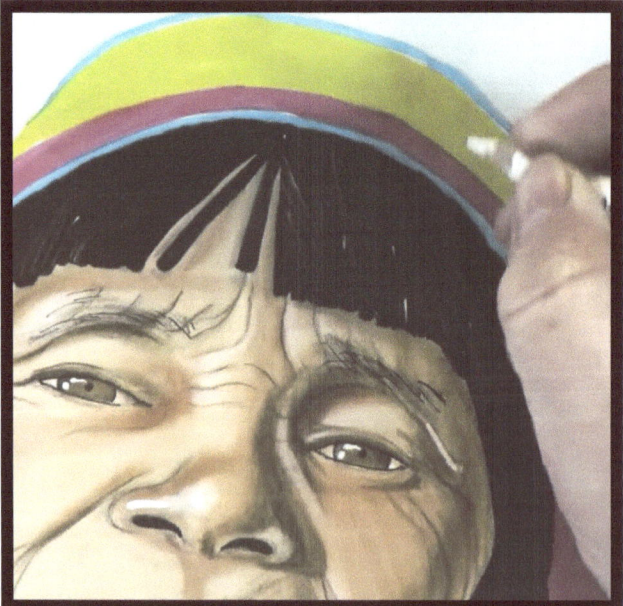

Step 16. Use the white pencil to add white strands of hair.

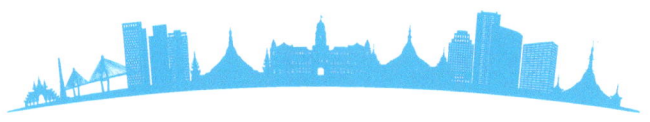

Myanmar (Burma)

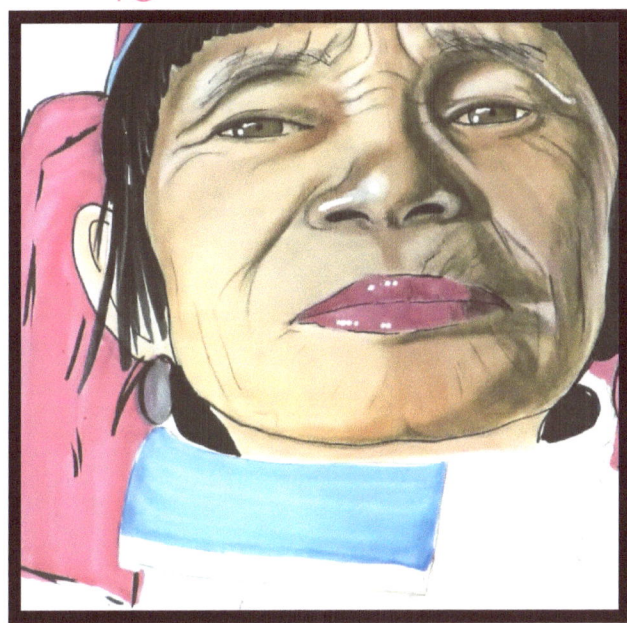

Step 17. Use a blue color to fill in the fabric as shown (same color as in headpiece).

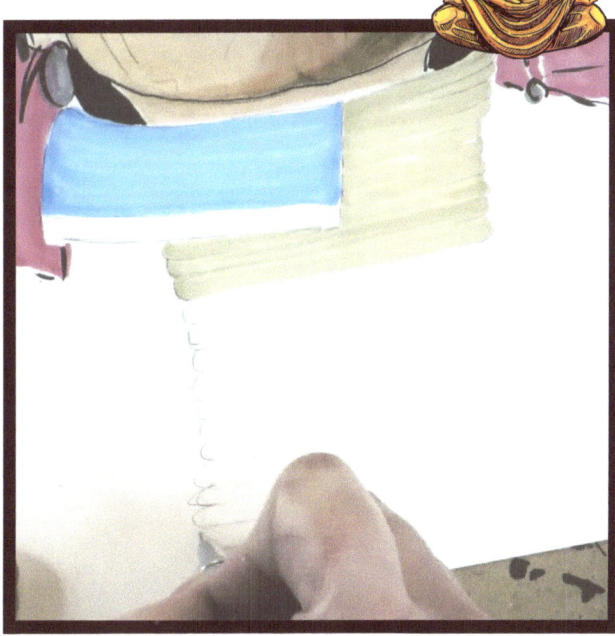

Step 18. Define the neck rings with pencil and color all of them with a metallic color.

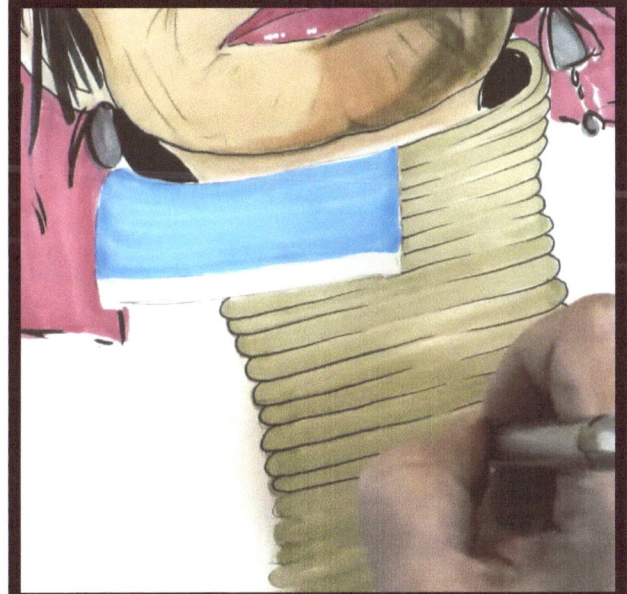

Step 19. Outline each ring with a fine liner but leave some spaces open.

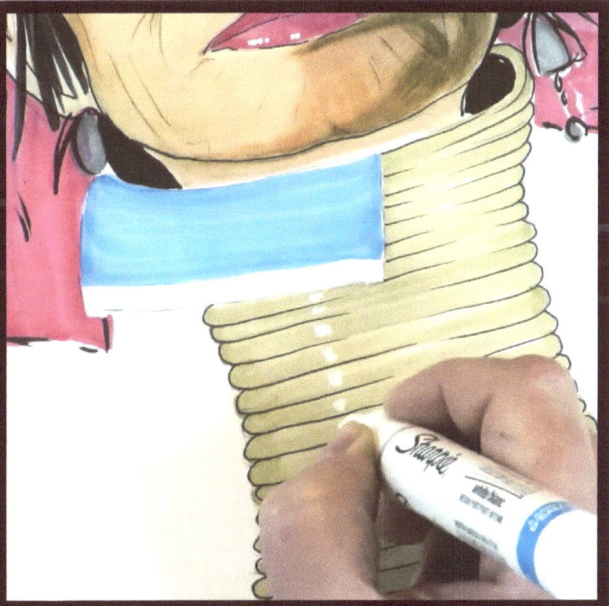

Step 20. With a white paint pen, add highlights all the way down one side.

Myanmar (Burma)

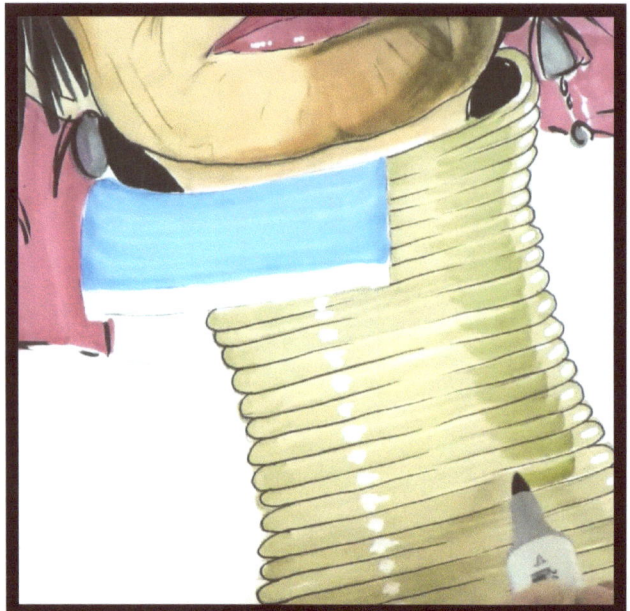

Step 21. Use a darker shade of the metal color to add shading all down one side.

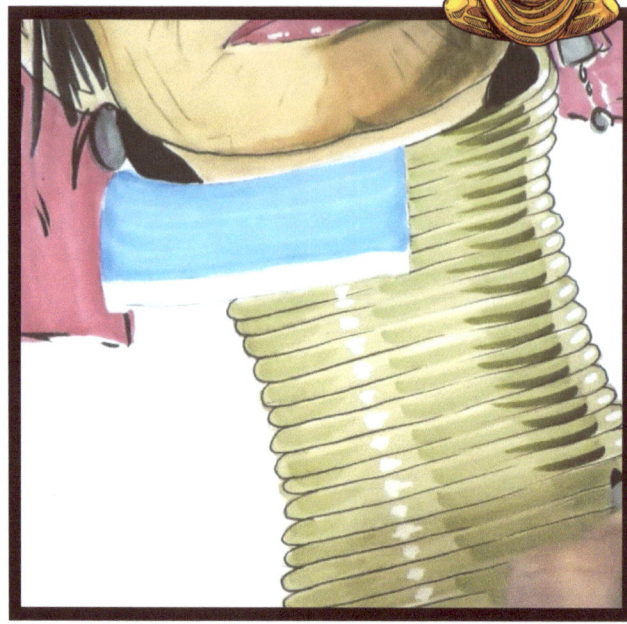

Step 22. Use a 3rd darker shade still and repeat that again.

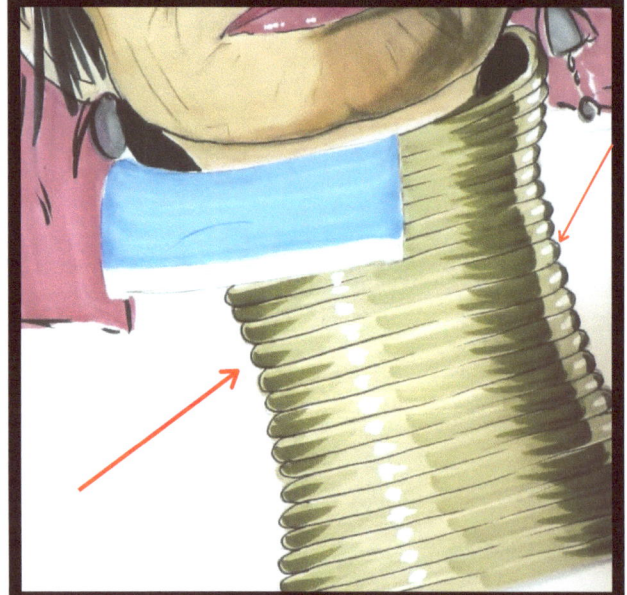

Step 23. Apply that 3rd darker shade to the far left and far right side.

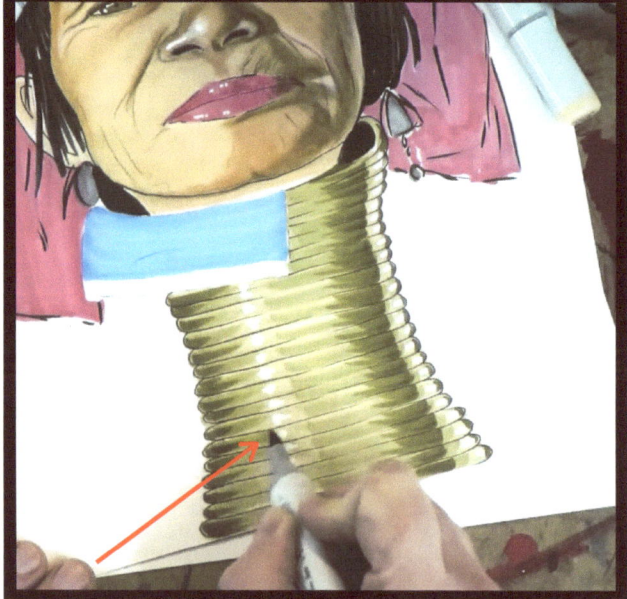

Step 24. Go back to the 2nd shade and use it to blend the darkest (3rd shade) with the lightest across all the rings.

Myanmar (Burma)

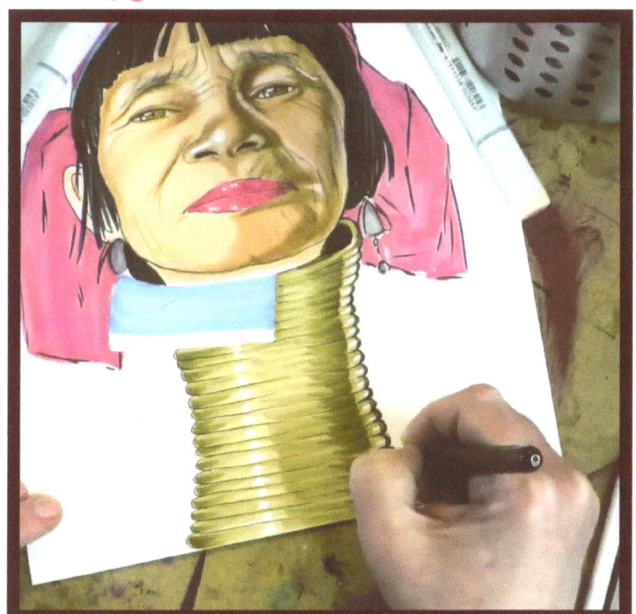

Step 25. Use a brush pen to outline the individual rings on both sides.

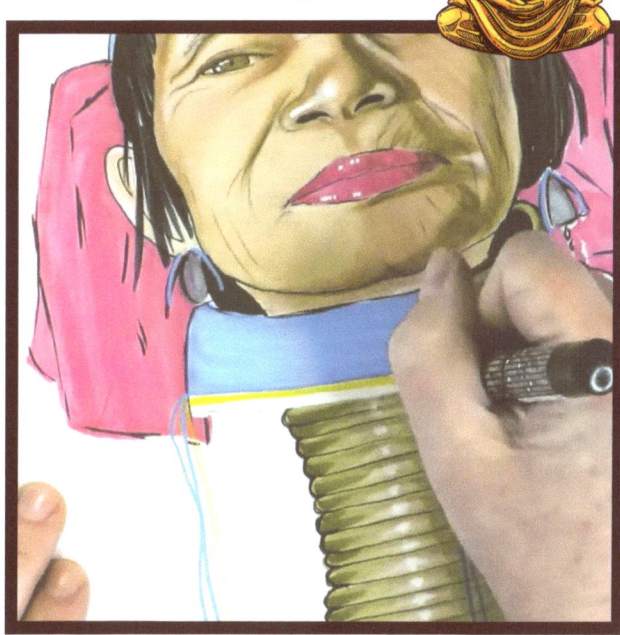

Step 26. Use paint pens (like Posca) to draw the strings that hang down from the fabric flap piece.

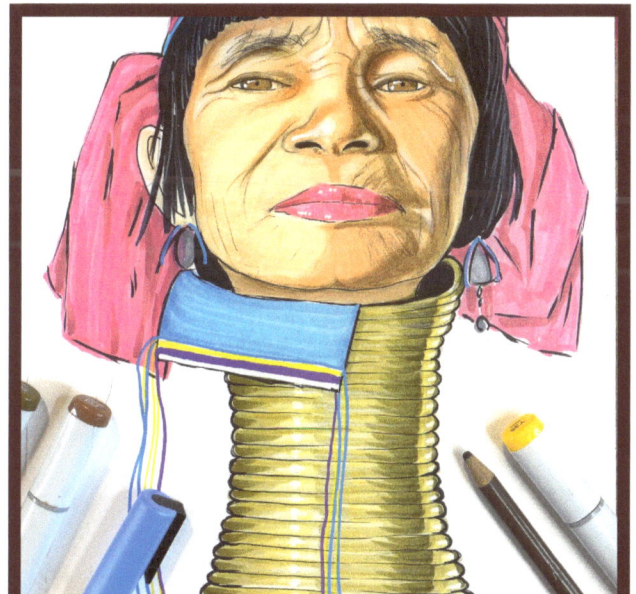

Step 27. Go around the entire face, eyes, nostrils, headpiece, hair and fabric folds and add gentle strokes of the black brush pen to tie it all together.

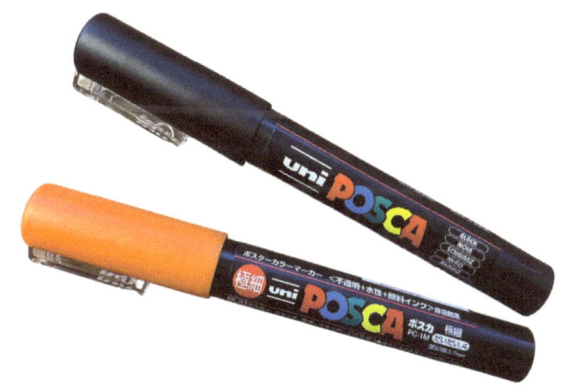

Posca Pens are markers that are filled with fluid acrylics. They are fantastic when you need some opaque coverage and come in really handy for creating the look of these life-like strings!

Student Spotlight

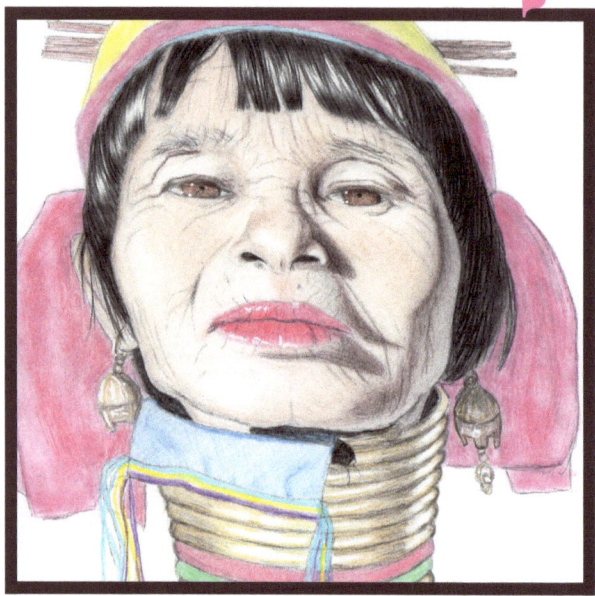

Lisa Hefley. Pencils and Pan Pastels. *"I enjoy colored pencils and my son bought me some light flesh tone pencils for Christmas."*

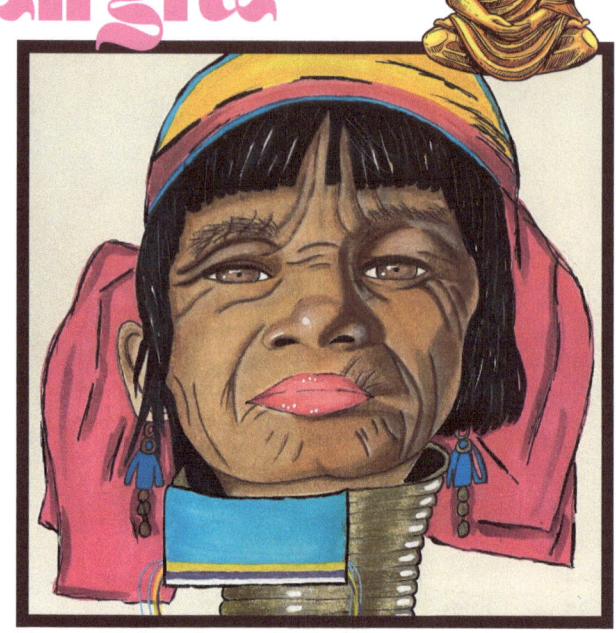

Karen Richardson. Copic Markers & Prismacolour Pencils. *"Materials are great to use and the prismacolour so smooth."*

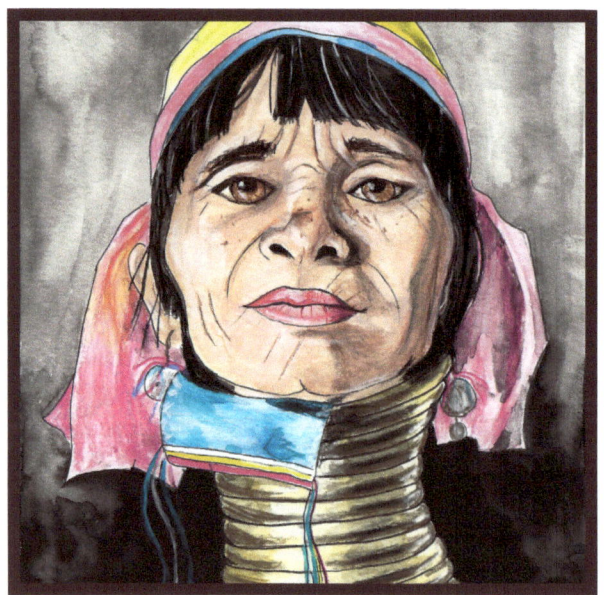

Jamie Drake. Prima watercolor confections Prismacolor colored pencils Art-n-Fly fine liners. *"This one was a real challenge but once I got her sketched and the first layer of water colors she was a real fun project to finish."*

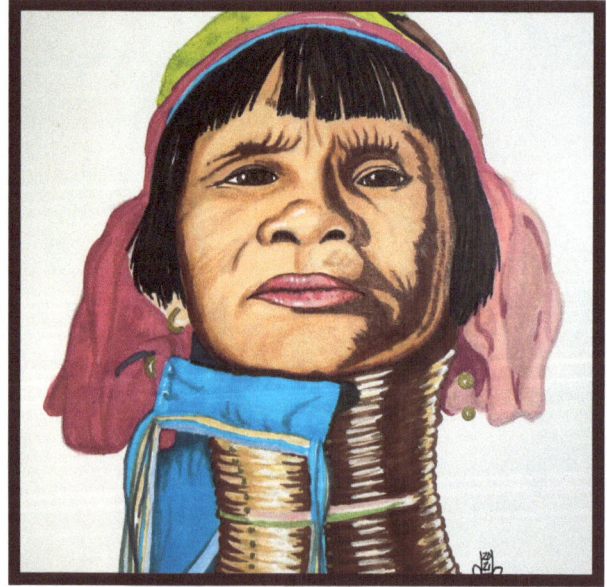

Deb Bratcher. Alcohol Markers. *"Out of all the whimsical paintings we've done in the series... I must admit she was the most challenging. She tooke me a couple hours of tweaking."*

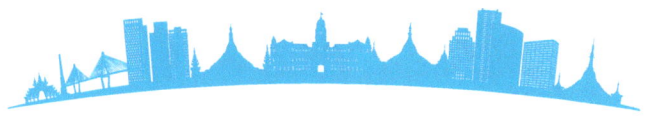

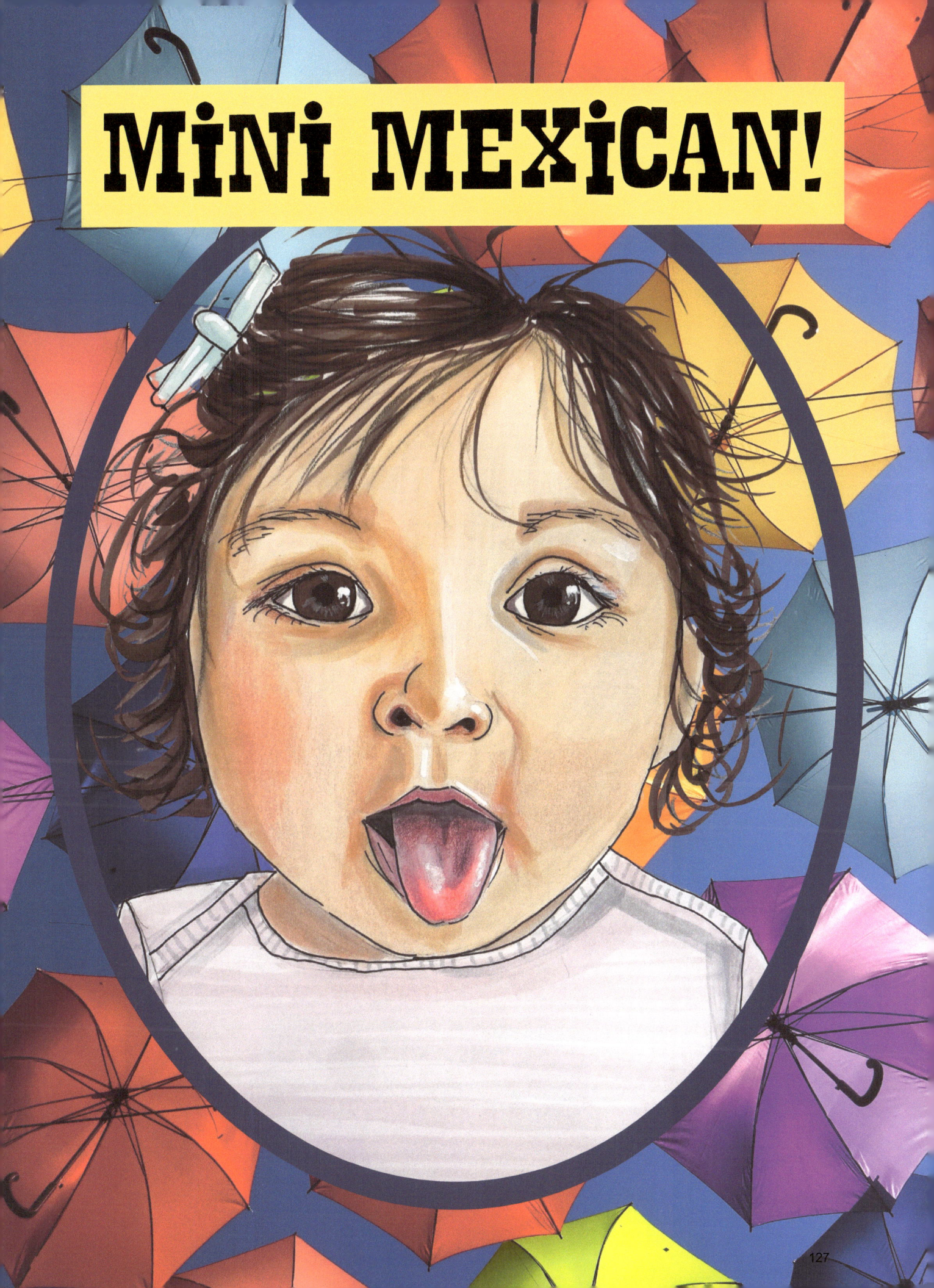

MEXICAN

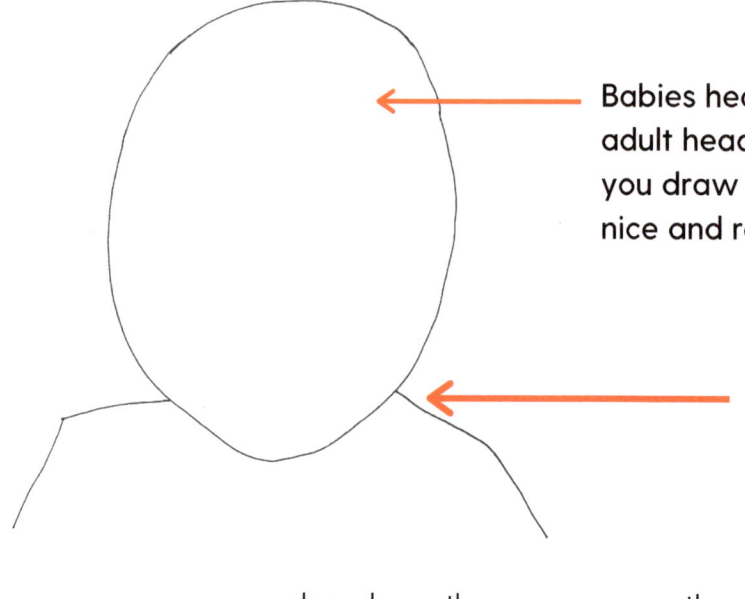

Babies heads are rounder than adult heads so this time when you draw your oval make it nice and round!

When you draw the neck, skip the neck lines and go right to the shoulders. Note how they are drawn directly off of the side of the face.

closed mouth head shape   open mouth head shape

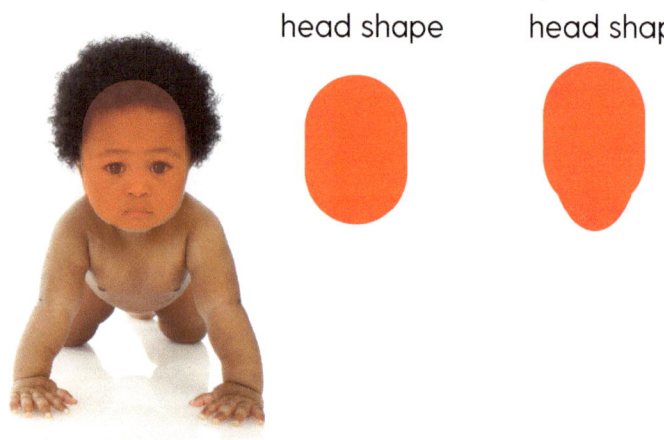

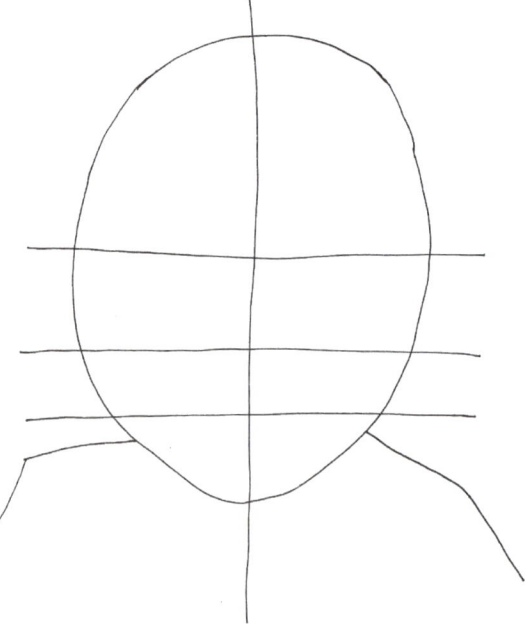

The guidelines for this baby are the same as they are for a normal adult.

NOTE: The baby we are drawing is a bit different though because of her open mouth. Her expression creates a longer oval face shape than a baby whose mouth is closed. A close mouthed baby's head is even rounder than what you'd see here!

MEXICAN

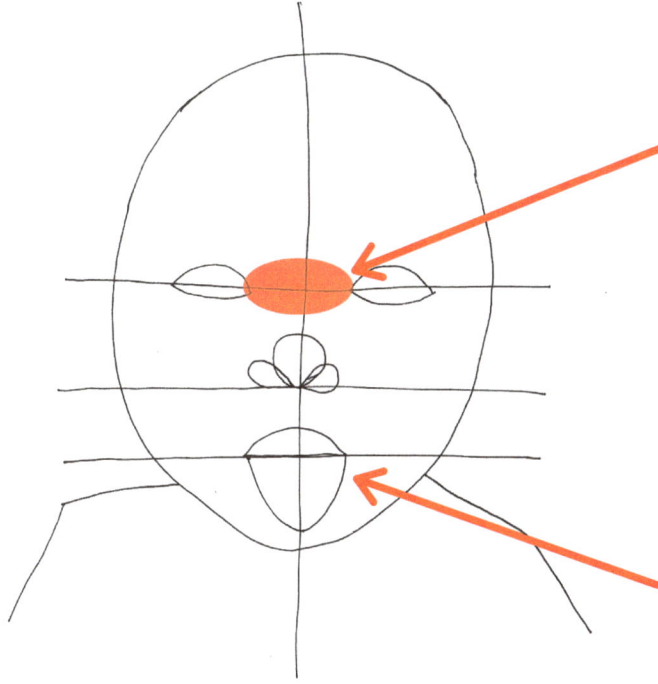

The eyes are *just slightly* farther apart than one eye-width (as is standard on adults) partly because of her adorable expression, and partly because she is growing so they aren't full size yet!

Use 3 circles for the nose. Make sure the ovals for the nostrils are still pretty big as she is laughing (squealing?) and so they are flared!

The mouth is open and tongue is out so use these general, rounded shapes as shown to mark those in.

Now you can lightly sketch the outline of the hair. It's a mess of curls so you can lightly draw in some curves to get started!

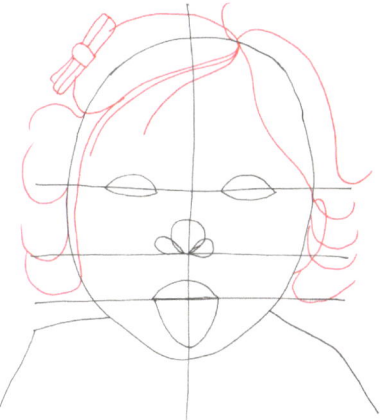

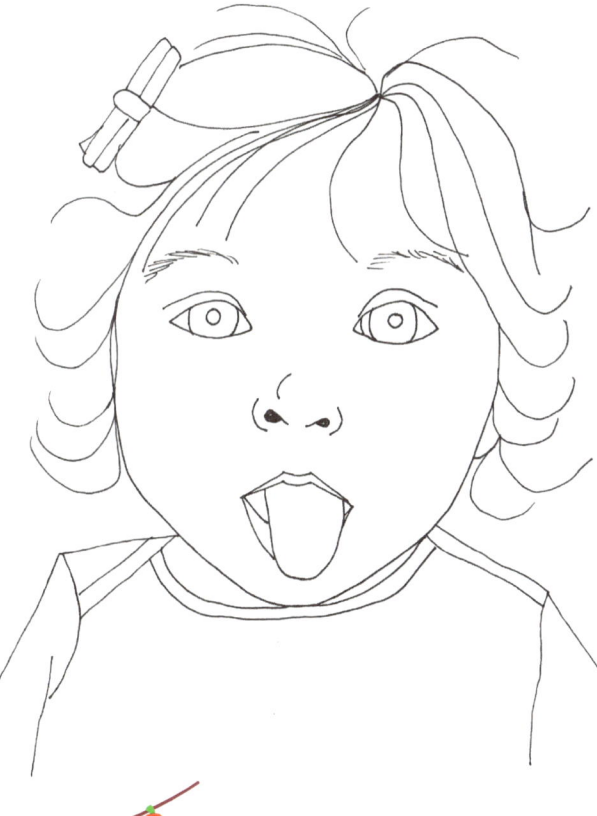

Now refine the facial features and define the details of the shirt and you're read to color!!

MEXICAN

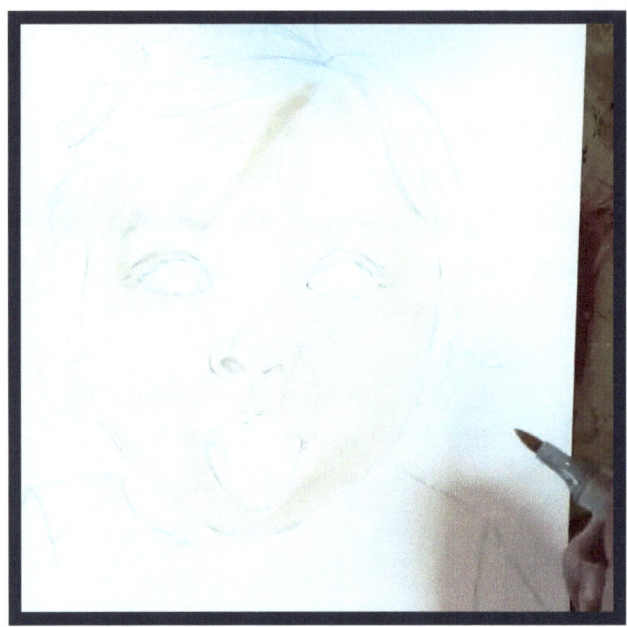

Step 1. Color the entire face with a very pale skin shade.

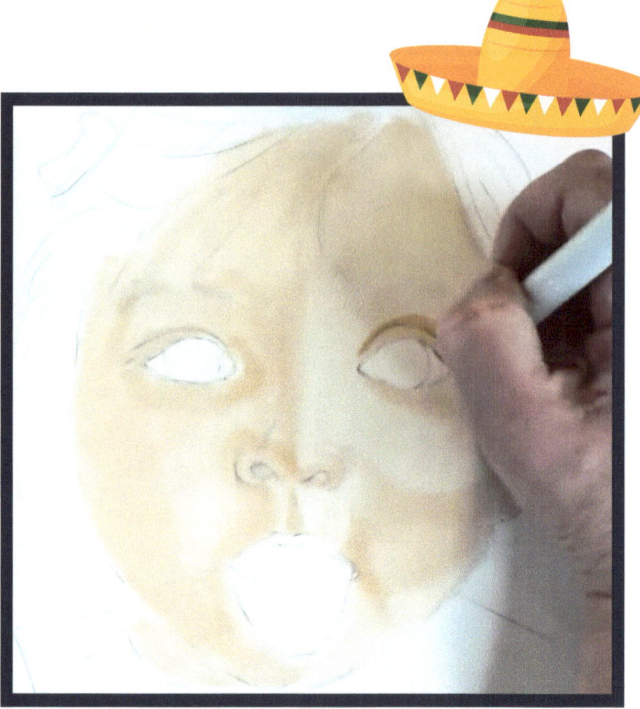

Step 2. Add a slightly darker shade to the areas as shown.

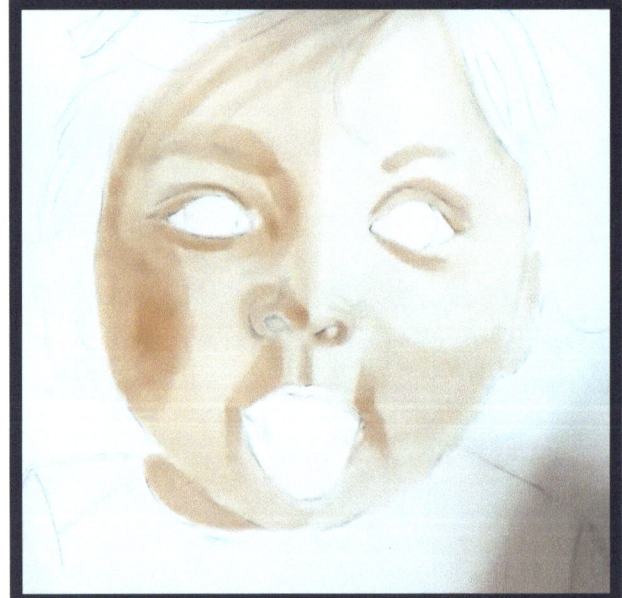

Step 3. Add a third darker shade to these areas: around the eyes, nostrils, sides of the mouth, left side cheek and under the neck.

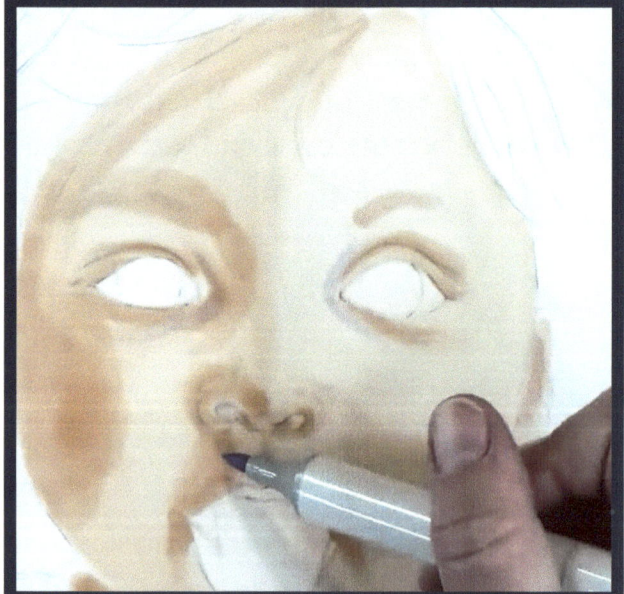

Step 4. Add a VERY pale violet to the inner corners of the eyes and around the nostrils.

MEXICAN

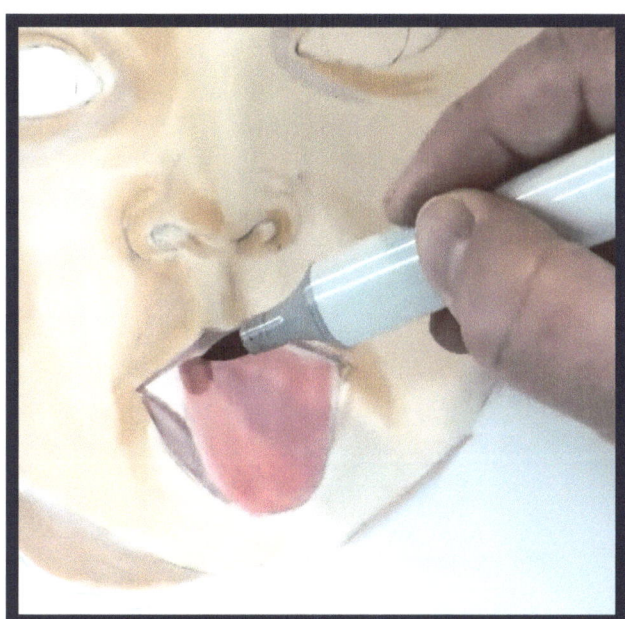

Step 5. Color the lips light mauve and the tongue a light pink.

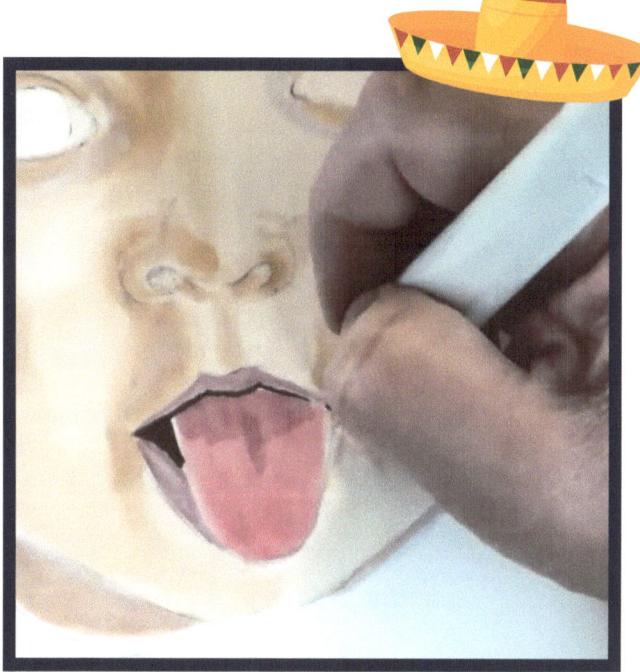

Step 6. Use black to fill in the mouth. Use a dark pink to the back of the tongue.

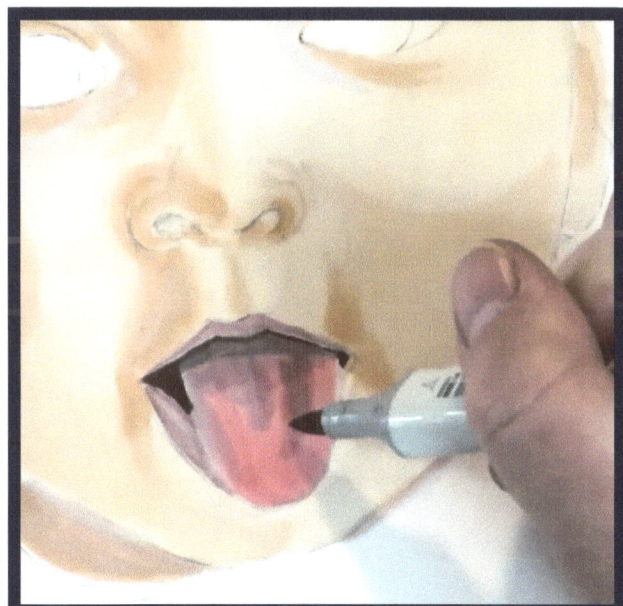

Step 7. Using a pale violet shade, add darker shades to the tongue along both sides. Then create a bit of shadow down the center.

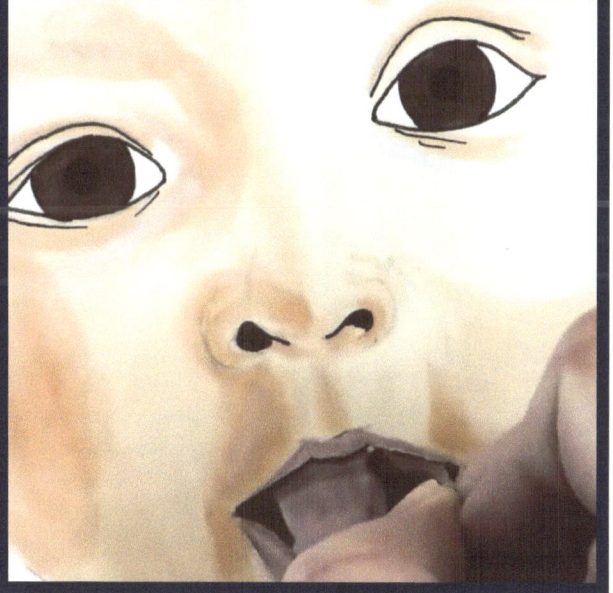

Step 8. Color the eyes brown. With a fine liner pen, outline all the facial features and add a pupil. Next, outline her shirt.

MEXICAN

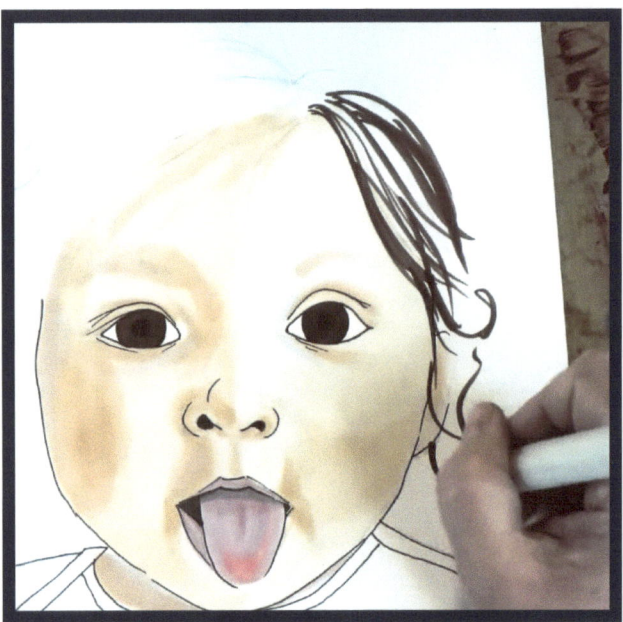

Step 9. Add each strand of hair from the scalp. Curl them up at ends as you go!

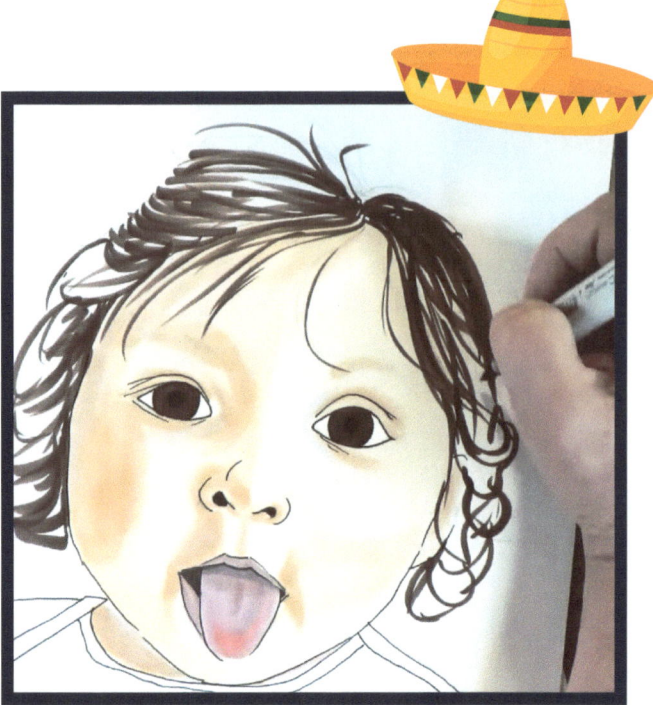

Step 10. Her hair is very fine so don't add too many strands or fill in the area too too much.

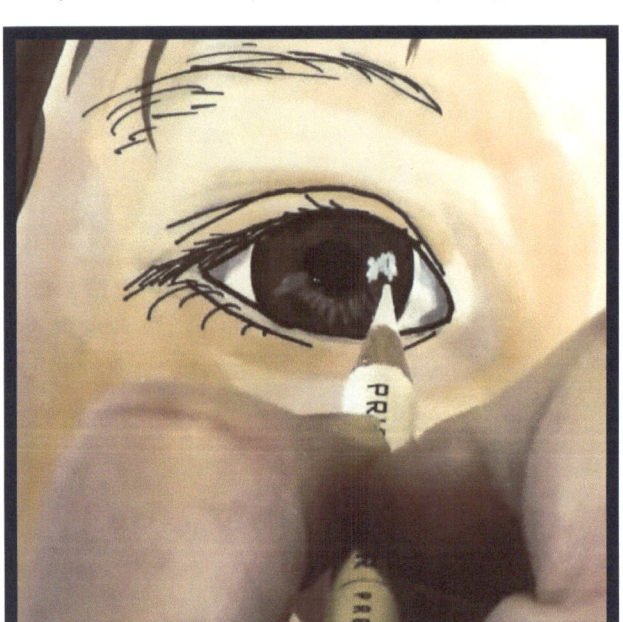

Step 11. Use a fine liner to draw the eyebrows and lashes. Use a white colored pencil and gel pen to add highlights of varying shades of white. Make those eyes sparkle!

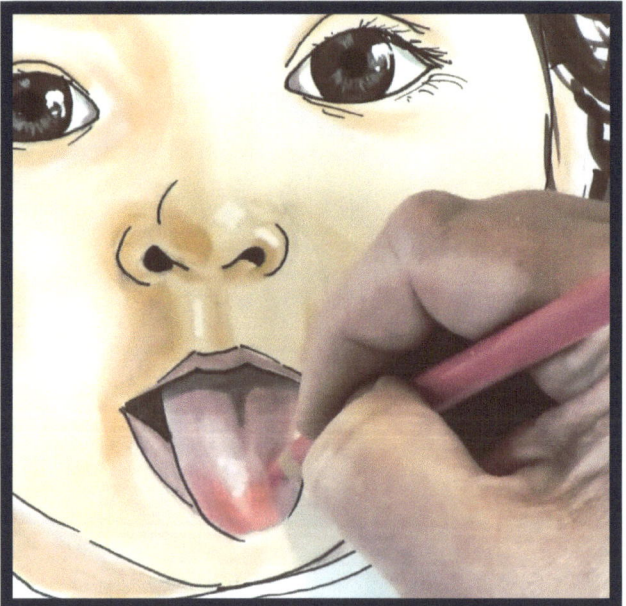

Step 12. Add white highlights to the nose, area between nose and mouth and tongue. Then use a pink colored pencil to color just the tip of the tongue.

MEXICAN

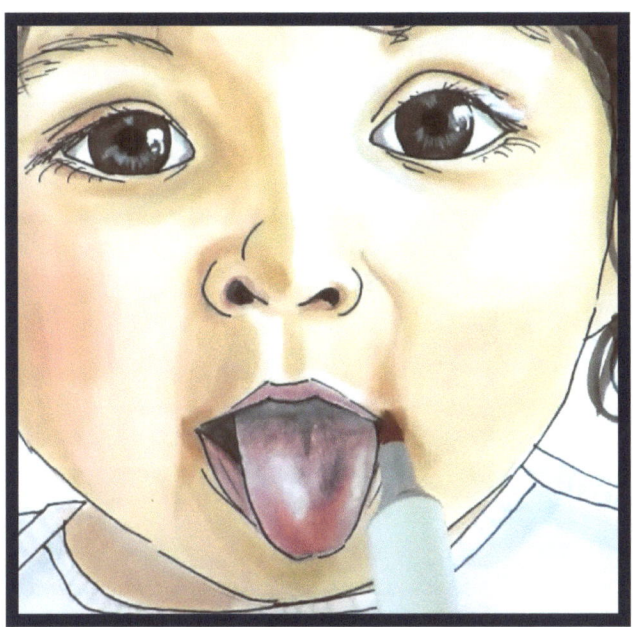

Step 13. Use a darker skin shade to accentuate the corners of the mouth.

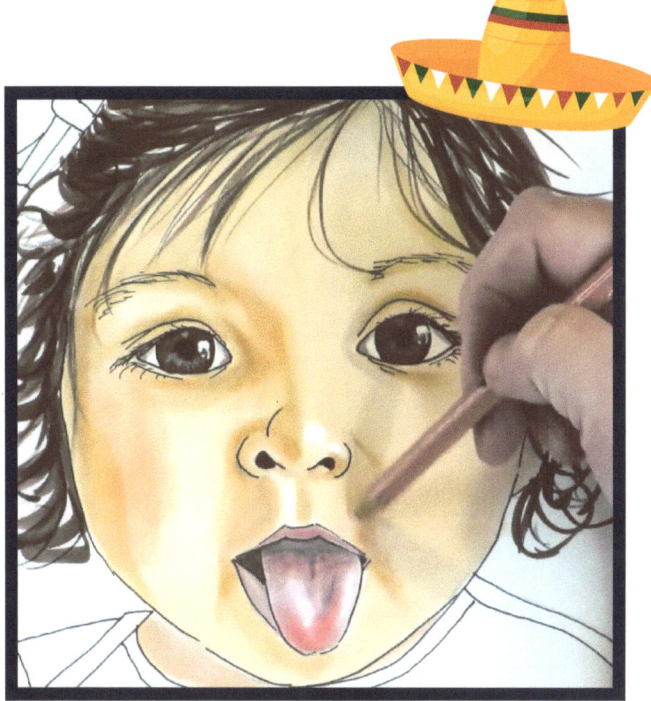

Step 14. Use colored pencils to smooth transitions between uneven skin shades.

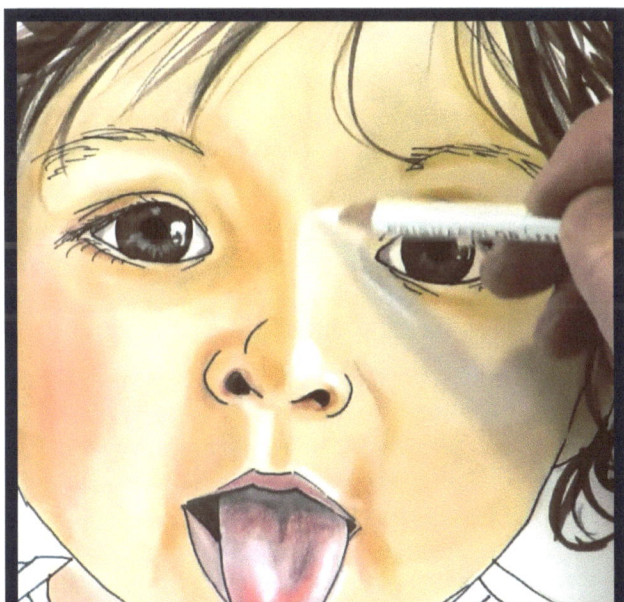

Step 15. Use a white colored pencil to add any last minute highlights (on nose bridge, brow bone, upper lip and nose)!

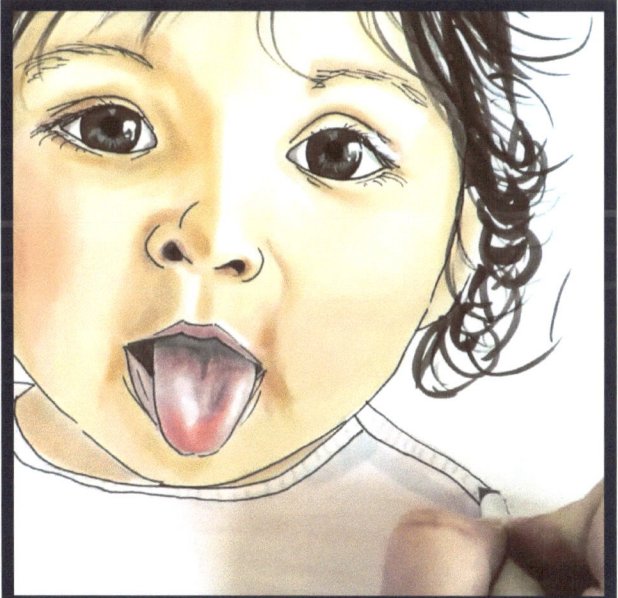

Step 16. Add color to the shirt and her cute barrette (I used pale pink and pale aqua). Congratulate yourself on a job SO WELL DONE!

STUDENT SPOTLIGHT

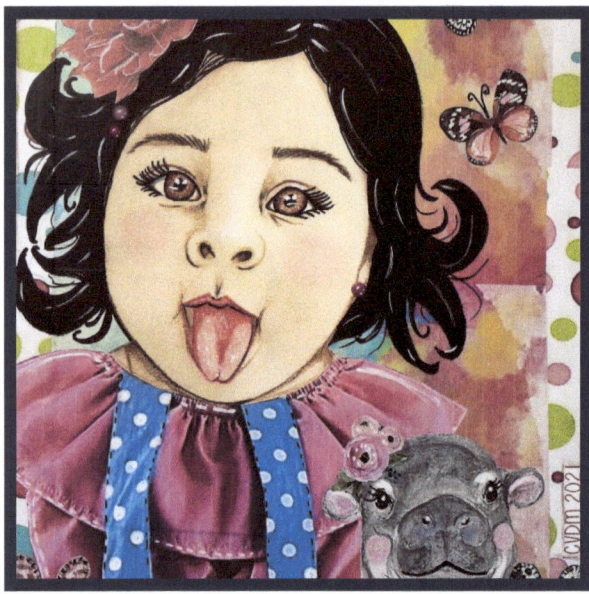

Cornelia Van der Merwe. Mixed media. *"I love how all the different types of supplies blend together to give the final product."*

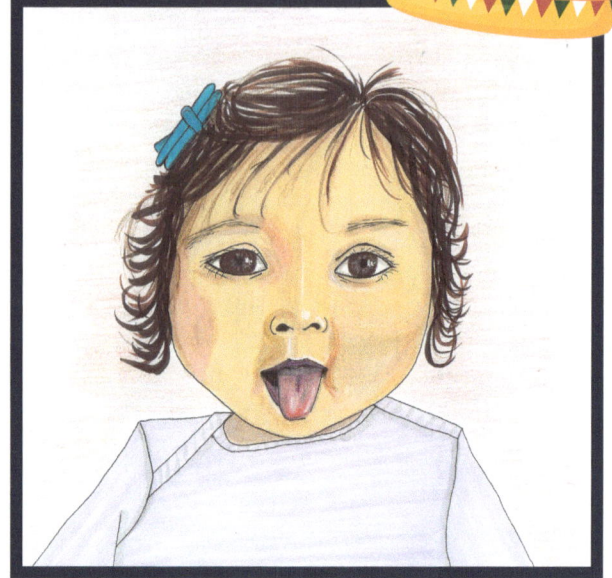

Caroline Scott. Copics, paint pens. *"I love the realistic affect of shadows and highlights that I was able to achieve by layering."*

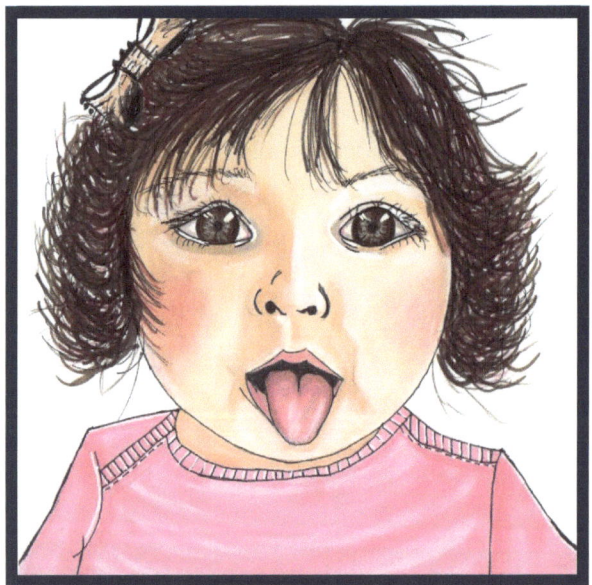

Jayne Charlton. Spectrum Noir alcohol markers and pencils, Uniball & Posca pens. *"These materials are high quality at affordable prices and do exactly what I want then to plus very large range of colour in alcohol markers."*

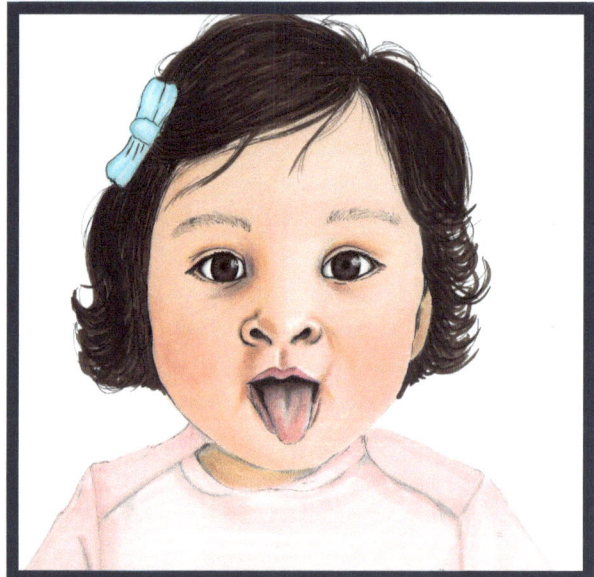

Deborah Palmer. Alcohol markers, palette pastel, fine liner, color pencil, and white gel pen. *"I used these materials to give the smooth look of baby skin."*

Acknowledgements

I'd like to thank ALL the artists who continue to draw along side me each week, both on YouTube and at Awesome Art School. Drawing and learning together is what makes this journey so fulfilling and so so fun! I'd also like to give special thanks to the following talented artists for their contributions. Keep up the FABULOUS work!

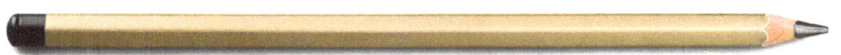

Karina Aguirre
Marie Arvin
Beverley Barclay
Julie Bédard
Zsuzsanna (Suzy) Bimbo
Rose Bloom
Felicia Boros
Deb Bratcher
Shellene Brooks
Iris Bruce
Pam Burns
Lynn Buchi
Vikki Burgett
Jayne Charlton
Denise Cheng
Viki Colonna
Junirose De Armas
Debby Delpopolo
Maria Despotis-Kadas
Adrienne Dinos
Jamie Drake
Patti Dutton
Leigh-Ann Evans
Norma Favela
Linda Fitch
Denise Flick
Bonnie Friesen
Abbe Glassman
Darlene Hanna

Lisa Hefley
Donna Holmes
Lena Holt
Jessica Hubbard
Liliana Hurst
Kate Ivester
Jhilmil Jain
Mary Jesse
Roxenne Kendall
Oxana Kimmel
Jackie Klassen
Debi Ledford
Michelle Leslie
Suzanne Levis
Janet Link
Giovanna Lo Grasso
Deborah Ludin
Sirkku Mannegren
Judie Martinez
Tamatha Mavraides
Judy Middleton
Nancy Moncada

Mary Mullins
Ramona Myers
Bryn Nguyen
Cindy Nijssen
Sharon Nilsen
Joanne Oliver
Deborah Palmer
Victoria Pearman
Ofelia Perez
Karen Pulfer
Donna Rega
Karen Richardson
Veronica Schlett
Maryna Schreuder
Candice Schwark
Caroline Scott
Karen Serna
Anette Severinsson
Kathy Snyder
Susan Spinnato
Debbie Starmer
Melanie Stringer
Kathryn Thomas
Janet Toto
Ursula Uzcategui
Cornelia Van der Merwe
Patricia Veneman
Kirsten Weidinger
Isabel Yuvienco

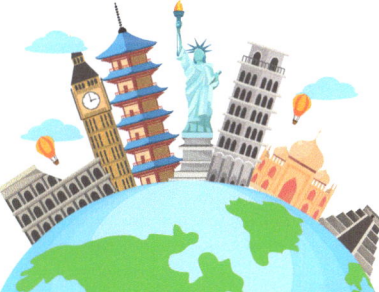

About the Author

Karen Campbell is a Boston area native who lives in North Carolina with her husband, three kids and four fur babies! She is a full time artist, instructor, business owner and is the author of many fun drawing and mixed media art books.

She started teaching art in 2011 and founded her online art school, Awesome Art School, in 2016. Thanks to her school and 2 art-based YouTube Channels, Karen has had the pleasure of impacting the lives of tens of thousands of adult learners across the globe with fun art lessons.

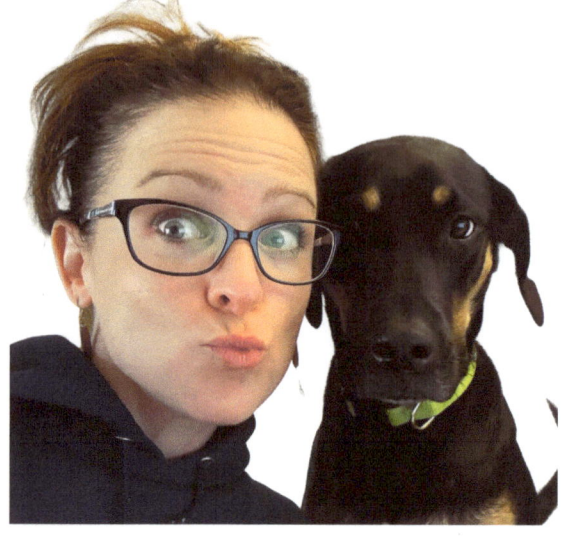

Karen's primary goal is to make art easy and accessible to anyone. Besides techniques, she focuses her students attention on becoming better artists through the practice of having pure, unadulterated FUN!!! Subscribe to her drawing YouTube channel for your own weekly dose of fun! www.youtube.com/karencampbellDRAWS

- awesomeartschool.com
- karencampbellartist.com
- youtube.com/karencampbellDRAWS (drawing)
- youtube.com/karencampbellartist (mixed media)
- facebook.com/karencampbellartist
- instagram.com/karencampbellartist
- pinterest.com/karencampbellartist
- amazon.com/author/karencampbell
- etsy.com/shop/karencampbellartist
- patreon.com/karencampbellartist

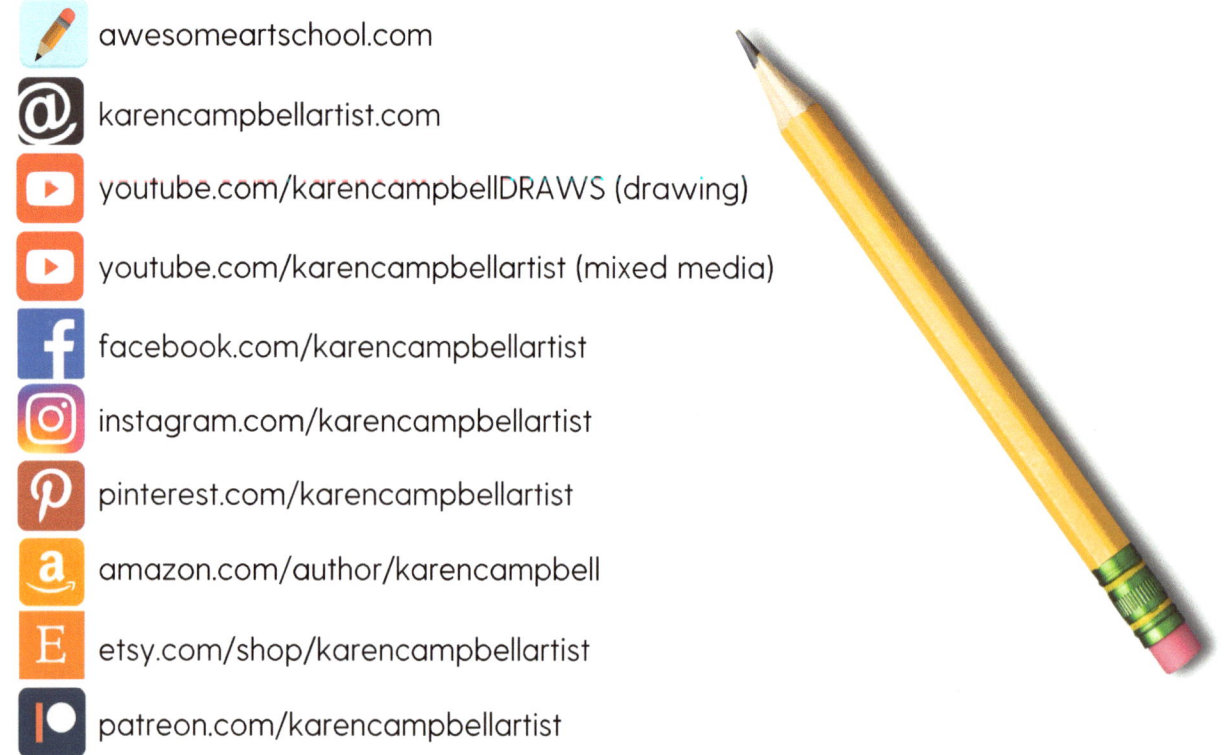

More Books by Karen Campbell

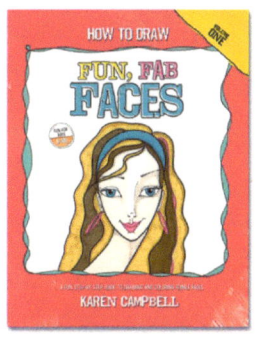
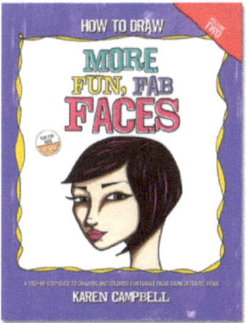
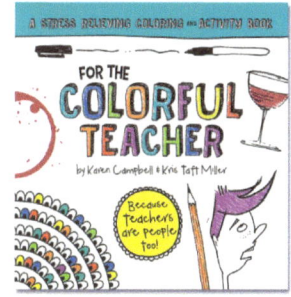
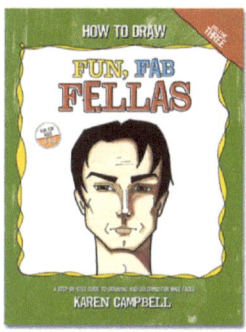
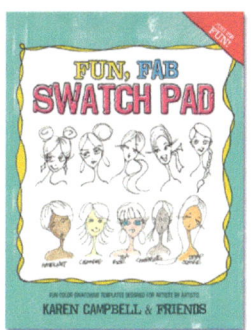
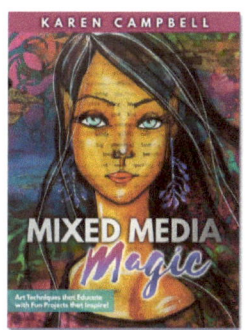
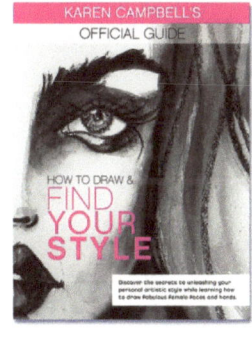
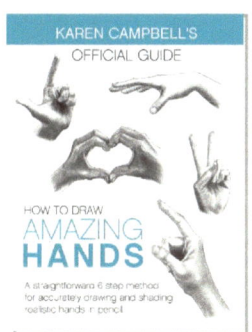
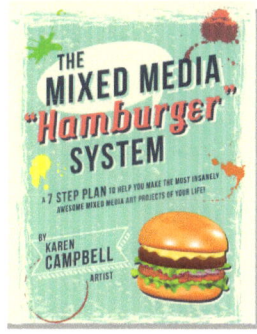
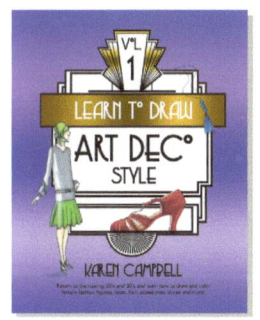
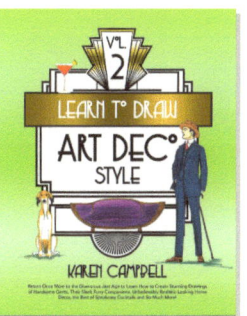
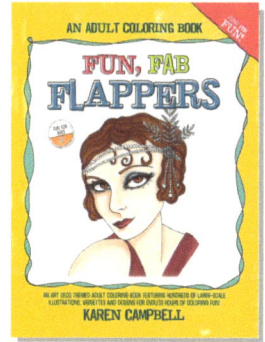

Available on Amazon

www.ingramcontent.com/pod-product-compliance
Lightning Source LLC
Chambersburg PA
CBHW051149220526
45473CB00003B/709